29/10/99
With love,

THE LIFE AND WORK OF
CHARLES BELL

Charles Davidson Bell (1813–1882). Self portrait.
Crayon on paper. 70 x 57 cm. William Fehr Collection

THE LIFE AND WORK OF
CHARLES BELL

by Phillida Brooke Simons

Including

THE ART OF CHARLES BELL:
AN APPRAISAL

by Michael Godby

FERNWOOD
PRESS

Fernwood Press
P O Box 15344
8018 Vlaeberg
South Africa

Registration no. 90/04463/07

First published 1998

Text (Chapters 1 to 10) © Phillida Brooke Simons
Text (Appraisal) © Michael Godby

Edited by Leni Martin
Designed and typeset by Abdul Amien
Picture research by Leonie Twentyman Jones
Map by Red Roof Design
Production control by Abdul Latief (Bunny) Gallie
Repro co-ordinator Andrew de Kock
Reproduction by Unifoto (Pty) Ltd, Cape Town
Printed and bound by Tien Wah Press (Pte) Ltd, Singapore
Collectors' and Sponsors' editions bound by Peter Carstens, Johannesburg

Standard Edition   ISBN 1 874950 34 2
Collectors' Edition   ISBN 1 874950 35 0
Sponsors' Edition   ISBN 1 874950 36 9

The engraving included in the Sponsors' Edition
was printed on a hand press by Cecil Skotnes and
Roderick Sauls from the original endgrain wood
block cut by Charles Bell in 1846.
The paper used is Zerkall Buetten.

The painting by Charles Bell included in the Collectors'
Edition depicts rhinoceros hunting in the Magaliesberg.

CONTENTS

It has been a pleasure and privilege to research and write the text and captions of *The Life and Work of Charles Bell*. In doing so, I had the support, advice and help of many people and institutions and, while there is not sufficient space here to thank them all personally, I must place on record my gratitude to those who have made a notable contribution to the creation of the book.

First I must express my deep appreciation to Old Mutual, the generous sponsor of this publication, without whose support it would have been difficult indeed to produce it. My special thanks are due to Frans Davin, a former managing director of the sponsor, and to Trevor Janse, Manager, Events & Heritage Management.

Most of the superb artworks on which the book depends for its visual appeal are held by the John and Charles Bell Heritage Trust Collection which is on loan to the University of Cape Town's Libraries. To Dr Frank Bradlow, chairman of the Trust since its inception in 1978, I owe my most profound gratitude for his patience, warm friendliness and encouragement. Professor Brian Warner, also a Trustee, was extremely helpful, as was Professor Michael Godby. I must also thank Lesley Hart and her staff at Manuscripts and Archives, UCT Libraries. They have been of immense help to me.

The assistance of Leonie Twentyman Jones, formerly in charge

Rhinoceros shooting.
Watercolour. 13.5 x 21.5 cm.
Bell Heritage Trust Collection,
UCT

of these Manuscripts and Archives, has been invaluable and my thanks for all she has contributed know no bounds. Leonie has applied her knowledge of the Bell Heritage Trust, her skill as a researcher, her ability to work with people and her meticulously orderly mind to assisting with the demanding picture research and photography required for this book.

My gratitude, and also that of all who appreciate the book's appearance, is due to the photographer Kathleen Comfort and her husband Geoff Grundlingh, and also to the skilful designer of the book, Abdul Amien. Their combined artistry and originality served to create a book that in itself is a reward for their efforts.

During the year-long preparation of the text, I haunted the corridors of the South African Library to whose staff in the Reference Department, Special Collections and Reading Room I owe my grateful thanks. Arlene Fanarof, Cathy Drake and Jackie Loos deserve special mention. Their ready assistance at all times and their cheerful friendliness added enormously to my enjoyment of this project. My gratitude is also due to the staff of the Cape Archives.

Assistance from Bell's native Scotland was also graciously given. My special thanks are due to Sue Bradman, honorary curator of Crail Museum, who freely shared invaluable information with me and provided illustrative material. I am also grateful to Sheila Brock and the staff of the National Museums of Scotland, as well as to Fionna Ashmore of the Society of Antiquaries of Scotland.

I must thank Helene Volgraaff and Sue de Beer of the South African Cultural History Museum; Lalou Meltzer, director of the William Fehr Collection; Jackie Baker, librarian of the South African Museum; and the staff of the Brenthurst Library, of MuseumAfrica, of the National Cultural History Museum, Pretoria, and of The Historical and Literary Papers, University of the Witwatersrand – all of whom provided illustrations or made it possible to take photographs.

I owe particular thanks to Robin Fryde, doyen of antiquarian book dealers in South Africa, who gave his painstaking and much appreciated advice regarding the text. Robert Goldblatt provided invaluable information regarding Bell's famous Cape triangular stamps; Michael Stevenson, Antonia Malan, Ethleen Lastovica, Mona de Beer, Gillian Falconer, Cathy Wheeler and David Rhind all contributed in various ways. I appreciate their help; it added enormously to the interest and appearance of the finished product.

No. 39. Medicine Man administering the Charm to Barolong Warriors when going to battle. 1834

To the staff of Fernwood Press – Pieter Struik and his wife Pam, and also to Bunny Gallie, I am grateful for their encouragement and friendship throughout the project. Leni Martin, reliable at all times, edited the manuscript with her customary quiet meticulousness, and to her go my personal thanks. I hope they all, like me, have found the entire undertaking to be a source of both pride and joy.

Finally, my affection and appreciation are due, as ever, to my family, particularly to my husband, Richard Simons, who patiently and unfailingly provides me with practical help and moral support.

PHILLIDA BROOKE SIMONS
Rondebosch, July 1998

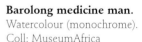

Barolong medicine man.
Watercolour (monochrome).
Coll: MuseumAfrica

The publisher gratefully acknowledges
the generous contribution of the principal sponsor of this book,
OLD MUTUAL.

Table Bay in a southeaster. *c.* **1838.**
Watercolour. 15.5 x 22 cm. Bell Heritage Trust Collection, UCT

SPONSOR'S FOREWORD

In surveying the broad sweep of history, there is little more engaging than the opportunity to examine in detail the life of an individual who in small but often important ways has had an influence in shaping that history.

In the history of South Africa, Charles Bell was such a man. What makes his story – and this book – so intriguing is that so little has been written about him before. At Old Mutual, we knew of him as our third Chairman and, enduringly, as the designer of Old Mutual's three-anchor emblem. That this elegant design has remained with us to this day – although modernised to take account of changing tastes – is a tribute to Charles Bell's creative qualities.

Phillida Brooke Simons has finally elevated Charles Bell to his rightful place: as an artist who deserves to be recognised alongside Baines and Bowler; and as a citizen whose 'restless activity' contributed in no small measure to the development of nineteenth-century South Africa. Her entertaining and perceptive approach has resulted in a volume with which Old Mutual is pleased to be associated.

M.J. Levett

M.J. LEVETT
Chairman, Old Mutual
July 1998

FOREWORD

Charles Davidson Bell was one of the most talented and certainly the most versatile of the artists who worked at the Cape in the mid-nineteenth century. Yet, until recently, his name was scarcely known in artistic circles. To philatelists, however, he is familiar as the designer of the sought-after Cape triangular stamp.

In an article that appeared in *Africana Notes & News* in 1953 (Vol. XI, No. 3, pp. 81–87), Anna Smith, later director of the Africana Museum – now MuseumAfrica – observed:

> It was exactly one hundred years on 1 September 1953 since the Cape Triangular stamp was first used and in preparing an exhibition to mark this event an attempt was once again made to discover some details about the life of the designer of this famous and beautiful stamp; but with little success – Charles Bell, Government Surveyor and versatile artist, remains almost as elusive as ever.

There was more than one reason for this lack of knowledge about Bell, especially as an artist. For one thing, his works seldom, if ever, came on the market, unlike those of other nineteenth-century artists like Thomas Bowler, Thomas Baines and Frederick I'Ons. Despite the large collection of watercolours in the Africana Museum which had been assembled mainly by the late Dr John Gaspard Gubbins, the famous Africana collector, and despite the two well-known oil paintings in the South African Library depicting the landing of Van Riebeeck and the raising of the Holy Cross, few members of the public were aware of Bell's work and talents. Another reason for the lack of public knowledge about Bell was that the largest part of his work was in private collections in England.

It was therefore with great pleasure that I learned from the late Jack Manning, in 1975, that Professor Charles Manning, his half-brother and a grandson of Charles Bell, owned a large collection of Bell's sketches and other items, such as wood blocks engraved by Bell in England. The collection included works by Charles Bell's uncle, John Bell. Charles Manning wanted to bring the collection to South Africa and appoint a board of trustees to look after it. Subject to my agreement, I would be chairman of such a trust.

When I saw the collection I was thunderstruck at its wealth. In due course the John and Charles Bell Heritage Trust was formed. At one stage I suggested to Professor Manning that he should make an outright gift of the collection to the University of Cape Town, but he felt that no institution would give it the care that a board of trustees, created for the express purpose of looking after the collection and carrying out his wishes, would do. The trustees decided to house the collection in the Manuscripts Department of the University of Cape Town Libraries, and the works have been magnificently restored by the University's restorer, Mr Johann Maree.

The trustees appointed by Professor Manning were obliged, among other duties, to 'encourage research into John and Charles Bell and into items in the Collection; to publicise, not least among persons visiting the Cape, the presence, location and accessibility of the Collection; and to kindle and sustain proper pride and pleasure in the "heritage" among the citizens of Cape Town'. In accordance with his wishes, a postgraduate student, Michael Lipschitz, was encouraged to write an MA thesis based on the collection, and items from it have been exhibited in Cape Town, Grahamstown, Bloemfontein and Bellville.

Professor Manning would have been delighted to see the collection as it is today. He would have been even more delighted to read Phillida Brooke Simons's *The Life and Work of Charles Bell*. This informative, interesting and balanced account has brought to life again the multi-faceted Bell. Moreover, Phillida has presented the results of her research in an eminently readable style. Through her efforts Charles Bell is no longer elusive, but is shown as the many-talented man he was, truly a 'man for all seasons'. This book will earn a high place in the hierarchy of South African art books, and in doing so will fulfill Charles Manning's wish to 'kindle and sustain proper pride and pleasure in the [Bell] Heritage among the citizens of Cape Town' – and, I might add, among all South Africans. The trustees of the Bell Collection are grateful to the Old Mutual for the part it has played in the production of this excellent book.

Lastly, it is my opinion that the work of Charles Bell is, as

Malay fisherman.
Watercolour. 14 x 21.5 cm.
Bell Heritage Trust Collection,
UCT

Phillida Brooke Simons has shown, to be judged in the context of his times and intentions. I feel sure that his satirical and humorous sketches were not made by him with any intention to belittle the people he portrayed. He was merely showing what his observant eye saw according to the mores of the times.

Frank R Bradlow

DR FRANK BRADLOW
July 1998

LIST OF ILLUSTRATIONS

All artworks are by Charles Bell unless otherwise indicated.

**Neptune's visit to the good
ship *Lady East.* 1830.**
Watercolour. 25 x 33.5 cm.
Coll: MuseumAfrica

Chapter 1

The IMMIGRANT

Charles Davidson Bell, *energetic and alert, blessed with an enquiring mind, an ebullient sense of humour and a prodigious artistic talent, was two months short of his seventeenth birthday when he first stepped onto the shores of Table Bay in the spring of 1830. Son of Alexander Bell, a tenant farmer of the parish of Crail in Fifeshire, and his wife, Isabella Davidson, Charles had left his native Scotland earlier in the year, made the long journey southwards to Weymouth and, on 3 June, boarded the barque* Lady East, *bound for the Cape of Good Hope.[1] Almost three months of foul weather and fair lay ahead for Charles Bell and his fellow passengers — mostly army personnel of various ranks bound for duty in India — but at last the hazy blue outline of Table Mountain rose on the horizon, signalling that landfall was all but imminent.*

figure 1
Table Bay and Cape Town, from the foot of Table Mountain.
Watercolour. 13 x 21 cm.
Bell Heritage Trust Collection, UCT

This scene, showing Cape Town and Table Bay beyond, was painted by Charles Bell from a vantage point on the lower slopes of Table Mountain.

figure 2
Table Mountain etc from the beach of Table Bay.
Watercolour. 14 x 22 cm.
Bell Heritage Trust Collection, UCT

The wide sweep of Table Bay, as Bell would have seen it on his arrival at the Cape. In the absence of a harbour, sailing vessels plying the sea route between east and west are obliged to lie at anchor in the roadstead. On the beach a stranded vessel attracts the interest of 'Malay' fishermen.

To many a prospective settler at this time, the sight of Africa's southern extremity would have aroused certain pangs of apprehension, but for the youthful Bell there was no need for any such sense of alarm. In Cape Town to welcome him was his uncle, Colonel John Bell, who for the past four years had held the office of colonial secretary and was thus second only in importance to the governor, Sir Lowry Cole. Moreover, there must have been an added sense of confidence in the knowledge that Colonel Bell's wife, Lady Catherine, was the elder sister of Lady Frances Cole, chatelaine of Government House. Shortcomings and discomforts there would undoubtedly be in a colonial town so far removed from the sophistication of London and Edinburgh, but Charles was little acquainted with the pleasures of these great cities and at the Cape, in the company of his uncle and aunt, he would undoubtedly have the opportunity to enjoy whatever entertainments were available. Besides, to a young man of adventurous spirit there was always the thrilling possibility of an excursion into the exciting, mysterious and largely unexplored interior.

figure 3 **Charles Bell as a young man. 1833.**
Pencil. 12.8 x 10 cm. Coll: MuseumAfrica

This sketch of Charles Bell as a young man was executed by Sir Charles D'Oyly, an official in the Indian civil service who spent part of 1832 and 1833 at the Cape on sick leave. Bell and D'Oyly would have met at Government House and it is possible that they went sketching together on the Cape Peninsula. Bell, according to his friend Piazzi Smyth, was at this stage, 'a handsome-looking fellow … not very tall, but broad-built and muscular'.

Cape Town boasted no harbour in those days. Ships lay at anchor out in the bay and passengers, transported by rowing boat across the lurching waves, clambered ashore by means of the rickety jetty close to the grey bulk of the Castle of Good Hope. A sprawling slate structure, with five 'points' or bastions named after the titles of the Prince of Orange, the Castle had been erected in the mid-seventeenth century by the Dutch East India Company to protect its small but strategic refreshment station at the Cape from rivals intent on grasping for themselves its precious trade with the 'gorgeous East'.[2] Yet, martial though the Castle's function might have been, never a hostile cannonball had been fired from those bastions, not even on the two occasions – 1795 and 1806 – when the British took possession of the Cape to forestall any attempts the French might make to get there first.

The Castle, then, would have been the first building at the Cape observed by Charles Bell, though he would have recognised that it was the curve of three mountains – Devil's Peak to the east, Lion's Head to the west and, linking them, Table

Mountain itself – that dominated the little town. The carriage bearing Colonel Bell and his young nephew homeward would have swept them past the Grand Parade with its marching red-coated soldiers and its fluttering Union Jack; past the massive, tumble-down Great Barracks occupied by the British garrison; past the Keizersgracht's elegant, tree-shaded private houses; and, with a clatter of hooves, into the town's main thoroughfare. It was grandly known as the Heerengracht, or gentleman's walk, though there was little that was gentlemanly about the filthy, evil-smelling canal that ran its length, carrying Cape Town's rubbish and effluent northwards to the sea. But at the street's southern end, the canal was left behind and the carriage, horses stepping nimbly now, would have entered the Government Avenue roofed by the dappled leafiness of Cape Town's oaks in their first flush of spring green. To the left there was Government House, hardly an impressive residence for such an important official as the governor, and certainly not to be compared with edifices fulfilling a similar function in other, more significant, British colonies. On the right stretched the Government Gardens, planted by the Dutch East India Company almost two centuries earlier with vegetables and fruit for the succour of passing sailors but now, shady with exotic trees and shrubs, the casual meeting place of Cape Town's high society on fine Sunday mornings.

At the very top of Government Avenue, on its east side and almost a mile from the town, stood Hope Mill,[3] a long, low house, so named because of an adjoining watermill, its wheel driven by a mountain stream. Surrounded by an extensive garden which included 'a vineyard full of fine grapes',[4] Hope Mill was to be Charles Bell's new home for it was here, in the fashionable quarter of the town, that Colonel Bell and Lady Catherine had made their home. Very agreeable and convenient it was, too, with Sir Lowry and Lady Frances Cole a mere stone's throw away at Government House. The two titled ladies were daughters of the first Earl of Malmesbury,[5] whose name had recently been granted to a town newly founded in the wheat-growing Swartland northeast of Cape Town. Originally plain James

Harris, the Earl had been raised to the peerage in recognition of the successful diplomatic negotiations he had conducted on behalf of Great Britain while serving as ambassador in various European capitals. In fact, he had named his eldest daughter, born in St Petersburg, after Russia's empress, Catherine the Great, whose goddaughter she was.

In June 1821, Lady Catherine Harris, then approaching middle age, had married Major John Bell, at thirty-nine her junior by a year or two and a distinguished and much decorated veteran of the Peninsular War. Son of David Bell, a farmer of Bonnytoun north of Dundee, John Bell had joined an uncle's ship-owning and mercantile business on leaving school, but in 1805, at the age of twenty-three, had abandoned the commercial world to enlist in the 52nd Regiment of Foot as an ensign. It was Bell's bad luck to be in America at the time of the Battle of Waterloo on 18 June 1815, but two months later he joined Wellington's army in Europe where he continued to perform his duties with distinction. Undoubtedly, John Bell was not only a brave and handsome soldier, but also a polished and cultivated gentleman, an accomplished artist and an entertaining *raconteur*. His family may not have been a noble one, but the Bells could proudly trace their ancestry back to Andrew Bell, laird of Sandihills and Kilduncan, whose descendant Thomas, born in 1687, was last chief of the clan before it broke up.[6]

John and Catherine had been married only a year when, in 1822, Colonel Bell (as he now was) took office as deputy quartermaster of the forces at the Cape. He soon began to make an important contribution to the affairs and society of the town and was rewarded six years later with his appointment as colonial secretary. The Cape, British since it had been captured from the Dutch twenty-two years earlier, was ruled by a governor whose autocratic powers were curtailed by a council of advice established in 1814. Colonel Bell served on this body and during the nineteen years that he was to live and work at the Cape, no fewer than five governors or their deputies came to rely upon him for his unquestionable integrity, his wisdom and his experience. Now, as brother-in-law of Sir Galbraith Lowry Cole, governor since September 1828, he was entirely within the gubernatorial circle. Lady Catherine, outspoken in opinion and enterprising in action, proved an able but certainly not submissive helpmeet to him, leaving her mark on Cape Society by, among other things, founding one of the first so-called 'mission schools' in the Peninsula.[7]

Not surprisingly at their age, the Bells had no children and it may have been because of this that they so readily made the Colonel's young nephew at home with them in Africa. Their influence was to be profound: it was probably through John Bell's guidance that the youthful Charles, so far untutored as an artist, rapidly improved his technique as a draughtsman. At the same time, the high level of conversation and debate to which the young man was exposed in the company of his uncle's friends and colleagues must have proved an exciting stimulus to his impressionable mind.

The Cape, both socially and topographically, was so different from the Scotland that Charles had been familiar with since he was born on 22 October 1813. The Royal Burgh of Crail, most easterly of the fishing villages strung along the rocky coast of the East Neuk of Fife, was – and still is – a quaintly picturesque town where seventeenth- and eighteenth-century cottages, their roofs crow-stepped and red pantiled, huddle round the old harbour. Narrow, winding lanes lead upwards from it to Marketgate, broad and tree-lined, while from the lofty stone tower of the parish church of St Mary, founded in the twelfth century, there is a splendid view across the Firth of Forth to the coast of Lothian. When Charles Bell was a boy, herring fishing provided Crail with its main livelihood, and a very satisfactory one it was at that time, though farming on the good soil inland proved almost as profitable.

About four miles north of Crail itself lay East Newhall, farmed and occupied by Alexander Bell at the time of Charles's birth, while a two hours' coach journey to the northeast would bring the traveller to St Andrews, once the ecclesiastical capital of Scotland and the site of its most ancient university. Charles probably attended the school at Kingsbarns,[8] a village a mile or thereabouts beyond East Newhall, and later studied at St Andrews University[9] where, according to family tradition, he read physics and chemistry, mathematics and advanced Latin – subjects that provided an excellent background to his later studies. To the south of Crail, across the Firth of Forth, was Edinburgh, Scotland's vibrant social, legal, cultural and scientific centre, and something of these two renowned seats of learning must have rubbed off on Crail, geographically remote as it certainly was.

If Charles Bell's birthplace had anything at all in common with the Cape it was in the fierce winds that battered their coastlines, for not for nothing was the Cape Peninsula known to mariners the world over as 'the Cape of Storms'. As for Crail – 'Round it the wild storms of winter raged,' wrote an old-timer a century after Charles Bell left home for Africa. 'The briny winds blew through its venerable Market Gait and Nether Gait; the sea haar enveloped it for days together.'[10] Besides, according to this

figure 4
Lt Gen Sir John Bell, KCB.
Mezzotint. 41.7 x 32.7 cm.
Bell Heritage Trust Collection, UCT

Sir John Bell, seen here in the uniform of a lieutenant general some years after he gave up the office of colonial secretary at the Cape in 1841. A witty raconteur and gifted artist and draughtsman, John Bell undoubtedly had a powerful and stimulating influence on his young nephew, Charles. Painted by John Lucas and engraved by Henry Cousins, this portrait was commissioned by the States of the Island of Guernsey of which John Bell was governor.

learned chronicler, 'whales and other wonders of the deep' were as familiar to the town's inhabitants as sheep and cattle were to crofters inland. Young Charles could well have been reminded of such tales when, for the first time, he witnessed spouting southern right whales cavorting in the waters washing the coast of the Cape Peninsula.

He was an immediate success with his new family. 'John finds him but little altered from what he was as a child,' wrote Lady Catherine to her father-in-law, David Bell, on 24 August 1830, the day after Charles's arrival. She declared that he had 'already made a most favourable impression on us both – I trust he will be as happy & comfortable under our roof as it is my warmest wish to make him – & I feel too much for a young person first leaving a kind home not to try to make this his second home as much as I can'. Colonel Bell was equally charmed by Charles: 'I have not seen him more really happy and delighted than in the company of his nephew,' ran Lady Catherine's letter, '& hearing a good account of you all.'[11]

Charles himself, according to his aunt, was busily engaged in writing home at the same time and it is disappointing that this letter – like most of those that he subsequently wrote to his family – has not survived to place on record his impressions of Cape Town and its extraordinary diversity of people. Nevertheless, he was soon busy with pencil and brush and from his lively sketches it is not difficult to assess his reaction to what one nineteenth-century visitor called 'the most motley crew in the world'.[12] For, in addition to the Dutch, well settled after almost two centuries, Bell would have soon seen about him slaves (for slavery at the Cape did not end until December 1834), whose roots were in both West Africa and the East, 'Free Blacks', as well as 'Cape Malays' in their colourful dress. Running errands and performing the most menial of tasks were the few remaining Hottentots,[13] while mostly at the other end of the social scale there lived an assortment of people of European stock.

They all appeared in Bell's sketches, from which one can see that he must have supported the opinion of another contemporary traveller who described Cape Town as 'this half-way house,

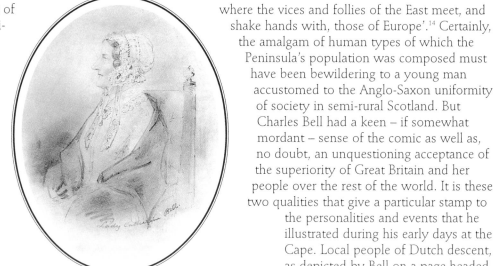

figure 5 **Lady Catherine Bell.**
Pencil. 26.5 x 18.5 cm. Bell Heritage Trust Collection, UCT

Lady Catherine Bell, as sketched by her nephew by marriage, Charles Bell, to whom she was hostess during his early years in Cape Town. The elder daughter of the first Earl of Malmesbury and the goddaughter of Catherine the Great of Russia, Lady Catherine was born in St Petersburg while her father was British ambassador in that city. As the wife of the colonial secretary at the Cape, she was dedicated to 'good works' and was respected for her forthright personality.

where the vices and follies of the East meet, and shake hands with, those of Europe'.[14] Certainly, the amalgam of human types of which the Peninsula's population was composed must have been bewildering to a young man accustomed to the Anglo-Saxon uniformity of society in semi-rural Scotland. But Charles Bell had a keen – if somewhat mordant – sense of the comic as well as, no doubt, an unquestioning acceptance of the superiority of Great Britain and her people over the rest of the world. It is these two qualities that give a particular stamp to the personalities and events that he illustrated during his early days at the Cape. Local people of Dutch descent, as depicted by Bell on a page headed 'The Boer', were seen as uncouth, greedy and dirty. On the other hand, dark-skinned slaves struck him as having a great capacity for merriment and a delight in music and dancing – despite their bare feet. And the town's élite, dressed in their colonial best at a race meeting at Green Point, were victims of Bell's ridicule when he sketched their carriage (with its passengers) overturning in the mud.

At this stage in his life Bell was not above creating 'types': his sketches show that, to him, Coloured women were perpetually embroiled in fights with one another while the men were invariably drunk. He observed people at work – washerwomen, knee-deep in a stream; convicts chopping wood; vegetable vendors hawking their wares through the town; 'Malay' fishermen in their *toerings* and pointed sandals – nothing escaped the notice of this observant young man or the piquancy of his pen.

While Bell drew others as they appeared to him, he, in turn, was sketched as an attractive young man with firm features and tousled hair. The artist was the visiting Indian civil servant, Charles D'Oyly – 'one of the most elegant, gentlemanlike, handsome and accomplished men of his day'[15] – to whom, almost certainly, Bell had been introduced by the Coles. Many years later, his friend Charles Piazzi Smyth, describing Bell as he was in his youth, wrote: 'He was a handsome-looking young fellow . . . not very tall, but broad-built and muscular, with a rather brown complexion, regular features of a refined and sculpturesque character, piercing black eyes, and dark lank hair.'[16]

How Charles Bell occupied his time when he was first at the Cape – other than by committing what he saw about him to paper – is uncertain, although Piazzi Smyth records that he spent 'a period of service' working for his uncle in the colonial secretary's office. This was situated in the government building,[17] formerly the slave lodge, which stood at the southern head of the Heerengracht and was thus in pleasant walking distance from Hope Mill. Interesting men came and went through the doors of those offices when Charles Bell started working there – fellow-Scotsman John Fairbairn, editor of the *South African Commercial Advertiser*, the Cape's first independent newspaper; Chief Justice Sir John Wylde, admired for the objectiveness of his judgments but censured for his scandalous private life – especially when it was rumoured that he had fathered a child by his own daughter.[18] Hard at work in the same building was Major Charles Cornwallis Michell, surveyor-general and artist, builder of bridges and designer of mountain passes, while the Rev. Abraham Faure, controversial but much respected minister of the Groote Kerk, had his office across the street. Altogether Cape Town had much to offer any young man of Charles Bell's calibre. Under the English the Colony remained a bastion of European culture and a centre of commerce, with such prosperous merchants as John

Bardwell Ebden[19] and Hamilton Ross[20] making their mark in every facet of the town's existence. In addition to a vibrant Commercial Exchange, meeting place of anyone of status in the town, it had, by 1830, spawned a free press, a public library, literary, philanthropic and medical societies, a natural history museum and a scientific institution.[21] In 1828 Sir Lowry Cole had officially opened the new Royal Observatory, and in October 1829 a group of dedicated citizens founded what was to become one of the country's most renowned educational institutions, the South African College.[22] For the physically active, there was hunting with horse and hounds on the Cape Flats – though in the absence of genuine foxes a luckless jackal had to suffice. And, from time to time, there were balls and receptions both at Government House and the Commercial Exchange with all the glitter and glamour that the Colony could muster. All in all, for an active and intelligent young man, it was a stimulating – albeit microcosmic – society in which to find oneself.

But of all the Cape Peninsula's many attractions, the magnificence of its natural surroundings has always appealed most strongly to anyone with an eye for beauty and the artistic skill with which to depict it. This was certainly true in 1832 when, it appears, eighteen-year-old Charles Bell set off, probably on

figure 6
At the races.
Ink and wash. 7.2 x 23.8 cm.
Coll: The Brenthurst Library

At the races: punters involved in minor but mortifying calamities as depicted by the lively pen of Charles Bell. Introduced by the British soon after their arrival at the Cape in 1795, horse racing provided entertainment for people of all walks of life and meetings were regarded as gala occasions. Unfortunately, the horses, both on the track and off it, were somewhat unreliable and Green Point Common, which provided the venue, became a veritable mud bath when it rained.

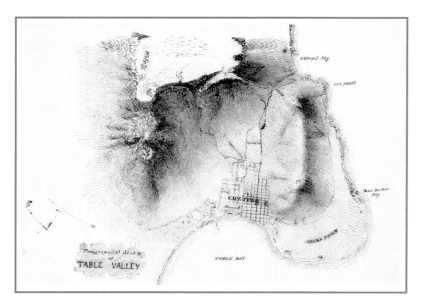

figure 7
Topographical sketch of Table Valley.
Pen and wash. 16.5 x 23.8 cm.
Bell Heritage Trust Collection, UCT

Early on in his life at the Cape, Charles Bell showed an interest in topography which was to reach fulfilment in his profession as a land surveyor. His sketch of Table Valley shows Cape Town, designed on the orderly grid system, with Devil's Peak, Table Mountain and Lion's Head forming an arc behind it. Table Bay lies at its northern boundary and the farmlands of lower Table Mountain are to its south. Green Point Common lies to the west of the town.

horseback, on an extended journey from Table Bay to Cape Point, and recorded what he saw in a sort of visual diary in the form of an album. Inscribed 'Cape Sketches' on the title page, the volume contains the earliest dated pictures by Charles Bell in the Bell Heritage Trust Collection and, by following them in sequence, it is possible to trace his movements as he travelled from place to place. Bell's chosen medium was pen and ink, and on some of the sketches he made notes regarding the topographical features of the landscape he depicted. Sometimes he gave details of colour and to several pictures he added small arrows, possibly to indicate wind direction.

It was at this time – and on the sketches in the Cape album – that Bell began to sign his works with a 'squiggle' that for almost 150 years remained an indecipherable mystery. It was only in the late 1970s that this signature, seen on a collection of sketches of unkown authorship acquired by the Brenthurst Library, began to puzzle and fascinate the well-known Johannesburg antiquary, Robin Fryde. By a fortunate coincidence, at about the same time, Fryde was visited by Father (now Monsignor) Donald de Beer of St Mary's Cathedral, Cape Town, who happened to be an enthusiastic student of early systems of shorthand. After careful study, Father de Beer identified the signature on the Brenthurst sketches as being written in a system of shorthand devised by a certain Samuel Taylor in the early nineteenth century.[23] In this system there were no vowel signs, but De Beer read the outlines as 'KRLS BL' or possibly 'CHRLS BL', a solution that indicated that the author of the Brenthurst sketches was Charles Bell. Even then he was well known to art historians, although most of his works were still in England. Also appearing on this collection was a longer inscription in which it seemed Taylor's shorthand was also

used. This Robin Fryde submitted to Geoffrey W. Bonsall, director of the Hong Kong Press and also an authority on old shorthand systems. He deciphered the outlines as reading 'FR LDY FRNSS KL', interpreted by Fryde as 'For Lady Frances Cole' – a solution that made sense in view of Charles Bell's relationship by marriage to the governor's wife. On the strength of information received from both Father de Beer and Geoffrey Bonsall, Robin Fryde was thus able to recognise the signature and to decipher other legends in Taylor's shorthand that appeared on the 'Cape Sketches'. All in all, the unravelling of the mysterious signature was an exciting discovery.

Charles began his pictorial journey on the eastern shores of Table Bay from which he sketched the town cradled by the three mountains. Then he travelled westwards along the shore to depict the Chavonnes defence battery built in the early eighteenth century and named after the governor of the time. He turned inland to Table Valley where Leeuwenhof[24] and Hope Mill proved subjects worthy of sketching; then he travelled along the Atlantic seaboard, depicting more houses, as well as views and seascapes, until he reached Hout Bay. Over Constantia Nek rode Charles, when the balmy autumn weather was at its best, and down into what are now Cape Town's southern suburbs, obviously to stay at – and sketch – Protea,[25] then the country house of Sir Lowry and Lady Frances Cole. Here, for the first time, he wrote the date, Monday 9th April 1832, on one of his pictures – an interesting detail for only a few days earlier Charles D'Oyly, who was also to sketch Protea on numerous occasions, arrived on a prolonged visit to the Cape. By 17 April Charles Bell had struggled through some forty kilometres of fynbos and crossed rocky mountains to reach Cape Point. On what appears to have been a calm day, he took to a boat, the *Curlew*, from which he sketched the glassy smooth sea and a scattering of houses along the coastline. Turning his back on the Peninsula's southernmost point, and possibly travelling by sea, Bell headed for Slangkop on the west coast and the great, silver sweep of Noordhoek beach which he reached, and sketched, on 19 April. Three days later – Sunday, 22nd – he was drawing the elegant homestead on the historic Constantia wine farm, Alphen, and then, dropping in on Protea and sketching it on the way, he headed back to his home at Hope Mill in the Gardens. There is no way of knowing whether Charles had any companions on his excursion, nor of precisely how long it lasted. However, in approximately a month he had recorded seascapes, landscapes and houses in 31 sketches which reveal him to be an acutely observant young man with an interest in geology and topography and a strong sense of form.[26] In the course of his travels he had covered the full length of the Cape Peninsula and, like so many others before and since, he became totally captivated by it for the rest of his life.

No 176 - The Merchant's Store - Cape Town 1839

figure 8
The merchant's store, Cape Town. 1839.
Pen and ink. 20.5 x 30 cm.
Coll: MuseumAfrica

Many of the merchants of Cape Town, including such well-known personalities as John Bardwell Ebden and Hamilton Ross, made fortunes and were therefore regarded as the 'aristocracy' of the Colony. They were welcome members of the society which met at Government House and among whom the Bells would have mixed. The top-hatted merchant whose store is depicted here clearly dealt in Cape wines and employed a 'Malay', complete with toering hat, as his driver.

figure 10
Hottentots dancing – Grahamstown. 1843.
Pencil. 18.5 x 23 cm.
Coll: MuseumAfrica

Once again Bell conveys, with a few deft strokes of his pencil, the inborn jauntiness of the Khoikhoi people and their love of merry-making. Despite their poverty, their ragged clothes and their clumsy physique, the women dancers, as seen by Bell, are both graceful and joyful.

figure 9
Hottentot.
Watercolour. 16.5 x 10.5 cm.
Bell Heritage Trust Collection, UCT

'Hottentot' is Charles Bell's simple caption for this painting of a drunken Khoikhoi, bottle in hand. Judging from his numerous depictions of these indigenous people, he saw them as being almost perpetually inebriated – cheap Cape wine being responsible for this condition. Nevertheless, by means of the rakish, feathered hat and the angle of foot and hand, he conveys the irrepressible, homespun humour which never fails to characterise the Cape Coloured people, no matter how ragged or oppressed they might be.

figure 11 **Coolies – Market Square.**
Watercolour. 14 x 22 cm.
Bell Heritage Trust Collection, UCT

Charles Bell captures a conversation between the bearded 'coolie' and his turbaned friend on the steps of the Town House,
headquarters of Cape Town's local government in those days. Their companion, a picture of indolence, lies asleep behind
them. The square, as its name implies, was for many years the scene of the town's fruit and vegetable
market to which 'coolies' employed as messengers would bring fresh produce from the farms in Table Valley.

figure 12 **Fruiterers.**
Watercolour. 13.5 x 21.5 cm.
Bell Heritage Trust Collection, UCT

In his paintings, Charles Bell records such familiar sights as the 'Malays' who plied their various trades in the streets and squares of Cape Town. They included the water-carrier with his pair of small barrels suspended from a pole balanced across his shoulders, while the fishmonger would carry his wares in twin baskets. Here a fruit seller passes the time with two women selling sweets.

figure 13

Malay washerwomen. 1833.
Ink and wash. 9.3 x 23.8 cm.
Coll: The Brenthurst Library

Charles Bell's early Cape sketches give a spirited picture of social life at every level. Here he depicts 'Malay' women engaged in one of their customary tasks, as they slap and thump their employers' dirty linen against the rocks in the process of washing it in the clear waters of a mountain stream. After ironing the dry washing at home, they would tie it up in a sheet and, bundle on head, carry it back to the house where it belonged.

figure 14

Malay family.
Watercolour. 14 x 21.5 cm.
Bell Heritage Trust Collection, UCT

Shown against shadowy Cape mountains, this elegantly dressed 'Malay' couple and their small child are depicted in clothes typical of their culture. The man wears a toering, jacket and waistcoat; the woman, her hair coiffed in sophisticated style, is in a graceful full-length muslin dress. Bell clearly saw these people as gracious and highly civilised – in fact, as superior in every respect to their 'Hottentot' neighbours.

figure 15 **Carbonatjie tents – Market Square.**
Watercolour. 13.5 x 21.5 cm. Bell Heritage Trust Collection, UCT

*Like so many other European newcomers to the Cape, Bell was fascinated by the exotic appeal of the 'Cape Malays'.
Here he shows them sheltering under an umbrella from the sun and the prevailing southeast wind while they sell
'carbonatjies', a favourite 'Malay' dish consisting of small mutton steaks grilled over red-hot coals.*

figure 16 **Travelling bullock wagon.**
Watercolour. 14 x 21.5 cm. Bell Heritage Trust Collection, UCT

In his years in South Africa, Charles Bell made many journeys in bullock-drawn wagons of this kind. Much was expected of the draught animals which, on occasions, had to be coaxed and goaded over the most rugged and dangerous of mountain passes. The narrow, covered section of the wagon often provided an uncomfortable 'home' for the passengers for weeks on end.

figure 17
**Elderly woman in a *doek*.
1841.**
Watercolour. 10.2 x 8 cm.
Coll: MuseumAfrica

*Bell captioned this small painting
'Malay in Cape Town'; perhaps it
would be more accurate to label it
'The Matriarch', for dignity and
wisdom are inherent in every line.
The elderly lady wears a turban,
a spotlessly starched fichu and
a full skirt over many petticoats –
an outfit obviously kept for
special occasions.*

figure 18
Untitled.
Watercolour. 18 x 24 cm.
University of the Witwatersrand
Library

*Bell's sense of the incongruous
frequently led him to capture a
moment of absurdity with a few
strokes of pen or brush. Here,
a rickety vehicle drawn by four
recalcitrant horses and with a
'Cape Malay' in the driving seat
appears to be taking its passengers
to some national celebration.*

Chapter 2

TOWARDS CAPRICORN

The Cape civil service, during the nineteenth century, was an excellent training school for a young man intent on rising to a position of responsibility and status in the community. Loyalty and absolute integrity were required of him, and all official business had to be dealt with both quickly and efficiently so that no arrears could gather dust in silent pigeonholes. The yearly issues of the Cape Almanac *reflect the steady rise of many a young man destined to make his name in the Colony and Charles Bell was no exception. In November 1832 he was transferred from his uncle's office to that of the Master of the Supreme Court and a year later was moved to the Colonial Audit Office where, as second clerk, he earned an annual salary of £100. He became 'a favourite everywhere,' wrote his contemporary, the astronomer, Charles Piazzi Smyth, 'until it seemed as if his friends intended the young man for a future of nothing but a quiet, resident, jog-trot official life in Cape Town itself, and no further'.[1]*

Charles Bell, however, thought otherwise and there were times when his musings ranged far beyond the cramped confines of the Cape's government offices and into an exciting world of discovery and high adventure. Travellers to the interior brought back tales of breathtaking experiences and marvellous sights, but there seemed little likelihood, at first, that Charles Bell would have an opportunity to see all these wonders for himself. At last, in June 1833, when he had been at the Cape for almost three years, there was talk of official plans for a journey of exploration into Central Africa on a grander scale than anything so far attempted. This was just the sort of enterprise guaranteed to capture Charles's imagination and as soon as he learnt of it (according to Piazzi Smyth) 'the internal fires of [his] spirit broke forth' and instantly he determined that he would be among the selected few destined to penetrate 'the great unknown'.[2]

It had all begun on 5 June 1833 when, at a meeting of the South African Literary and Scientific Institution, a paper was read describing a recent trading excursion that had penetrated the interior as far as the Tropic of Capricorn. The leaders of the party, two traders named Hume and Millen, had brought back to the Cape the first reliable account of the region where the vast and enigmatic Lake Ngami could be located and where the Matabele (Ndebele) warrior king, Mzilikazi, a fugitive from Shaka's bloody offensives, had established a realm of his own. The paper aroused such interest among the audience that an official and scientific expedition into the areas described by Hume was

immediately proposed and unanimously accepted. Within days, the Cape of Good Hope Association for Exploring Central Africa had been established, its objective to expand geographical knowledge; to 'obtain Scientific Information, especially as regards Meteorology, Geology and Magnetism; to collect Botanical Specimens and those of Natural History; and to ascertain what prospects the productions of the Country and the disposition the Native Tribes [held] out to Commercial Enterprise'.[3] To these official objectives, Sir Lowry Cole personally added a mandate that the expedition should 'confer with the chiefs of the principal tribes in order to induce them to give up their barbarous practices, to accord a more favourable reception to traders, and protection to Christian missionaries'.[4] Needless to say, there was one serious stumbling block – 'inadequacy of the pecuniary means of the Institution available for such an undertaking'.[5] The solution was one commonly resorted to at the Cape: the project would 'go public' and make shares at £3 each available to interested parties. By February 1834, when the required target of £1000 was reached and plans could go ahead,[6] Sir Lowry Cole had been succeeded as governor by Sir Benjamin D'Urban. His immediate task was to establish the Cape's first legislative council, but he also found time to give the expedition his unqualified support.

Ever since the latter years of the fifteenth century, when Africa was first rounded by Portuguese mariners bent on discovering a sea route to the East, the subcontinent's mysterious southern interior had presented an irresistible challenge to men in search of adventure. Undaunted by its rugged mountains, its rivers and deserts and its seemingly impenetrable bush, they had set forth cheerfully for the unknown – the hunters and the missionaries, the botanists, the traders, the prospectors for gold and the seekers after the elusive empire of Monomotapa. Some had returned sick, weary and crestfallen; others had come back laden with precious ivory or rare plants. And there were those, of course, who had disappeared without trace. Any further disasters of this kind should be avoided at all costs, declared the organisers of the expedition, and to ensure its success it was vitally important to select a suitable leader. Fortunately the choice was an obvious one, for nobody doubted that a dynamic and enterprising Scotsman named Dr Andrew Smith would be the right man. Born in 1797 and son of a shepherd turned market gardener, Smith's high intelligence had secured him a place at Edinburgh University where he qualified in medicine before joining the British Army. In 1820 he was ordered to the Eastern Cape to serve the needs of newly arrived British Settlers – a fortunate move for him, since it gave him the opportunity to develop his interest not only in the natural history of southern Africa, but also in the culture of the local indigenous people. Indeed, Governor Lord Charles Somerset was so inspired by Smith's enthusiasm for his

figure 1
Sir Andrew Smith.
South African Museum

Dr Andrew Smith (1797–1872), destined to be knighted by Queen Victoria for his achievements as an army surgeon, dedicated naturalist, explorer, government emissary and author, was leader of the expedition to Capricorn. The original portrait, probably painted by Bell during the expedition, has not been traced and may be in the possession of Smith's descendants in Scotland.

figure 2
The outspan.
Watercolour. 12.5 x 18 cm.
Old Mutual Collection

Dr Andrew Smith (the bearded figure on the left), his party and their horses relax during their journey towards the Tropic of Capricorn in 1834.

hobbies that in 1825 he ordered the establishment of a museum in Cape Town and released the doctor from his military duties so that he could take over as superintendent.

Meanwhile, as 1834 progressed, preparations for the expedition went ahead. Stores had to be assembled; scientific instruments were borrowed or bought; elephant guns and other weapons arrived from England as did beads, mirrors and other

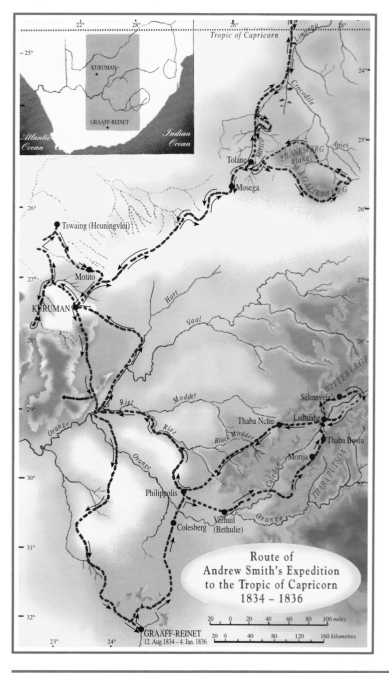

Route of
Andrew Smith's Expedition
to the Tropic of Capricorn
1834 – 1836

objects intended as gifts for the indigenous tribes they expected to meet. At least five sturdy wagons and 120 oxen had to be acquired – Dr Smith, fortunately, was able to provide his own transport. Then there was the difficult matter of selecting the men who would make up the party, for not only was it essential that they have disparate skills, but it was important that they should prove good companions during a sojourn in the wilderness expected to last almost two years. By the end of June, Smith had chosen his team. It included, among others, Captain William Edie of the 98th Regiment as his deputy; John Burrow, only eighteen years old but entrusted with the considerable responsibilities of astronomer and surveyor; George Ford, a talented draughtsman known to Smith since his childhood, who was to make a pictorial record of the fauna of the region; and, to investigate the possibilities of establishing commerce with the interior, a trader named Benjamin Kift. The more menial tasks were assigned to a handful of rough-and-ready men, both civilian and military, while a number of Khoikhoi were employed to drive the wagons and care for the animals.

From his office in the Heerengracht, Charles Bell watched the hectic activity with keen interest and envy. Now in his twenty-first year, he was a personable young man who had impressed the renowned astronomer, Sir John Herschel, newly arrived from England, as having 'much good information & desire for more – [and] with decided pursuits and industry to make progress in them'.[7] Herschel was not alone in his opinion of Bell, for his colleague, Thomas Maclear (he had recently been appointed His Majesty's Astronomer at the Cape), wrote of him at much the same time: 'This young man's extraordinary talents added to his energetic courage would secure, I am told, success in any undertaking he might embark in'.[8] Surely, one would think, Bell was an obvious candidate for such an expedition, but the party was complete and it seemed there was no room for him. However, when plans were all but settled, Andrew Smith decided to include Bell as a second draughtsman, entrusting him with the task of keeping a pictorial diary of the African landscape and of the customs and appearance of the indigenous people encountered in the interior. Only a day or two before the expedition was due to leave, Bell was told of his appointment and was instantly caught up in such a whirligig of euphoria that he mounted his horse and galloped with 'wild excitement through the streets of Cape Town to dash off preparation for an instant start.'[9] No matter that his rank in the expedition would be the lowest; to be included at any level was his dearest dream come true. But first, he had to compose himself sufficiently to write to the auditor-general informing him that 'being desirous of accompanying the Expedition for Exploring Central Africa ... I have to request you will be pleased to assist me in obtaining His Excellency the

Governor's Leave of absence for that purpose'.[10] Sir Benjamin D'Urban was away on the Eastern Frontier but his deputy, Baron de Lorentz, seems to have been perfectly agreeable to the request and the young man got his way.

All Cape Town joined in the expedition's tumultuous send-off. It included a 'sumptuous banquet'[11] at which the skirling of bagpipes aroused feelings of nostalgia within every Scottish breast – and there were several present besides those of Andrew Smith and Charles Bell. Some of the heavier ox-wagons, as well as stores and equipment, had been sent ahead to the expedition's official starting point at Graaff-Reinet. On the morning of 3 July, after a substantial breakfast at the Observatory, the explorers themselves set off on the first stage of their journey. Travelling grandly in horse-wagons, they crossed the Hex River Mountains and the fringes of the Great Karoo, arriving at Graaff-Reinet on 18 July. Here several 'passengers' joined the party, among them the surveyor-hunter, Andrew Geddes Bain[12] and three German missionaries.[13] Inevitably there were problems and delays but at last, on 12 August, the silence of the Karoo dawn was cleft by the crack of whips, and men, horses and oxen, their breath steaming in the wintry air, set off towards the north. The hearts of the youngest of the explorers must have thudded with excitement – none more so than that of Charles Bell.

He had already shown signs of a remarkable desire for knowledge in a variety of disciplines, including astronomy,[14] and now he began to acquire from John Burrow – a high-spirited youth who soon became his boon companion – basic information concerning land surveying. There was plenty of time for the young men to talk as they plodded across the Karoo. Ravaged by drought, it was a dreary sight,[15] but on 22 August there was some relief when the caravan rolled into the newly established village of Colesberg. To the explorers' amazement they discovered themselves in company with what seemed a vast multitude of people and wagons closing on the little town from every direction. This, as it turned out, was the weekend set for the quarterly celebration of *nagmaal*, or Holy Communion. 'Each wagon,' wrote Andrew Smith in his diary, 'disgorged a small tent which was pitched close to the vehicle, and in that the family resided during its stay.'[16] Local shopkeepers hastily capitalised on the occasion by organising a kind of fair,[17] while many of the visitors,

taking advantage of the unexpected presence of a doctor, pestered Andrew Smith with requests for medical treatment.

Nagmaal over and the assemblage scattered, Smith led his party on towards the Orange River, northern limit of the Cape Colony, which they reached on 26 August. Though not as impressive as Smith had expected, the river was 'a noble stream for South Africa in the month of August'.[18] Among the trees on the bank opposite to Smith's camp site, someone spied a somewhat tumble-down Bechuana kraal and, emerging from it, the first real 'natives' Bell and Burrow had ever seen. 'I assure you I stared...' wrote Burrow,[19] 'for they were wrapped in karosses and their faces and bodies were well rubbed with red stone and grease.'

On trundled Smith's wagons and, two days later, the explorers were heartened to see the Union Jack fluttering in welcome as they entered the village of Philippolis. Named after the missionary, John Philip, it had been founded eleven years earlier as a refuge for displaced Griquas under the leadership of Adam Kok II.[20] Since then it had become the capital of Griqua territory whose

figure 3
The Orange River near Buffel's Vlei. 1834.
Watercolour (monochrome).
17.3 x 23.5 cm.
Coll: MuseumAfrica

When Smith's party reached this point towards the end of August 1834, they found the river to be (in Smith's words) 'a noble stream'. Bell's depiction of it here shows it to be much as Smith described it in his Journal. *'The beauty of its limpid waters,' wrote Smith, '[was] skirted on both sides by fine verdant foliage, and either gliding in a gentle current over a stony channel or apparently motionless in large pools.'*

inhabitants, during the fortnight that the party spent there, Bell had ample opportunity to observe and sketch. At Philippolis the party split up; the German missionaries had decided to remain there for the time being, while Andrew Bain and his party went off to capture live animals for export to America. Later Bain was to dispatch a letter to John Centlivres Chase, secretary of the Literary and Scientific Institution in Cape Town, reporting on the 'order and harmony' that had prevailed throughout the entire period he had travelled with the explorers. 'Dr Smith is the most indefatigable man I ever met with,' ran his letter. 'Nothing comes amiss to him; he sees everything done himself and trusts nothing to others.'[21] According to Bain, every member of the expedition knew exactly where his responsibilities lay, and both Bell and Ford had already revealed their talents as competent artists. 'The graphic and Cruikshankian labours of Mr Bell,' wrote Bain, 'with the delicate and minute products of Mr Ford's pencil were the subject of daily admiration of all.'

Their wagons repaired and their animals refreshed, Smith's party bade farewell to Philippolis and travelled on towards the southeast. They halted at Verhuil (now Bethulie), a station run by the Paris Evangelical Missionary Society, and then set off hoping to discover the source of the Caledon River. This part of the country, as Bell depicted it, was a seemingly interminable plain covered with waving blond grass interrupted only by flat-topped

figure 5
Sikonyela chief of the Mantatees. 1834.
Watercolour. 22.5 x 14.5 cm.
Coll: MuseumAfrica

Bell described Sekonyela as chief of the 'Mantatees' but, more correctly, he was chief of the Tlokwa. Unlike Moshoeshoe, he did not welcome the arrival of Smith's party. In fact, John Burrow describes him as having 'a thorough bad countenance, and every action was so suspicious that we were always expecting the worst'. Bell shows him with his customary kaross thrown over his shoulders, although Andrew Smith was later to present him with a cloak and a medal as tokens of friendship.

hills, their rocky sides scattered with a stubble of small thorny bushes. The travellers soon reached the river and followed its course which, in this area, was fringed with lush green trees rich in birdlife – a temptation to any man with a gun on a fine spring day. Corporal George McKenzie, one of the soldiers in the group, loaded his weapon and fired at a wild duck – but, in attempting to retrieve it, was caught in a tangle of weeds and dragged under the water. His companions were horrified to see him disappear, and for hours Charles Bell, perched on a frail raft, searched frantically for the man's body. All attempts were in vain: the unhappy McKenzie had vanished for ever. 'It is much to be feared that he was ill fitted for so sudden an end,' wrote Andrew Smith in his diary. 'He professed to be a disbeliever of our Saviour, and, poor fellow, he had at last little time to think and get rid of such horrible notions.'

October came and with it the rains. Heading northwards through the long grass, the wagons jolted along the mountain fringes of what had, in recent years, become the realm of King Moshoeshoe, founder of the Sotho nation and its first paramount chief. Somewhere in this region, on 8 October, a male lion materialised from the bush and attacked an unsuspecting Khoikhoi. Fortunately Burrow, with (in Smith's words) 'a coolness and intrepidity extraordinary in a youth eighteen years of age', dispatched the animal with a single shot and rescued its terrified victim literally from the jaws of death.[22]

Morija, a mission settlement lying at the foot of the magnificent Thaba Putsoa, or Blue-grey Mountain, was the travellers'

figure 4
A day's sport with Moshesh. Jacob runs the quagga to a standstill. 1834.
Watercolour (monochrome).
11.5 x 17 cm.
Coll: MuseumAfrica

While Smith and his party were visiting Moshoeshoe, king and founder of the Sotho nation, they joined a quagga hunt. Bell's companion, John Burrow, wrote of it: 'They are the only tribe I ever saw that hunted with horses; and it was a beautiful sight to see them galloping after the Quaggas . . . until they came up alongside the one they had singled out, when they generally brought them down with two or three stabs.'

next important stopping-place. The station's director was the Rev. Jean-Eugène Casalis of the Paris Evangelical Mission Society,[23] a man held in such great respect by the local people that their king, on hearing of the arrival of Smith's party, mounted his horse and galloped some thirty kilometres from his isolated mountain stronghold at Thaba Bosiu[24] to welcome them to his kingdom. 'We all agreed,' wrote John Burrow, 'that [Moshoeshoe] was the picture of a Chief, although he wore, in honor of us, dirty European clothes and a large broad-brimmed hat.'[25]

Heartened by Moshoeshoe's friendly approach, Smith decided to return his visit and travel to his hill-top citadel. With Bell and Burrow leading the way, the party started out on 22 October on a daunting mountain climb to Moshoeshoe's palace. Here the king, surrounded by his headmen, greeted them warmly, offering them 'an enormous wooden bowl full of meat cooked in no despicable manner'.[26] Smith, in return, presented his host with a medal and a cloak, at the same time obtaining his assurance that

he would continue to encourage the work of Christian missionaries among his people.

Their spirits cheered by their reception by one of the region's great kings, the explorers set off again, travelling through magnificent country which, at this season, was teeming with game of every kind. There were flocks of ostrich, various types of antelope roaming free, herds of zebra and quagga seemingly under no threat from man, as well as an occasional prowling lion. Across the Caledon River at Lishuane – also known as New Boetsap – they stopped for a few days at a Wesleyan mission station run by the Rev. John Edwards before setting off for the country of the Tlokwa. Here they arrived on 7 November but, much to their disappointment, they found the people suspicious both of them and of the gifts they offered. Their chief, Sekonyela, could scarcely be described as hospitable, though, after some persuasion from Smith, he did grudgingly agree to 'abstain from aggression'.[27] Perhaps it was a spectacular – and to

figure 7 **A grand hunt – game driven by the Barolong of Thabe Unchoo. 1834.**
Watercolour (monochrome). 14 x 24 cm. Coll: MuseumAfrica

Bell's impression of a 'grand hunt' which he and his companions were invited to join near Thaba 'Nchu in November 1834. Smith's party never ceased to be amazed by the teeming game that they witnessed roaming over an area of Africa as yet largely unexplored and certainly unspoilt. Nevertheless, John Burrow, for one, was sickened by the gross slaughter that was inflicted on quagga, antelopes of all kinds, wildebeest and other game on this occasion.

him, terrifying – display of fireworks that Smith's men organised that persuaded him that it would be wise to treat his visitors with respect.

Meanwhile, Captain Edie had suffered an unpleasant accident.

This occurred when he woke in his wagon one morning to see three lions ambling along the bank of the river. In his panic and haste to fire at them he somehow mishandled his gun and shot himself in the hand with such force that the ball passed right through it and whizzed past his whiskers.[28] Fortunately for him, Smith's immediate and professional attention saved what remained of his hand.

On rolled the cavalcade of wagons until, on 27 November, it reached Thaba 'Nchu – or Black Mountain – site of another Wesleyan mission station. Here Bell was hard at work sketching the Barolong, depicting them both dead (their burial customs were interesting) and engaged in a variety of occupations. The principal excitement of this visit was a hunt organised by the local chief, Moroka II, for the benefit of his guests. He took them to a wide plain where there were tremendous herds of antelope of various kinds grazing peacefully in the grass. His huntsmen rounded them up by closing in on them until they were closely packed in a circle three-quarters of a mile wide. Then, wrote Burrow, 'We began to chase and kill as much as we could, and all that were driven to the edge were stabbed while endeavouring to break through the ring'.[29] Eventually, even Burrow was sickened by the slaughter. 'The amount of what we shot, or rather murdered, I forget,' he wrote, 'but it was enormous.'

Heading southwest, the explorers crossed the Black Modder River where, for the first time, they encountered a group of Bushmen. 'A more miserable group of human beings could scarcely be conceived,' commented Andrew Smith in his *Journal*. 'They were besmeared from head to foot by what *we would call* filth, but which they consider convenient and essential to their comfort.'[30] Charles Bell sketched them dancing and hunting and he drew their weapons. He depicted the Modder River in water-colour and the explorers' outspan beside it – but the beauty of the landscape as he portrayed it was deceptive. Burrow records that by day the heat was unbearable and that throughout the night he and his companions were tormented by mosquitoes.[31] Occasionally, in this remote region, the explorers encountered families of wandering trekboers in their dilapidated wagons; these, too, Bell sketched and painted, conveying with both skill and humour their austere lifestyle.

At last, a few days before Christmas 1834, Smith's wagons, now much travel-stained, arrived back in Philippolis and any weariness the travellers might have been feeling was dispelled by the sight of the pile of letters awaiting them. There was one addressed to Charles Bell from his mother and even though it had been written the previous May, he was overjoyed to receive it. 'You cannot imagine with what pleasure I read over the news from East Nook,' he wrote to his mother the following day in his clear, cursive script, 'for even though valued much in Cape Town [letters] are even ten times more so when rec[d] in this far away land & they bring back the thoughts & remembrance of home more strongly when there is nothing to distract the mind & prevent it from dwelling on them.' Bell writes fondly of various members of his family – aunts and uncles, his grandmother, sister Christina and brother David. He mentions, too, his uncle, John Bell, in Cape Town from whom he had received 'a very kind letter letting me know that had he been in Cape Town I would never have come on this pleasure jaunt by his leave & had I thought it possible he would have objected I should never have thought of it for a moment'.[32]

To his parents, far away in Scotland where a black face was seldom if ever seen, Charles's reaction to the indigenous people he had encountered on the expedition must have been both comforting and interesting. 'We have found the Natives civil, hospitable & kind,' he told his mother, '& have met with more assistance from them than we could have got for nothing had we travelled as long in the Land o' Cakes[33] & yet these are the people of whose cruelties, barbarity, & ferociousness travellers write & traders tell.' Charles assured his parents that he had never before been in better health despite 'heat, cold, sun & rain – night watching & daily fatigue'. He told them that all the members of the party got on 'good-humouredly together' and that Smith was 'an excellent fellow in every way'. Yet why, one wonders, did he did not tell them that it was he whom Smith had delegated to take the Sunday services while on trek, even though (Burrow excepted) he was the youngest member of the party?[34] And why did he not once allude to the numerous drawings, paintings and sketches that he had made during the course of the journey? However, some shirts Mrs Bell had sent her son were deemed

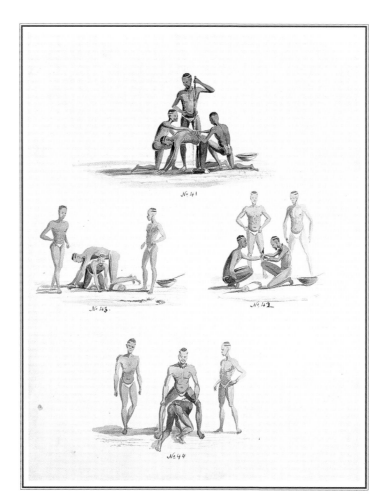

figure 8
Barolong purification of a warrior who has slain a man in battle. 1834.
Watercolour (monochrome).
26 x 19.5 cm.
Coll: MuseumAfrica

In the detail of this series of drawings showing a Barolong warrior undergoing purification, Bell is obviously mindful of his particular responsibility, as a member of the Expedition into Central Africa, to illustrate the manners and customs of the indigenous people they encountered.

worthy of comment, even though 'at present you could see few symptoms of dandyism about me, for we can take but few clothes to load the wagons … & then the thorn bushes make sad work of everything but leathers'.

Another letter that reached Charles Bell in Philippolis came from twelve-year-old Christina, and his affectionate reply is another among the few personal letters that have survived.

> I rec^d your nice little tidy short letter here a few days ago, having just arrived from far on the other side of 'the back of beyont' … I think you would have laughed to see your Brother paying visits of ceremony to the Chiefs & supping thick sour milk & cold porridge with them – King Moscheshe (sic) of the Basothos took a particular fancy to me & would have made me his son in Law I dare say – he presented me to his daughter who kissed my hand in a sweet gracious manner & brought me corn & Caffre beer – She paid me a visit afterwards at the waggons & I painted her cheeks green & her brow red & I tipped her nose with gold leaf & she told me through the Interpreter that she thought me a very sweet young man. But I had not the least ambition to become the son in law even of the Basuto king for all his cattle & herds & tribes of naked Savages.

Clearly the expedition was living up to all Charles had hoped. He was seeing wild animals in their thousands against their own rugged, African background, besides having the opportunity to enjoy 'excellent shooting & hunting'. The 'Eiland' was the biggest of all the creatures, 'larger than an ox', he told Christina, but none was more appealing than the 'beautiful & graceful Springbuck'. It was all novel, marvellous and exciting, yet he confessed to Christina that sometimes he longed to be sitting in the parlour at home, 'listening to my Father's Fiddle, or telling

Mama and you long stories of what I saw in the Centre of Africa & I assure you I will tell long ones of dreadful dangers & hair-breadth escapes, of savage beasts & more savage men, but whether they are true or not you must never inquire'.[35]

But, the oxen were being inspanned and it was time for the party to leave Philippolis and continue on its northward journey. Unfortunately Captain Edie's injured hand did not improve and he was obliged to return to Cape Town for more sophisticated treatment than any Smith and his first-aid box could provide. For some distance the captain rode alongside the wagons and then, 'wishing us success,' wrote Burrow, '[he] left us with a heavy heart amidst firing and cheering'. Edie had taken charge of the impressive collection of museum specimens that had been assembled *en route*. Carefully packed for delivery to the Association for Exploring Central Africa were 491 birds, 59 quadrupeds and 188 reptiles, besides quantities of geological specimens and ethnic curios. In addition Edie took with him no fewer than 131 drawings and paintings executed by George Ford and Charles Bell.[36]

Over four months had passed since Smith's men had left Graaff-Reinet and their objective now was New Latakoo, or Kuruman as it was more properly known. This mission station was a veritable oasis on the arid northern boundary of the Cape Colony and headquarters, since 1824, of Robert Moffat of the London Missionary Society.[37] During this lap of the journey it rained almost ceaselessly, forcing the wagons to wait for days on the banks of the overflowing Vaal River. As last the water-level dropped, but even then the explorers had to wade, chin deep, across the torrent while the oxen were forced to swim.[38] One of the wagons stuck in the mud; another overturned, washing away 'our small stock of necessaries' (Burrow's words), including a quantity of precious gunpowder.

On 30 January 1835, Smith's wagons, more than a little battered by now, reached 'the long wished-for Latakoo … the most perfect Station we had yet seen'.[39] They found an orderly village dominated by a fine church and with neat stone houses surrounded by beautiful, well-stocked gardens. Smith was greatly impressed by what had been achieved; the mission station served to confirm his belief that 'religion and civilisation go hand in hand with rapid strides'.[40] However, the visitors' joy at finding themselves among friends was somewhat subdued when they learnt that Moffat himself was desperately ill with fever, and that his wife, Mary, was at 'the very gates of death' after having given birth to a son.[41] Smith, whose arrival Moffat later described as 'a dispensation of mercy, ordered by that gracious Providence, without whom a sparrow cannot fall to the ground', immediately attended to his hosts' needs and before long both Robert and Mary were restored to health.

figure 9
Pack oxen crossing the Vaal River. 1835.
Watercolour. 9 x 17.8 cm.
Coll: MuseumAfrica

When Smith's party reached the Vaal River early in January 1835 they found it in flood and were obliged to wait almost two weeks before the water subsided and they dared to make the crossing. The pack oxen were launched into the raging current and eventually landed safely on the other side. According to Smith's Journal, 'the oxen swam for nearly the whole distance, the depth of the water being from five to five feet ten inches'.

One of Smith's most important projects was to survey the uncharted region bordering present-day Botswana, but for this he required permission from the Matabele king, Mzilikazi, in whose territory it lay. Moffat, who was fortunately on excellent terms with the monarch, immediately dispatched a messenger – he was promised the gift of a cow for his labours – to travel to the royal village of Mosega, about a week's journey north of the mission station, and arrange a meeting. While the man was away, Smith, taking Bell, Burrow and some others with him, set off to survey the edge of the Kalahari desert northwest of Kuruman. It proved to be an exhausting expedition. Intense heat alternated with violent, drenching thunderstorms. Smith's horse, his faithful companion since his days in the Eastern Cape, contracted a fatal disease and died in what Burrow described as 'great torture'. On one occasion, Charles Bell and a soldier named Tennant somehow lost touch with the wagons and were forced to spend an entire night clinging precariously to the branches of a thorn tree while rain pelted them from above and lions roared threateningly below. Youthful resilience was on their side, however, and once safely on the ground they managed to rejoin their companions. Together they travelled on until they reached a dry saltpan, today known as Heuningvlei. Game abounded in the vicinity, and it was in this region that the travellers saw giraffe for the first time.

On 10 May 1835, the returning party reached the French mission station at Motito where they met Moffat's messenger on his way back from Mzilikazi's kraal. The king, he said, was prepared to receive the party as long as they had 'clean hearts' – but woe betide them if they dared to lay hands on a single one of his cattle![42] Fortunately, they were joined by Robert Moffat himself soon afterwards; he was the ideal person to act as intermediary between Smith and Mzilikazi, for a sincere friendship already existed between the missionary and the monarch.[43] Wagons were inspanned immediately and the long-suffering horses were saddled (Bell's had also succumbed to horse disease by this time and Burrow's luckless mount was to die soon afterwards), and once more the explorers were on trek.

This area was untamed Africa. There were no defined roads for the wagons to follow and travellers, struggling over rocky terrain abounding with snakes and other wild creatures, had to make their way from one waterhole to the next. But the scenery was savagely beautiful, and a drawing that Charles Bell made of the explorers' outspan on the banks of the Great Choai saltpan gives a graphic idea of both the landscape and the encampment.

It was at this place that Smith's men had the exciting experience of seeing and hunting down their first rhinoceros – an incident that Bell illustrated, stage by stage. Burrow's diary records that there were two known species of rhino – the black and the white – but 'with ourselves, lies the merit of the discovery of an

entirely new sort … having two horns of equal length. If this had been the only discovery we made, natural history could not have complained of the Expedition.'[44]

When, at the end of May, the explorers reached the approach to Mosega they were met by one of Mzilikazi's *indunas*, a man named Mklapi, who had been sent to accompany them to the royal village. Their fame, it seems, had gone before them, and hardly had Mklapi arrived at the camp when he begged to see the sketches made by Ford and Bell. At the sight of them, his astonishment was unbounded, for pictorial art, so it seems, was unknown to his people. 'He closely surveyed each drawing,' Andrew Smith wrote in his journal, 'and after having done that he closely inspected the back of the paper expecting to find appearances of the actual objects themselves, but observing them to be perfectly smooth and white, his wonder appeared tenfold.'[45] Mklapi was then introduced to the two artists whom he inspected solemnly from head to foot, no doubt seeking some indication of the extraordinary powers they possessed.

Early in June Smith led his men into Mosega – but Mzilikazi was nowhere to be seen! Smallpox was rife in the land and in terror of contracting it, the king had fled to one of his most

figure 11
First reception by Matzelikatzi. 1835.
Watercolour (monochrome).
11.5 x 17.8 cm.
Coll: MuseumAfrica

Bell's record of the first meeting with Mzilikazi, in June 1835. Seated on stools which they had judiciously provided themselves, Smith's party gaze with respect on the founder of the Matabele nation. The meeting was held in a cattle kraal, and there was nothing in the king's appearance, Smith commented in his Journal, 'save his nakedness which was calculated to excite disagreeable impression . . . He is rather low of station,' continued Smith, 'and embonpoint giving every evidence of there being no want of beef or beer where he resides.'

remote kraals. Undaunted, the expedition pressed on, and in a kraal beside the Tolane River they came across the mighty king of the Matabele hidden away in an insignificant hut. Nevertheless, the meeting was a friendly one: Mzilikazi ordered his warriors to honour his guests with war dances and to demonstrate their skills at praise-singing, both of which diversions Bell – judging by his sketches – found extremely entertaining. The explorers, unable to repay the king in like manner, showed Mzilikazi their scientific instruments in which he took considerable interest, as his people did in their clothes and other possessions. Then, after an amicable parting, Smith and his men headed off towards the southeast to explore the Magaliesberg.

Herds of white rhinoceros ranged freely in this area and once more Bell depicted a hunt, this time with almost grisly humour. Here, too, hippopotamus grazed in vast numbers and the explorers, unable to resist such an easy target, immediately fired at the defenceless creatures. Within three hours no fewer than seven had been slaughtered and the river ran red with their blood. 'The whole camp soon became a scene of cooking and eating,' wrote Burrow; the meat had an interesting taste and he, personally, found hippopotamus foot roasted on an ant-heap to be 'a great dainty'.[46]

On went the caravan, heading in an easterly direction, but when the wagons arrived at the confluence of the Magalies and Crocodile rivers the wagons were too wide for the narrow *poort* through which the mingled waters flowed.[47] Smith then turned towards the northwest and, travelling along the slopes of the Pilanesberg, reached their former outspan at Tolane at the end of July. Here, they parted with Moffat, who was understandably anxious to return to his wife in Kuruman, and pursued their journey towards the northern limits of Mzilikazi's territory. Charles Bell appears to have revelled in the splendour of the landscape, depicting the bold colours of rock and grass that changed as variously as the patterns in a kaleidoscope. But his paintings were not limited to scenery: among other things, he recorded a variety of brutal punishments meted out by Mzilikazi to people supposed to have committed offences.

Unfortunately, the explorers' brief stop at Tolane was not a peaceful one. Rumbles of discontent among the 'lower orders' turned to open protest when the men learnt that Smith, instead of turning homewards at this point, intended to continue towards the Tropic of Capricorn and so fulfil his pledge to the shareholders. A few fierce words from the director diffused the ugly situation, though one of the mutineers, Andries Botha, remained stubbornly recalcitrant. This man was reputedly an excellent shot and for this reason Smith had included him in his party, even though it meant obtaining his release from prison where he was serving a sentence for murder.

Now it was the beginning of August and the expedition had been on trek for over a year. Reluctantly, Smith's men once more inspanned their oxen and set off towards the north, making their weary way along the course of the Marico River until it joined the Limpopo. Leaving most of the party and the exhausted oxen at this point, a group consisting of Smith, John Burrow and ten of the men, continued towards the Tropic. Thorn bushes blocked their paths and ripped their clothes; tumbled rocks almost upset their wagon, but they pressed on, even though the river was running dry and there was scarcely any grass. At last, on 6 September, Dr Andrew Smith and his men triumphantly reached the Tropic of Capricorn, surveyed their surroundings with joyous hearts, and set off to rejoin the rest of the party before gratefully turning for home.

The journey back to the Cape took the travellers through Mosega where Mzilikazi again welcomed them warmly and announced that one of his chief *indunas*, a man named Mkumbati, and his suite would accept their invitation and accompany them to Cape Town in order to consolidate the king's relations with the British government. Then, taking leave of their host and loaded with gifts, the explorers continued towards Kuruman and their friends, the Moffats. From there they travelled southwards, on the way fording the flooded and turbulent Orange River on a rickety pontoon. By now the relentless demands of the long journey and the unremitting hostility of the African terrain had become too much for their weary animals. One by one the faithful oxen were overcome by sickness or exhaustion, and the travellers grieved to see them dropping dead beside the track. Then there followed the horrifying experience of the irresponsible (and, according to John Burrow, tipsy) Andries Botha, who was clawed to death by a lion – no doubt fair punishment for having betrayed Smith's trust in him.

At last, the travel-weary explorers reached the borders of the Cape Colony and on 4 January 1836 they staggered into Graaff-Reinet, their mission accomplished and their sponsors' faith in them justified. But still they had to endure a wagon journey to Port Elizabeth and eight days at sea cramped in a small brig before they and their precious cargo – not to mention Mzilikazi's envoys – sailed safely into Table Bay. An enthusiastic crowd of friends and relations greeted them, none more welcoming than Colonel John Bell and his wife. They must have been proud indeed to learn that Charles, who had left nearly two years before as the least important member of the group, had returned as its second in command.[48] Hardly more than a boy when they

last saw him, he had developed into a confident young adult, his skin tanned by the African sun, his intellect sharpened and his emotions matured by all he had experienced. During the excursion he had recorded, in some two hundred sketches and paintings executed with lively and steadily improving skill, sights and scenes of an Africa and its people until then unknown and undreamt of by the rest of the world.

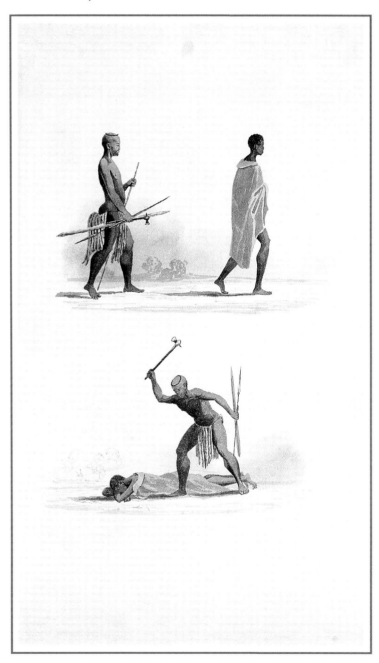

figure 12
Prisoner conducted to execution. The penalty for witchcraft. 1835.
Watercolour (monochrome).
28 x 20.5 cm.
Coll: MuseumAfrica

Anyone suspected of plotting against the life of Mzilikazi could expect a horrible death in retribution, as depicted here by Charles Bell. As many as ten malefactors could be brutally killed in a single day, and on one occasion Mzilikazi sentenced to death two of his brothers whom he accused of using medicines to murder him. According to Smith, the king could not forget that Dingane had killed his brother Shaka to deprive him of the Zulu kingdom.

figure 13 **The Great Choai – on the way from Kuruman to Motselikatzi's country. 1835.**
Watercolour. 14 x 24 cm. Coll: MuseumAfrica

Smith's tents, with their cavalcade of wagons outspanned beside them, on the shore of what Bell called 'The Great Choai'. Other travellers referred to it as 'The Barolong Chui' or 'the Great Tswaing'. Be that as it may, it was an enormous lake (six miles long and two broad, according to John Burrow) which was almost dry when Bell and his companions first saw it on their journey north from Kuruman.

figure 14 **Thaba Bosigu (mountain of darkness) stronghold of Moscheshwe chief of the Bassootos. 1834.**
Watercolour. 19 x 31 cm. Coll: MuseumAfrica

Bell has painted Thaba Bosiu, Moshoeshoe's impregnable stronghold, with Smith's party camped at its foot. Shortly after their arrival on 21 October 1834, he and Burrow ascended the 120-metre-high mesa to attend an audience with Moshoeshoe. A single path led to the summit where there was an arch so narrow that only one man at a time could pass through it. Once at the top, the two young explorers had to negotiate a veritable labyrinth through thousands of huts before they reached the king's palace.

figure 15 **Bushman – method of creeping on game.**
Watercolour. 14 x 21.5 cm. Bell Heritage Trust Collection, UCT

A Bushman camouflages himself with branches of a camelthorn tree in order to creep up stealthily on game before shooting the animal with poisoned arrows. Bell was charged with the duty of recording the scenery and customs of the indigenous people encountered on the expedition, but he managed to include animals – the preserve of his fellow artist, George Ford – in many of his sketches.

figure 16 **Bushman – another method.**
Watercolour. 13.5 x 21.5 cm. Bell Heritage Trust Collection, UCT

*Disguised as ostriches, Bushmen make use of another method by which to creep up on unwary game. Bell here shows
how the wily hunter makes use of the feathers, neck and head of the dead bird – a stratagem which seems to bewilder the
small buck in the middle distance, while the wildebeest continue to graze peacefully.*

figure 17 **Quagga and gnu hunting.**
Watercolour. 13.5 x 20.5 cm. Bell Heritage Trust Collection, UCT

*The wide open spaces of Transorangia (as the Free State was known when Bell visited it with Smith's expedition) gave a
great advantage to the hunter bent on slaying game. While the wildebeest, or gnu, remains relatively common today, the
graceful quagga, once so numerous, has been completely shot out.*

figure 18 **Cameleopard blown or flaauw.**
Watercolour. 9 x 16 cm. Bell Heritage Trust Collection, UCT

A giraffe – or in Charles Bell's words a 'cameleopard' – provides a hunter with an easy target. The seemingly innocent
expression on the animal's face serves to emphasise the trust with which southern Africa's teeming game regarded the
invading white men with their guns. Even the horse has a disconsolate air about it.

figure 19 **The unbidden guest.**
Oil on paper. 7 x 11.5 cm. University of the Witwatersrand Library (A29 D'Urban Papers)

Here two men relaxing beside the campfire snatch up their guns to dispatch the unwelcome intruder, while a terrified ox kicks up its heels and makes for safety. Encounters with lions were frequent on Andrew Smith's expedition into the interior, and one at least was fatal. Even in potentially disastrous situations, the youthful Bell's sense of humour did not desert him.

figure 20 **Bushwomen.**
Watercolour. 9 x 16 cm. Bell Heritage Trust Collection, UCT

Two Bushwomen as Charles Bell saw them during the Expedition to Central Africa. Despite what Bell must have considered the curious physique of these people, he imbues them – particularly the woman in front – with a kind of dignity. Adorned with beads and a fez-like headdress, and carrying stick and spear, she appears to be a woman of status, while her companion could be an attendant.

figure 21
**The tom tom dance –
Mozambiques & mixed race.**
Watercolour. 13.5 x 22 cm.
Bell Heritage Trust Collection,
UCT

*Bell captures the grace and liveli-
ness of these dancers – people who
originated in Mozambique and
clearly brought with them to the
Cape something of the Portuguese
tradition of that colony. In the background is a typical* kapstylhuis *– a
simple thatched shelter which often
provided a home for the trekboer or
itinerant farm labourer.*

figure 22
Hottentot woman.
Watercolour. 16.5 x 10.5 cm.
Bell Heritage Trust Collection,
UCT

*Unlike the two Bushwomen, this
Khoikhoi female is allowed neither
beauty nor dignity in this painting.
Her stance and demeanour – not to
mention her grotesque shape – suggest defiance and insolence, while
the pipe conveys a certain lack of
femininity, to the artist's biased eye
at least.*

Chapter 3

CIVIL SERVANT

Much of interest *had occurred at the Cape since Charles Bell had waved goodbye to his well-wishers at the Observatory on that chilly morning in 1834. Letters reached the travellers only intermittently once they had left Graaff-Reinet, but somewhere on his journey Bell had probably learnt that, at the Cape, the freeing of slaves on 1 December 1834 — according to an Act of Parliament passed some three years earlier — had not been without its problems, that of the lack of adequate compensation being uppermost in the minds of the erstwhile masters. On a more cheering note, there had been the ceremonial opening, in December 1834, of the new English church — later St George's Cathedral — in the presence of Sir Benjamin D'Urban and a host of other dignitaries.¹ It was the first Episcopalian place of worship to be erected in Cape Town itself and the ground plan of the handsome colonnaded building had been designed by none other than the versatile Colonel John Bell.² But with the end of 1834 news ceased to reach the expedition almost entirely for communications were severely affected by the outbreak of war — for the sixth time — on the Eastern Frontier.*

Once he was back in Cape Town, Charles would have heard, for the first time, the epic saga of how his uncle's friend, the dashing and popular quartermaster-general, Colonel Harry Smith, had galloped out of Cape Town on New Year's Day 1835 and covered the 600 miles – almost 1000 kilometres – to Grahamstown in less than six days in an attempt to restore order out of the chaos in that area. He was, on the whole, successful but even so, much suffering, pillage and bloodshed had to be endured by both sides before hostilities ended in August 1835. This was followed by the implementation of Sir Benjamin D'Urban's new frontier policy which included the annexation of the land between the Keiskamma and Kei rivers as the province of Queen Adelaide. In the eyes of the white settlers, the scheme had certain virtues but any positive effects were nullified in December 1835 when Lord Glenelg, the philanthropically inclined British colonial secretary, issued a despatch completely at variance with D'Urban's policy. As if this were not enough, the general unrest already prevailing among the Xhosa on the Frontier and beyond the Kei was being steadily exacerbated by pressure from the powerful Zulu nation to their northeast. Remote as the Cape Peninsula certainly was from all this turmoil, the insecurity it caused eventually filtered southwards, and of this Charles must have become aware soon after his return.

Yet, despite all these alarms and disturbances, 1835 had proved a time of prosperity at Cape Town itself. There had been

a considerable import of capital; Government revenue was increasing and, paradoxically, optimism regarding the economic future of the Colony was high among the local merchant class.³ Perhaps it was the sense of permanence engendered by a feeling of financial security that, during 1835, led Colonel Bell to buy a property of considerable size in the leafy suburb of Rondebosch, on the eastern side of Table Mountain, and to build a house on the foundations of the Dutch dwelling that had stood there.⁴

Possibly political events mattered less to Charles Bell, on his return to Cape Town at the end of January 1836, than the revival of old friendships, particularly with two exceedingly interesting families whom he had met at the Cape not long before the expedition set off. First there were Thomas and Mary Maclear who, with their five young daughters, had arrived at the Cape on 6 January 1834 and swiftly established a firm and lasting friendship with the Bells. Thomas Maclear, a medical doctor by profession, had recently been appointed astronomer in charge of the Cape's Royal Observatory, a fine neoclassical-style building erected six years earlier. The easy hurly-burly in which his lively young family lived must have provided Charles with a pleasant relief from his clerical duties in the government offices. At all events, on Thursday 11 February, less than a fortnight after his return to Hope Mill, Charles paid a call on the Maclears and may well have given his hosts a private view of some of the sketches he had made during the expedition. Another frequent visitor to the Observatory at this time was Bell's friend John Burrow who, according to Mrs Maclear, called on them almost every day.

Then there were the Herschels who, with Sir Benjamin and Lady D'Urban as fellow passengers, had sailed into Table Bay aboard the *Mountstuart-Elphinstone* on 15 January 1834.[5] Son of Sir William Herschel, reputedly the most celebrated astronomer of the day and from whom he had undoubtedly inherited his skills, Sir John Herschel was visiting the Cape at his own expense to observe the heavenly bodies of the southern skies, and for this purpose had brought with him – in company with his charming and artistic wife, Margaret, their three small children, an assistant and a servant – a mass of impedimenta including a 20-foot telescope. This he set up in the garden of Feldhausen (or The Grove as a previous owner had called it), a rambling house in Claremont where Colonel John Bell, his wife and nephew were to be frequent guests during the four years that the Herschel family lived there.

There were new friends to be made, too, and possibly the most important of these was a young man with whom Charles Bell had much in common. This was seventeen-year-old Charles Piazzi Smyth whose surprising second name was the one by which he was generally known.[6] The two young men would have met soon after the return of the expedition, probably at the Royal Observatory where Smyth had been part of the Maclears' ménage since his arrival there on 9 October 1835. He had come from England to take up the post of assistant astronomer, and at the Cape Piazzi Smyth was to remain, loyally labouring under Thomas Maclear, until he was appointed Astronomer Royal for Scotland ten years later. Like Charles Bell, he was a gifted artist and, like Bell's, his sketches often reveal a lighthearted and quirky sense of humour. These two remarkable men were to remain close friends until the death of the elder of the pair – Charles Bell – almost fifty years later.

Meanwhile, Dr Andrew Smith was busily preparing his vast collection – including a hippopotamus and two rhinoceros specimens – for a local exhibition. The mind boggles at the thought of

figure 1 **Sir John Herschel.**
Engraving. University of Cape Town Libraries

Sir John Herschel (1792–1871), a renowned astronomer, arrived at the Cape in 1834 to study the skies of the southern hemisphere. He bought the estate Feldhausen in Claremont and set up his 20-foot reflecting telescope in the garden. His friendship with Colonel Bell brought him into close contact with the young Charles Bell, whose life must have been considerably enriched by his wide interests and enquiring mind.

the logistics and other problems incurred in transporting these great carcasses across the subcontinent and then (as Smith planned) to England, but doubtless the science of taxidermy was included among his many skills. Conscious as he was of the necessity to exhibit the fruits of his labours to the shareholders who had sponsored the expedition, he nevertheless felt that his immediate duty was to Mzilikazi's two visiting envoys. Having entertained them in Cape Town and shown them the sights of the bustling town, on 3 March he invited the Matabele ambassador to sign a treaty he had drawn up with the purpose of ensuring peace and friendship between the colonists and Mzilikazi's people. Both Sir Benjamin D'Urban and Smith appended their signatures to this document, after which it was formally ratified by the addition of the official seal.[7] The ceremony concluded, the two visitors, lavishly provided with gifts as well as with safe conduct to the border of the Colony, returned to their home territory.

The shareholders did not have to wait long to see the results of Smith's expedition. At a meeting of the Association for Exploring Central Africa opened by Sir John Herschel on 19 March 1836, they listened attentively as Smith informed them that his party had learnt much about the hitherto unknown tribes of the interior and that friendly relations had been established with their rulers. He was also able to tell them that many new zoological specimens had been discovered and identified and that, for the first time, the precise positions of numerous places and topographical features had been correctly determined and marked on the map. Their hopes of trading with the interior, however, had been disappointed, for the indigenous people had little to offer in exchange for European goods. The sponsors, while regretting that the expedition had failed to provide

figure 2
Charles Piazzi Smyth (self-portrait). 1847.
Illustration in Warner, B. *Charles Piazzi Smyth*; A.A. Balkema for UCT, Cape Town, 1983. History of Science Museum, Oxford

Charles Piazzi Smyth (1819–1900) was first assistant astronomer at the Cape from 1835 until 1845, when he was appointed Scotland's Astronomer Royal. An eccentric of varied talents, he became a close friend of Charles Bell, with whom he shared many interests and activities both at the Cape and later in Scotland. When Bell died in 1882, Smyth wrote his obituary, a perceptive account of his friend's character and achievements. It was published in the Proceedings of the Royal Society of Scotland, 1886–1887.

figure 3
Shooting hippo in the Marico River. 1835.

Watercolour (monochrome).
12.7 x 17.8 cm.
Coll: MuseumAfrica

When they were exhibited in 1836, the sketches and paintings of the Expedition for Exploring Central Africa by Charles Bell and George Ford opened a window on the hinterland for the ordinary citizens of Cape Town. Bell's contribution included a number of hunting scenes, such as this one in which members of the exploration party despatch a hippo. This 'cunning and cautious' creature (as described by Andrew Smith) was highly sought after by indigenous people both for its flesh (for eating) and for its tusks (for commerce).

them with even the hope of financial gain, appreciated its scientific merits and agreed that the most valuable specimens and objects should be sent to London for exhibition without delay. Smith's report was duly published by the Cape Government Gazette and a copy despatched to the Royal Geographical Society, which not only discussed it at a meeting in London on 10 August 1836, but reprinted some sections in its Proceedings.

Meanwhile, in Cape Town Smith's exhibition of zoological specimens had been mounted at the museum in Looyer's Plein (in 1851 to become the site of St Mary's Roman Catholic Cathedral), while the drawings made by Charles Bell and George Ford were displayed round the corner at No. 2 Hope Street.[8] Ford rapidly capitalised on his success as an artist by inserting an advertisement for his services as miniaturist and drawing instructor in the *South African Commercial Advertiser*, strategically placing it alongside a notice announcing the display of his – and Bell's – sketches.

The exhibition created a considerable stir among the people of Cape Town. Even if there were those who could not appreciate the scientific significance of the zoological exhibits, they must have been struck by the singularity of the animals and by the beauty and spectacular colour of the birds' plumage, as well as by the minute detail in which the paintings had been executed. There were also numerous ethnological exhibits on show and these, together with Charles Bell's spirited depictions of the

appearance and customs of the indigenous people of the subcontinent, must have opened up a world unknown to ordinary colonists in those days before the Great Trek had got fully under way and before photography was known at the Cape. Certainly not least appreciative of the importance of the expedition was Sir John Herschel, who brought his wife to visit it although she had been confined only three weeks earlier with their fourth child, a boy to be named Alexander. Herschel found the drawings of Ford and Bell to be 'uncommonly beautiful' – a compliment indeed, coming as it did from a man who was no mean artist himself.[9]

Perhaps the visitor most impressed by the exhibition was Piazzi Smyth, who described it in a letter written at the time to his mentor, the English lawyer and antiquarian, Dr John Lee.[10] He had found the meeting of the Association for Exploring Central Africa to be 'most interesting from the magnitude & richness of the collections which it brought home', while 'the drawings about 500 in number ranked first, from their *truth* & exquisite workmanship: the natural history is by Mr Ford a most indefatigable & talented artist'. The landscapes and figures, he wrote, were by Charles Bell, '& are about as well executed in their line as the others in theirs: his pencil has a peculiar twist & he has hit off the manners and customs of the natives to a t.'[11] Piazzi Smyth never forgot that exhibition. Nearly fifty years later, in an obituary to his friend he wrote, in a torrent of admiration:

Everyone was astonished, delighted and instructed at finding the walls of the room decorated by nearly three hundred of C.D. Bell's drawings . . . There, in those matchless drawings, was the peculiar country the expedition had passed through, in its minuter as well as its larger features; unadulterated, moreover, artistically, by any methods of drawing taught at home on English trees and hedges and shady lanes; for C.D. Bell had taught himself in South Africa on exactly what nature presented to him there. Hence was the great interior's physical geography, geology, and vegetation, too, where there was any, depicted again and again, either in brilliant colour, or *chiaro-scuro* force of black and white, and almost perfect truth of outline; with the very atmosphere also before one to look into, it shimmered and boiled in the vividness of solar light, and over stony surfaces heated to 140° or 150° Fahr. but yet garnished with episodes of the wild animals of the region – generally gigantic animals of South Africa today, but of other parts of the earth only in some past geological age; and with lifelike examples of the natives of every tribe, whose lands the expedition had traversed, depicted in their most characteristic avocations.[12]

What is particularly interesting, though, is that, according to Piazzi Smyth, Bell 'drew as much, or more, from memory in the silent watches of the night, as by sketching direct from nature through the day'.[13]

It is not certain when Charles Bell returned to his humdrum

duties in the Audit Office, but he must have worked diligently for before long he was promoted to the lofty post of first clerk which brought with it a salary increase of £30 a year.[14] It seems that the work was tolerable and the company in the old government offices pleasant – despite the prevailing and noxious smells emanating from the canal in the Heerengracht outside.

Any shortcomings in Charles's daily labours would have been more than compensated for by the interest provided by his social life and, in particular, by his expanding circle of friends. On at

Following his brief as one of the artists for the expedition, Bell depicted, among other things, the different hunting methods of the local people he and his companions encountered. With its tough hide, ferocious nature and sheer bulk, the rhinoceros was clearly no animal to be trifled with. Nevertheless, Andrew Smith, in his Illustrated Zoology of South Africa, *not surprisingly disagrees with an early description of the rhinoceros by a missionary who stated that it had a flexible horn which 'when the animal is asleep … can be curled like the trunk of an elephant, but becomes perfectly firm and hard when the animal is excited, and especially when pursuing an enemy'!*

least two occasions during this period he was invited to dinner parties which he was unlikely to forget. The first took place on Saturday 9 April 1836.[15] His host was the wealthy merchant John Bardwell Ebden and, presumably, the venue was Belmont, the splendid house Ebden had built for himself in Rondebosch. It must have proved a stimulating gathering for the guests included the Herschels, Captain Robert Wauchope, captain of the flagship HMS *Thalia*, and his wife, as well as Major and Mrs Charles Cornwallis Michell. The Maclears and Dr Andrew Smith were there, as well as Colonel Bell and Lady Catherine. Another guest was Baron von Ludwig, apothecary, horticulturist and businessman of German birth who was renowned for the wonderful garden of both exotic and indigenous plants that he had created in Kloof Street. Not recorded, however, is whether Ebden included any of his many progeny, most of them already young adults, in the party. It would indeed be interesting to know whether this was the first occasion on which Charles Bell met the fascinating Martha Antoinetta, fifth of Ebden's six daughters. Be that as it may, the guests must have been somewhat distracted by the outbreak of a fire in Belmont's adjoining vineyard during the evening; fortunately the house, which still stands,[16] escaped the blaze.

The second significant dinner party which Charles Bell attended at this time was given by the Herschels, whose invitation was for 6 o'clock on the evening of Wednesday, 15 June 1836. On this occasion the guests were even more celebrated and the conversation must have been scintillating to say the least. One of those present was Captain James Edward Alexander, soldier and traveller, who had fought in various wars in such far-flung places as Russia, Turkey, Portugal and the Eastern Cape. Later he was to see service in the Crimea, Canada and New Zealand and to go exploring, to some extent in the footsteps of Andrew Smith (of whom he appears to have been unreasonably jealous) in the interior of southern Africa.[17] But even Captain Alexander pales in comparison with the two men who were probably guests of honour on that winter evening – the charming Robert Fitzroy, hydrographer, meteorologist and captain of HMS *Beagle*, at that time lying at anchor in Table Bay;[18] and, with him, the ship's naturalist, a young man named Charles Darwin, destined to become famous for his epoch-making theory of evolution. Of course, no one at that dinner table could have known that some twenty-three years from then he was to publish one of the most notable scientific works the world has ever known, his *magnum opus*, *On the origin of species*. And, when the book did appear in 1859, what, one wonders, was the reaction of that good Presbyterian, Charles Bell? Darwin recorded the occasion in a letter written to John Stevens Henslow, at that time professor of botany at Cambridge University. Of Herschel Darwin wrote: 'He was exceedingly good natured, but his manners at first appeared to me rather awful.'[19] Of Charles Bell, not surprisingly, he made no mention at all.

Stimulating as these events must have been to a young man with a mind as alert as Charles Bell's, there would have been times when he welcomed the opportunity simply to have fun. Such an occasion was the 'fancy ball' – an extremely popular and fashionable form of entertainment at the time – which Sir Benjamin and Lady D'Urban organised at Government House on 19 July 1836. Cape Town's society was there in force, including

several members of the expedition. Naturally, the Maclears were among the guests, and in her diary the observant Mrs Maclear writes that Lady D'Urban wore 'a very rich costume of the time of Queen Mary', and that a prominent medical man, coyly referred to as 'Dr L' but undoubtedly the well-known Dr Louis Liesching, had risked both reputation and dignity to appear disguised as Old Moses.[20] This old tatterdemalion, reputedly a discredited army officer turned money lender, with his 'nor-wester hat, chalk pipe, spurs and money-bag', was a familiar sight in Cape Town and the subject of an amusing sketch by Thomas Bowler.

But of all the fancy costumes on view that night, none aroused more amusement than those sported by 'Messrs B and B', as Mrs Maclear referred to them, but undoubtedly none other than Charles Bell and his fellow traveller, John Burrow. These 'two young rips' had rigged themselves up as Mzilikazi and his great wife and, in Mrs Maclear's words, 'were the most remarkable figures in their karosses of leopard skins and fringes. The chief had a curious collar round his neck (to grin through) and bore shield and assegais; his wife had a child at her back.' At all events, the general atmosphere in the ballroom of Government House was one of merriment and the music for the quadrilles, the waltzes, the gallopades and reels was provided with verve and enthusiasm by the bands of the 27th and 98th regiments. As if the impression made by the two 'Messrs B' on this occasion had not been enough, they repeated the performance at 'a Juvenile party' (Sir John Herschel's words) given by Colonel and Lady Catherine Bell only four evenings later to celebrate their nephew's homecoming. Attired in the same garb, they exaggerated their tomfoolery by 'dipping for apples in flour with the hands behind [and] grinning with orange peel teeth'.[21]

By September the exhibits were ready for despatch and a notice was placed in the *Commercial Advertiser*[22] calling for tenders for 'a number of Wooden Cases for packing specimens of Natural History for Transmission to England'. There is no knowing whose tender was successful, but the task must have been completed in time for the crates and their precious contents to accompany Andrew Smith when he returned to his military duties in England early in February of the following year. He lost no time in contacting the Royal Geographical Society and in making arrangements for an exhibition at which would be displayed not only the specimens and artifacts brought back from the Expedition into Central Africa, but the artworks of George Ford and Charles Bell too. The exhibition opened at London's Egyptian Hall in July 1837 and, at an entrance price of one shilling per visitor, ran for a year.[23]

Smith had every intention of publishing his expedition journal, copiously illustrated by Ford and Bell, as soon as possible –

indeed, a notice announcing its imminent appearance was printed on the back of the catalogue to the exhibition. However, this was not to be, probably because at the time Smith was preoccupied not only with his medical responsibilities and with what Piazzi Smyth referred to as 'curiosities in the way of undescribed snakes', but also with anxieties arising from the exhibition's complete failure to pay for its expenses.[24] Meanwhile, both Ford and Bell had been obliged to hand over their artworks to their former chief, who, after a lapse of some eight years, did publish what was to prove his masterpiece, the magnificent *Illustrated Zoology of South Africa* in five volumes. The illustrations – hand-coloured lithographs – were almost entirely by George Ford with the exception of one or two which may have been the work of Charles Bell, although the book does not give him credit for them. The fortunate Ford was thus allowed the pleasure of seeing his

figure 6 **Corythaix porphyreolopha.**
Watercolour. Illustration in Smith, Andrew. *Illustrated Zoology of South Africa*; Smith, Elder & Co., London, 1849.
South African Museum.

The purple-crested lourie, painted by Charles Bell's fellow artist George Ford, who accompanied the Expedition for Exploring Central Africa specifically to paint the wildlife of the subcontinent. This sensitive painting eventually appeared in the volume entitled Aves (Birds) in Andrew Smith's Illustrated Zoology of South Africa, *which was published in London in 1849.*.

works published within a decade; not so Bell whose 'brilliant collection of pieces of graphical information', according to Piazzi Smyth, 'never saw light again until, after twenty years, a few of them straggled out to illustrate later travellers' books'.[25] This is only partly true: in 1842 one of Bell's sketches appeared as the frontispiece to Robert Moffat's *Missionary labours and scenes*, and another was used as an illustration in David Livingstone's *Missionary travels and researches*, published in 1857. One of the 'travellers' books' Piazzi Smyth was referring to was probably James Chapman's *Travels in the interior of South Africa* which made an appearance in 1868. It was illustrated with a number of engravings based on drawings Bell had made during the expedition.

Back in the Cape Town of 1837, the Bells were by now comfortably settled in what Lady Herschel described as 'their pretty new house on the Camp Ground'.[26] Conveniently placed about halfway between their friends, the Herschels at Feldhausen and the Maclears at the Royal Observatory, the property had a superb view of Table Mountain's eastern buttresses. Most of the neighbours were prosperous merchants, some of whose spreading estates were still planted with vines and fruit trees established almost two centuries earlier. Colonel Bell had called his new home after Mount Canigou, a wildly beautiful area in the eastern Pyrenees where he had served during the Peninsular War, and had made it into 'an excellent, comfortable & very handsome *Gentlemanlike* Residence'. So at least wrote Charles Bell in a long letter to his sister, Christina, on 8 November 1837.

> He has excellent taste in Building, and planned the house in the Elizabethan manorhouse style and has succeeded completely in building the prettiest house at the Cape. My room is in the Garret – an excellent one with capital light for drawing and I have filled it with all sorts of natural curiosities etc. [I] have generally got a tame snake or two in it and all sorts of drawing, engraving and modelling tools.[27]

Unfortunately Christina's reply – if she wrote one – has not survived; it would be interesting to know how she felt about 'the tame snake or two'.

Life for the elder Bells must have been pleasant indeed once they had moved to Canigou. 'Lady Catherine is glad to club with

figure 7
Damalis (Strepsiceros) capensis.
Watercolour. Illustration in Smith, Andrew. *Illustrated Zoology of South Africa*; Smith, Elder & Co., London, 1849. South African Museum

George Ford's painting of a male 'koedoe' captures all the power and dignity of this lord of the antelope. It is an illustration in the volume Mammalia *in Andrew Smith's* Illustrated Zoology of South Africa.

me,' wrote her friend Lady Herschel to her brother Duncan, a doctor stationed in India, '& we drive & make visits together, or dine with them en famille.' Canigou boasted a splendid garden where both Colonel Bell and Lady Catherine spent many hours working among their plants, though most of their labour appeared to consist of superintending the gardener. 'This is an excellent thing for both of them,' wrote Charles enthusiastically, 'and the consequence is that it counteracts the bad effect of Our Uncle's close attendance at Office & prevents both of them from

Bell observed and drew every stage of the slaughtering of rhinoceros – a drawn-out process owing to the animal's stamina and extraordinarily tough skin. In his Journal Smith wrote: 'To attempt killing rhinoceri or elephants or hippopotami with bullets purely composed of lead is vain. Only those partially made of some harder metal being constituted to injure either of these animals. The bullets, therefore, commonly employed by the South African hunters are composed of one part pewter and two parts lead.'

being much troubled with ill health.' Every day Colonel Bell drove in his carriage from Rondebosch to the government offices in town and it is likely that his nephew accompanied him. For Charles, these six-mile journeys must have been highly entertaining for, as he wrote to Christina, his uncle was 'the most agreeable & amusing companion'. Dinner parties at Canigou, too, were highly diverting with Colonel Bell as host, for not only was he a man possessed of great funds of information, but he kept his guests in a 'constant fit of laughter' by telling funny stories and, according to Charles, 'talking Scotch'. Seldom did Charles see his uncle with what he called 'the ruffled temper', and Lady Catherine was unfailingly kind to him. 'Thus within our own home,' he informed his sister, 'I have a society which it requires some temptation to induce me to quit.'[28]

But, of course there comes a time and a situation when a young man must quit the security of his own comfortable home, though such temptation did not come Charles Bell's way for several years. He remained on in the Audit Office even though in September 1838 he was appointed to serve as relief to the clerk of the Legislative Council, a certain K.B. Hamilton, who was away in England on long leave.[29] On 31 January 1839 he wrote to his mother describing his work:

I have now had three months of trial and I like it very much. It is a position of considerable responsibility – and I have plenty of work during the sitting of Council but it is that sort of work that it is a pleasure to do because I feel that it is of some importance. I sit opposite the Governor in Council & note down all the proceedings, publish the Ordinances or Laws & if I do wrong not even the Members of Council can find fault with me except by a formal Complaint to the Governor in Council so that I am completely my own master.

Charles then goes on to give his parents some idea of Colonel John Bell's responsibilities as colonial secretary at the Cape:

My uncle has hard work of it. Everything depends on him, at least in the Civil Service, through this large extent of Country – he receives all communications through his Office to the Government & issues all orders from the Government – his health is wonderfully good. Lady Catherine suffers more from bad health than he do (sic) being very subject to violent Headaches – and a constant severe Cough. Their kindness to me is unchanged.[30]

Socially, the Bells continued to move in the governor's circle and Charles, in this letter, tells his parents how Sir George Napier, in office for the past year, had 'taken a country house'[31] only 300 yards from Canigou. 'Before [Sir George] left England,' wrote Charles, 'he fell in love with a very beautiful widow with £2000 a year and we hear she has sailed in the "Euphrates" to join him here. She is expected every day & our House is in preparation to receive her until her marriage so we'll have a grand wedding soon.' In fact, Sir George Napier – a gallant soldier who had lost his right arm during the Peninsular campaign – married Frances Dorothea Williams Freeman in St George's Church (later Cathedral), Cape Town, on 12 March 1839.

Somehow Charles managed to combine his duties in both departments, at the same time finding himself increasingly interested in land surveying. Experienced as a draughtsman and competent with figures, he had learnt something of what surveying involved from John Burrow during their travels with Andrew Smith. Now he made it his business to study the subject seriously and to qualify in it, taking the examination before the surveyor-general, now Colonel Charles Cornwallis Michell. 'Mr Bell has gone through every part of the examination with the highest credit to himself,' reported Michell, 'evincing throughout such superior ability that I feel it my duty to record the same in recommending him to His Excellency for nomination.'[32]

Charles Bell, aged twenty-four, was now a qualified land surveyor. He was duly transferred to the office of the surveyor-general and embarked on the profession that was to occupy him, and to which he would be a credit, for the rest of his working life.

Chapter 4

SURVEYOR

In more ways than one, *the late 1830s had proved a period of change and upheaval in South Africa. At intervals from 1835 onwards, groups of disgruntled Boer farmers packed their families and their possessions into their long, covered wagons, rounded up their sheep and goats, inspanned their teams of oxen and trundled off into the African wilderness. Besides trusting that they would find grass that really would be greener, they hoped that Africa's mountains, deserts and rivers would separate them for ever from what they saw as injustices imposed upon them by their British overlords, not to mention from the predations of their Xhosa neighbours. The activities of missionaries and philanthropists, too, had exasperated them, and the last straw had been the failure of the British government to make adequate financial compensation for the loss of their slaves. These, in simplistic terms, were the main causes of that watershed event in South Africa's history, the Great Trek, and although the inhabitants of Cape Town were aware of what was happening far into the interior, the creaking of the wagons and the grunts of the straining oxen were too distant to mean much to them — at first. Then, in February 1838, came the horrifying news of the slaughter of trek-leader Piet Retief and his companions at the hands of the Zulu chief, Dingaan, and, at the end of the year, of the equally violent retribution that the trekkers wreaked on the Zulus at the so-called Battle of Blood River.*

Whatever effect these terrible events may have had on Charles Bell, apparently he did not consider them worthy of mention in the letter that he sent his parents at the end of January 1839. However, something that must surely have held Charles's attention at this time was a project that had for some years been occupying the mind of his uncle, John Bell. Disturbed by the generally deplorable state of schools at the Cape – despite the successful establishment of that laudable institution, the South African College, in 1829 – Colonel Bell and two enterprising friends, newspaper editor and proprietor, John Fairbairn, and Sir John Herschel, had devised a new and efficient educational system for the Colony. With the support of Sir George Napier they approached Lord Glenelg, the colonial secretary in London, and convinced him of the urgency to appoint not only an able man to reorganise and supervise education at the Cape, but also to find competent teachers to serve under him. Fortunately the right man for the job was at hand, and in July 1839 James Rose Innes, a mathematician on the staff of the South African College, took up the new post of superintendent-general of education in the Colony; qualified teachers were brought out from

England and well-organised state-run schools were established throughout the land.

Meanwhile Charles Bell continued to work in the surveyor-general's office. He was fortunate that his chief, Colonel Charles Cornwallis Michell, was a man of many talents and tremendous industry whom he had known personally since his arrival at the Cape. Something of Michell's dedication and dynamic energy must have been contagious, for Bell quickly developed the skills of a surveyor and in July 1840 was promoted to the newly created post of second assistant surveyor-general with an annual salary, according to the *Cape Almanac* of 1841, of £300.[1] His immediate superior was the first assistant surveyor-general, Willem Frederik Hertzog, a forceful personality and a member of a well-known Cape family. At the time of Bell's promotion, Hertzog was confined to his office following a serious

riding accident on the Eastern Frontier,[2] so his new assistant could confidently expect to be sent out into the field before long.

In earlier times, the administration of land surveying in country areas had been undertaken first by the local *landdrost* and *heemraden* and later by whoever held the combined offices of resident magistrate and civil commissioner. In 1840, however, the responsibility for land surveying was transferred to the surveyor-general's department which consequently was burdened with a great deal of extra work – hence the creation of Charles Bell's new post. He did not wait long for his first commission for in October 1840, three months after his promotion, he was entrusted with investigating serious land problems in the Kamiesberg, a mountainous part of Namaqualand some 30 kilometres inland from the Atlantic Ocean and stretching between the little town of Garies in the south and the Richtersveld in the north.[3] Not surprisingly, since land delimitation in the past had been unreliable to say the least, considerable disputes had arisen between the various landowners in the area – mainly farmers and missionaries – and bitter litigation had frequently resulted.

Hertzog now instructed Bell first to make a study of all the documents and correspondence dealing with this matter, and then to travel up to the Kamiesberg and examine the entire area in question. He would then carefully investigate the merits of the various conflicting claims and report on them. Having completed this part of his task, Bell was to proceed in an easterly direction towards the Hantam mountains and by comparing three farms in

the area – Tyger Hoek, Ramskop and Vye Vallei – decide which would provide the most suitable site for a new magistracy with a small gaol attached. However, in making his decision, Hertzog reminded Bell, his most important consideration was to be the presence of a consistent and reliable supply of water. 'Finally,' wrote Hertzog, 'you will both going and in returning put yourself in communication with the Astronomer Royal for the purpose of obtaining from that Gentleman and for recording by notes and Sketches – all such information desirable from the measurements on which Mr Maclear is now engaged, as shall be requisite in proceeding hereafter with the general Trigonometrical survey of the Colony.'[4] These last instructions referred to work on the Arc of the Meridian on which Thomas Maclear had been engaged in much the same area since 1837.

The African landscape is seldom a hospitable one and the craggy, arid escarpment of the Kamiesberg is no exception. Jagged peaks reach towards the blue sky, their slopes scattered with lichen-encrusted rocks, some crudely carved into grotesque animal-like shapes by the relentless wind, others split asunder as if by some primordial cataclysm. During the greater part of the year this is a harsh land, bitter cold in winter and, in summer, scorched by a blinding sun. But in spring Namaqualand is miraculously transformed into a seemingly limitless paradise of flowers, their brilliance and variety unequalled throughout the world. So breathtakingly beautiful is this floral spectacle that Namaqualand has been aptly described as the garden of the gods. Bell, solitary but for a Cape Malay driver and a Khoikhoi servant, arrived there in his little ox-cart too late to enjoy the annual display of flowers, for it was November by the time he reached the Kamiesberg and summer had begun.

It had been a wretched journey. Bell, who well knew the exigencies of travel in the African wilderness, had done his best to make adequate preparations, but he could do nothing to improve the miserable condition of the oxen with which the government had provided him. Day after day, as the little party toiled northwards in increasing heat and drought, the unfortunate creatures became steadily weaker. Somehow, despite a prevailing lack of water, they eventually reached the foot of the Kamiesberg and, on 17 November, dragged themselves some 1500 metres up its slopes to reach the welcome respite of Leliefontein mission station.[5] Its name derived from the arum lilies that grew in a nearby stream, the station must have seemed like a veritable oasis in the desert to the young Scotsman – and an intriguing one too, with its *matjieshuise*, or rush huts, in which the local people lived. The first mission settlement established by Wesleyans at the Cape, it had been founded in 1816 by the missionary Barnabas Shaw, but the land on which it stood had been granted to the Little Namaqua tribe by the Dutch governor, Ryk Tulbagh, half a

figure 2
Watercolour. 11 x 17.5 cm.
Coll: Dr Frank Bradlow

Charles Bell's sense of the absurd – often at the expense of others – was clearly stimulated by observing this tussle between man and beast. The naked rider, mounted bareback on the leading ox, appears to be enjoying the fun. Not so his clothed companions or the man endeavouring to restrain the recalcitrant creatures. An identical engraving of this scene, captioned 'Koranna Pack-oxen', was reproduced in James Chapman's work, Travels in the interior of South Africa…, *published in London in 1868.*

Sketch in Little Namaqualand – Charles Bell

figure 3
Little Namaqualand. *c.* 1841.
Watercolour. 21 x 28 cm.
Coll: MuseumAfrica

*Bell's painting of a scene in Little
Namaqualand shows in the centre
a* matjieshuis *consisting of over-
lapping rush mats sewn together
with bark threads and stretched
over a hemispherical sapling
frame. These huts were made
by the Korana people who, on
moving home, would dismantle
them, roll up the mats and set up
the* huis *elsewhere.*

century before. Now the ownership of the land was in dispute
and it was Charles Bell's task to solve the problem, if possible to
the satisfaction of all concerned.

Bell was to remain at Leliefontein for some time for, as he
wrote to Willem Hertzog on 24 November, 'the great extent of
ground in the Occupation of the Hottentots of the Missionary
Institution, the ruggedness of the Country, the distances between
the places in dispute, and the necessity of making Sketches of
many of them in order to furnish an accurate report, will probably detain me here, notwithstanding my utmost exertions, until
the arrival of the next Post'.[6] In any case, the poor condition of
his oxen was of considerable concern to him and he asked for

permission to return to Cape Town on horseback by way of
Clanwilliam if they did not recover. Eventually, at the end of a
long, dry summer, he realised that further travel in his ox-cart,
now both ramshackle and unreliable, had indeed become impossible. Besides, swarms of locusts, through which Bell and his cart
had to struggle on at least one occasion, had caused such devas-
tation in the countryside between the Hantam mountains and the
Kamiesberg, that one of the oxen, weakened by starvation, had
collapsed and died.

Having waited impatiently for the arrival of the necessary
authorisation from Cape Town while his expenses mounted
daily, Bell eventually took it upon himself to hire the required

horses locally and set off for home. This decision amounted almost to impertinence in the opinion of his superiors, for when they heard what he had done they rapped him severely over the knuckles, particularly since he was unable to produce the receipts for his transactions. 'I have to state,' he wrote to Surveyor-General Michell in explanation, 'that it was not my intention to charge for either of those sums or for horsehire for my own horses until I discovered that the allowance of five shillings a day was inadequate to cover the additional expenses of the journey. Besides the expenses mentioned in these accounts there were several services rendered for which the parties would accept neither payment nor certificates.' He was referring to occasions when local inhabitants – three farmers, a field cornet and a dominee – had lent him oxen to draw his cart without thought of payment[7] – a clear indication of the respect in which he was held by the people he had come so far to serve. Years later Piazzi Smyth was to write: 'He settled [the land problems] so satisfactorily, and with so much calmness and wisdom, that the Dutch boers ever after that always addressed him, though still only twenty-seven years of age, by their title of highest honour, viz., "Old Mynheer Bell".[18]

Charles Bell returned to Cape Town in mid-March 1841 and less than three months later, on 3 June, he married Martha Antoinetta, daughter of John Bardwell Ebden. The ceremony took place at the Ebdens' splendid house, Belmont, in Rondebosch, and was conducted by the Colonial Chaplain, the Rev. George Hough, according to the rites of the Church of England. Among the guests was Thomas, the son of Governor Sir George Napier and an officer in the Cape Mounted Rifles, who signed the marriage certificate as one of the witnesses.[9] It must have been the society wedding of the year for it involved a union of two of the most highly respected local families. Due to sail for England on his retirement only a few days later, Colonel John Bell had, during almost twenty years at the Cape, proved a popular and able senior public servant. With his gracious and intelligent wife at his side, he had also played a prominent role in

figure 4 **John Bardwell Ebden. c. 1850.**
Lithograph. 20 x 18 cm. Coll: South African Library

John Bardwell Ebden arrived at the Cape by chance in 1806 when the ship in which he was travelling was wrecked in Table Bay. He remained to become one of the Colony's most respected inhabitants, distinguishing himself as a merchant, politician, banker and company director. When his fifth daughter, Martha Antoinetta, married the nephew of the Cape's colonial secretary, John Bell, he must have been more than satisfied. Charles Bell's portrait of his father-in-law conveys a sense of the solid respectability that the Ebden family seemed to represent.

a variety of spheres, not least Cape Town's social life. The building of 'Canigou' and the hospitable home he and Lady Catherine had made there had given an air of permanence to their sojourn at the Cape and there was considerable disappointment at their decision to leave the country.

For John Ebden, on the other hand, there was no question of returning to England. Born in Norfolk in 1787, he arrived at the Cape in a somewhat novel way when the ship in which he was travelling to India in 1806 was wrecked in Table Bay. There is a story – apocryphal no doubt but certainly symbolic – that after the ship had foundered nineteen-year-old Ebden swam ashore grasping a bag of golden coins in his hand. At all events, within ten years he was well established as a merchant successfully importing goods of various kinds from the East and despatching ships loaded with local wine to St Helena. Like many another English settler, he married a local girl, Antonia Adriana Kirchman, daughter of a fellow merchant, and fathered no fewer than six sons and six daughters.[10] Whatever pies there were at the Cape – financial, commercial or political – John Bardwell Ebden had a finger in each one of them, and certainly he was one of the dominating figures in the Colony's public life during most of the nineteenth century. At home, as might be expected, he was a patriarch, exerting a powerful influence over his large family, and it is probable that he regarded the marriage of Martha Antoinetta to the nephew of the distinguished Colonel John Bell with satisfaction. Perhaps it was in deference to the father of the bride that George Hough, in completing the marriage certificate, gave Bell's occupation as 'gentleman', not land surveyor, while he declared Martha Antoinetta – only nineteen years old – to be not a spinster as was customary but a 'lady'. Little did he suspect how unladylike her subsequent behaviour was to be!

The young couple settled in No. 4 Rheede Street in the Gardens, not far from Hope Mill and within a pleasant walking distance from Charles's office in town.[11] It was, of course, only a matter of time before he was sent away on a second commission, though ten months were to pass before Charles Michell, now promoted lieutenant-colonel, issued the anticipated instructions. 'His Excellency the Governor,' the memorandum began, '[has] been pleased to determine that the Second Assistant Surveyor-General shall proceed to the Eastern Districts for the purpose of investigating the various Claims for titles to Land reported to Government in compliance with Government notice dated 28th March 1840 ...'[12]

The land in question was situated in the district of Albany between the Sundays and Great Fish rivers and, according to Piazzi Smyth, the soil was of such a poor quality that it had been stigmatised by the local settlers as the 'zuurveld'.[13] Dutch Boer farmers had tried to cultivate it; so had the British settlers of 1820, but inevitably their efforts were in vain. To add to the farmers' difficulties, their properties had been delineated inaccurately in the past by the two officials responsible, Mr White and Mr Brown. Now it was Charles Bell's duty to put matters right, much as he had had to do in the Kamiesberg. His instructions, as detailed by Colonel Michell, were clear enough, but whether it would be possible to carry them out amicably (as Colonel Michell had requested) remained to be seen. It seemed that Mr White and Mr Brown had left things in something of a muddle.

First Bell had to make adequate preparation for the journey and for a long, hard stint of roughing it in the field. Having

figure 5
Crossing a mountain stream.
Watercolour. 18 x 25.5 cm.
Old Mutual Collection

Charles Bell would have known only too well the perils of travelling at the Cape during the nineteenth century, for it was in a wagon such as the one he depicts here that he and his young wife, Martha Antoinetta, made the long and hazardous journey to Grahamstown in 1842. The roads were no more than tracks and there were certainly no graded mountain passes. Not only did the travellers have to endure extreme discomfort, but the oxen on which they depended were subjected to every kind of wretchedness.

suffered in the past at the hands of a tight-fisted bureaucracy, he now had the temerity to make his needs known to his chief, following which Michell passed them on, in an extraordinary display of verbosity, to the acting colonial secretary. 'The Second Assistant Surveyor-General,' he wrote, 'being now ready to proceed to the Eastern Division and having been put to much expense in Outfit for the Service he is going upon, has requested me to solicit His Excellency that he will be pleased to Authorize an advance being made to him to meet the expenses of the journey.' The advance Bell required was £50, and this could be 'deducted out of any accounts that may become due to him *after* that which will be payable at the expiration of this month …'[14] One trusts that this – considerable – amount was forthcoming, but no records to this effect have been traced.

And so, on 2 April 1842, Bell once more packed up his belongings and his instruments, hitched his wagon to his inferior, Government-provided oxen and set off for the wilderness, ostensibly for a year on the Eastern Frontier.[15] The difference, this time, was that he had a wife with him – a wife who, presumably, had grown up accustomed to the comforts of her father's highly civilised home and to the solicitous attentions of mother and servants. Not surprisingly, it was a difficult journey. Bell started

off with ten 'government' oxen, to which two more were added from the depot at the foot of Sir Lowry's Pass. None of them proved satisfactory: one by one, as the wagon laboured along the rough and mountainous route to the Eastern Cape, they had to be exchanged for other, sturdier animals but, 'on about 6th or 7th May',[16] one of them collapsed and died. Hurriedly, the hired Khoikhoi stripped the dead animal of its skin – 'for the use of the wagon', wrote Bell – while another ox, which 'was dead lame', was exchanged free of charge for a fresh one. For three more weeks the wagon struggled on, two more oxen dying in harness while another had to be let loose in the veld to fend for itself. Such were the sufferings of the oxen. What, one wonders, did the unfortunate Martha Bell endure in such harsh surroundings where comforts were non-existent, where there were no made-up roads and every mountain pass presented new terrors? Eventually, at the beginning of June, the wagon heaved its way up to the summit of the last hill, and a cluster of small houses cupped in the folds of a green valley below proclaimed that this was Grahamstown at last. By then, Martha Antoinetta, sick not only from the endless lurching of the wagon, knew that she was pregnant.

Twenty-nine years had passed since Lieutenant-Colonel John Graham of Fintry in Scotland, founder of the Cape – or Hottentot – Regiment and British hero of the Fourth Frontier War of 1811–1812, had chosen the site of a Boer farmhouse razed to the ground during the recent hostilities as the military headquarters of the Eastern Frontier. He restored the ruins, converting the building into an officers' mess; he ordered a parade ground to be laid out in front of it and, on its far side, ordered a row of officers' cottages to be built. Soon afterwards, the governor of the Cape, Sir John Cradock, announced that this handful of buildings and their surroundings would become the nucleus of a civilian centre to be named Graham's Town 'in testimony of His Excellency's Respect for the Services of Lieutenant-Colonel Graham', and sites were chosen for the town's first public buildings.[17] But Grahamstown was still essentially a garrison town, and it was only after the British settlers of 1820 began to move in – finding it preferable to their allocated headquarters at Bathurst – that it began to show signs of real development. Attractive houses and cottages were built, as well as one of the finest churches in the country; trade with people across the border flourished, and by the mid-1820s Grahamstown could claim to be the most important commercial centre in the Eastern Cape. Nevertheless, the peaceful appearance of the town belied its true state. Almost incessant wars and rumours of wars on the Frontier made Grahamstown into a troubled place; it was, after all, difficult to forget the terror of Christmas 1834 when panic-stricken women and children sought refuge in the church and the town itself almost went up in smoke.

CAPE TOWN, CALEDON & SWELLENDAM
Royal Mail Coach.
1844. 1845.

This was to be the home of Charles Bell and his young wife for as long as his work kept him there. They found a small house in New Street[18] and although it was conveniently close to the centre of the town, Charles Bell found it excessively cramped.[19] This discomfort was aggravated by the necessity to convert one of the rooms into an office and to find space in it for all Charles's books and instruments, not to mention the vast collection of documents that had to be sorted out.

Altogether, Bell was quite overwhelmed by the state of affairs that awaited him: the amount of work to be done was enormous and no effort had been made to establish any sort of order in the so-called records. Some of the documents had been 'mutilated' while others were actually lost and attempts to find them naturally not only wasted his time but irritated him to a point of distraction. 'I have at last discovered a Copy of the document alluded to in my former communications respecting ... the claims of the Albany Settlers,' he wrote to Hertzog on 13 January 1843. 'I am astonished to find that the extract on which I had formed my opinions respecting the liability of Government bears quite a different meaning when read with the context.' Besides, he found himself 'out on a limb' as far as his head office was concerned. There were long delays between his submission of accounts and their payment from Cape Town, and then there were (as usual) constant quibbles about his claims for seemingly modest expenses. No one responded to his pleas for supplies of stationery and he was obliged to make use of his personal stock. 'Please send me 150 quills,' Bell wrote in near despair on one occasion.[20] And of course the necessity to leave Martha in her 'delicate state', and go into the field for days at a time could not have improved the situation.

The last straw was the receipt of instructions from the surveyor-general's office ordering him to stay on in Grahamstown for a second year, no doubt because of 'the great quantity of unexpected work' still requiring his attention. Immediately stung into action, Charles Bell picked up one of his 150 quills on 18 January and wrote to the surveyor-general, reminding him,

figure 7 **William Porter.**
Photograph. Coll: South African Library

Witty, handsome and gifted with a fine speaking voice and the legendary charm of the Irish, William Porter (1805–1880) was the Cape Colony's attorney-general from 1839 until 1865. In 1869 he entered the House of Assembly, but declined the offer of the first premiership in 1872 on the grounds of ill health. Porter became the first chancellor of the University of the Cape of Good Hope in 1876.

with remarkable restraint, that his agreed term in Grahamstown was for one year only and asking, with respect, to be allowed to return to Cape Town in April 1843 at the latest. It seems that his request fell on deaf ears, for the records show that he was to go on struggling with the complexities of land claims in the Frontier region for at least another year.

On 25 January 1843 a son was born to Charles and Martha Bell in Grahamstown, presumably in their New Street cottage. How much, one wonders, did Martha yearn for the comforts of her parents' home at Belmont and for the affectionate support of her many sisters while attempting to quell the wails of her newborn infant in the dead of night? And how much, at this time, did the frustrations of Charles's work and the strain of her new status as mother tell on their relationship? Unlike many another Victorian young lady, Martha apparently did not keep a diary – or if she did, it unfortunately has not survived.

At last, in March 1844 – the very month in which the new governor, Sir Peregrine Maitland, took office – Charles Bell, accompanied by Martha and the toddler, John Alexander (his names honoured both great-uncle and grandfather), arrived back in Cape Town. They soon settled into No. 4 Rheede Street once more[21] and Charles returned to his daily walk to work down the Government Avenue. However, before the year was out he received a letter from John Montagu, his uncle's successor as colonial secretary at the Cape, which could have disturbed the even tenor of his life: it offered him the post of surveyor-general at the newly annexed colony of Port Natal at a salary of £400 a year, plus expenses.[22] The recommendation had come from none other than the British secretary of state, Lord Stanley, who was no doubt inspired by the efficiency with which Bell had coped with the land problems on the Eastern Frontier. All was to no avail, however, for Charles turned down the promotion, preferring to remain at the Cape – perhaps because Martha wished to be close to her family. However, he did agree to join yet another expedition in May 1845, this time to investigate an ugly situation that had arisen in

figure 8 **Colesberg. 1845.**
Watercolour. 17.8 x 25.5 cm. Coll: MuseumAfrica

Colesberg, named after Charles Bell's uncle by marriage, Governor Sir Galbraith Lowry Cole, was founded in 1830 and by the time Bell visited it in 1845 it had grown considerably since he had first seen it with Andrew Smith's party eleven years earlier. The surrounding countryside was still largely unspoilt. On this occasion William Porter wrote: 'Crowds of springbok, wilde beasts, pouws, koorhaan, cranes, with quagga and other animals, all in one way or another obviously delighted with their lives. It was God's great menagerie. I have rarely been more struck.'

figure 9 **The skirmish at Driekoppen, near Zwaartkopjes.**
Lithograph. 34 x 51.5 cm. Old Mutual Collection

This battle scene was sketched on the spot by Charles Bell, although he had not been present to witness the event. The lithograph, which was made by P. Gauci, gives a complete panoramic view of the various stages of the battle. Lieutenant-Colonel Robert Richardson of the 7th Dragoon Guards, to whom the lithograph was presented, is presumably the mounted officer in the cocked hat in the left foreground.

an area north of Philippolis known as Transorangia. The party assigned to the task numbered seven and was led by Governor Maitland himself, then sixty-eight years old and something of a responsibility to his companions.

Since Bell's last visit to this region nine years earlier, considerable friction had developed between the Griqua people and Boer farmers who were moving into the area in increasing numbers. In August 1836 (six months after the return of Smith's expedition) the British authorities, disturbed by the deteriorating situation, had endeavoured to control white expansion by extending the jurisdiction of the Cape courts to the latitude 25°S.[23] Seven years later Governor Sir George Napier ratified a treaty which formally recognised the authority of the Griqua chief, Adam Kok III, in the region. The unrest escalated, eventually developing into an explosive situation. British troops were called in and on 29 April 1845, using the co-operative Griquas as a decoy, the cavalry emerged from behind a hill at a place called Swartkoppies and, attacking from the rear, routed the unsuspecting Boers. Determined to settle matters in Transorangia permanently and in person, Sir Peregrine Maitland summoned a handpicked group which included, among others, the attorney-general, William Porter, the staff surgeon, Dr John Forrest, and the second assistant surveyor-general, Charles Bell. The party, each member (including the governor himself) mounted on horseback, left Cape Town on 15 May 1845, its destination Touwfontein, 50 kilometres to the northeast of Philippolis and, until the skirmish, the site of the Boers' main laager.

An account of this expedition is to be found in seven letters written in a charming and light-hearted style by William Porter to his friend and clerk, Hugh Lynar, in Cape Town.[24] All of them interesting, the letters give a lively first-hand account of the various characters in the party, not least of Charles Bell, on what – because of the company he enjoyed – must have been one of the most pleasant excursions he ever made. Through Porter's eyes, we see Bell scampering after his hat – appropriately called a 'maitland' – as it somersaults down the Franschhoek Pass goaded by a fierce wind; we have him translating into Dutch one of Scott's epic poems (as recited loudly by the Governor when the going was slow) to the amazed wonder of the local field cornet; we join him, and the local regiment, at a singsong round their campfire at Cradock and admire his good voice as 'he comes out strong' in the chorus. We look on, too, as he reads William Porter to sleep by candle-light as the two men, huddled on mattresses, lie side by side on the floor of a Karoo farmhouse. But Porter's style is inimitable, so let it speak for itself:

Bell, as you know, is our mainstay. He is our interpreter, our manager, and I don't know what else besides. Now a matter by which he is sorely vexed is the payment of the Field Cornets. He is obliged to learn how far each horse has come and how long he has been detained, and then, taking the distance travelled, to draw out an account. This, I perceive, occupies a good deal of time, though Bell goes to it with a great deal of earnestness and assiduity. Now ... while the rest of us were discussing the Field Cornet's tiffin, Bell was discussing the Field Cornet's bill. Both discussions seemed to terminate about the same time, and the Governor desired Bell to fall to luncheon with what appetite he might. Feeling as a man placed under authority should do, Bell fell to accordingly; but before he had quite satisfied the rage of hunger, the Governor was in the saddle, and Bell having in a muffled tone with his mouth full of meat mentioned he would follow speedily, we were off once more.

Bell was left behind and, needless to say, lost his way while attempting to join the rest of the party. His companions spent a restless night worrying about him but fortunately he managed to catch up with them at about noon the following day.[25] The weather was hot and, according to Porter, he and Bell, riding in their shirt sleeves, presented a fascinating sight 'with unshorn beards, dirty breeches, battered hats, and boots which felt their latest brush in Cape Town'.[26]

The Governor and his companions reached Touwfontein early in June and a meeting was called with the various chiefs in the area. Sir Peregrine made the suggestion that each chief's territory should be divided into two, one section to become a tribal reserve while the other should be leased to white farmers. This seemed to satisfy Adam Kok but Moshoeshoe had reservations and time was to prove that the problems of Transorangia were by no means settled. Meanwhile, Charles Bell took advantage of his visit to sketch the site of the Battle of Swartkoppies, though the skirmish was long since over and an apparent peace reigned. Nevertheless, he drew on his imagination to insert its role-players as though he had actually seen them in action and took the liberty of raising the summit of the koppie in his sketch to give it dramatic emphasis.

Their mission more or less accomplished, the governor and his party returned to the Cape by sea from Port Elizabeth, reaching Simon's Bay in the steamer *Thunderbolt* on 23 July. For Bell, these last days away from home must have been anxious ones, for Martha was expecting her second child at any moment. Fortunately, he arrived home in time for the event, for on 1 August Martha gave birth to a second son. This one, to satisfy both families, was named Charles David Ebden Bell.

Chapter 5

The MIDDLE YEARS

On 17 May 1845, two days after Sir Peregrine Maitland and his party had set off for Touwfontein, there came into being in Cape Town an institution that was to play an important role not only in Charles Bell's life, but in the social and economic development of South Africa itself. Its name, at that time, was the Mutual Life Assurance Society of the Cape of Good Hope, and the leader of the group of gentlemen responsible for its founding was that doughty and enterprising Scot, John Fairbairn. Preoccupied as he might have been at the time by preparations for his expedition to Touwfontein, Charles Bell would have known of the plans afoot to establish the new society. A notice boldly signed by his father-in-law, John Ebden, and calling for the names of people prepared to pledge themselves as prospective policyholders, was displayed at the Commercial Exchange. Inaugural meetings had been well publicised in the press and the founders' intentions had been much discussed locally. Besides, Charles Bell would have known John Fairbairn personally as he had been a frequent guest at Canigou and one of Colonel Bell's closest associates throughout his years of service at the Cape.

For some fifteen years prior to 1845, several joint stock companies, their capital provided by shareholders' investments, had been doing business in such spheres as fire and marine insurance in Cape Town. Unknown locally as yet, but well established in Scotland, was the principle of mutual life assurance: in institutions based on this system there are no shareholders, only policyholders; their combined premiums form the capital and they are entitled to share any profits. Such an altruistic concept appealed strongly to the philanthropically minded John Fairbairn, for he appreciated that only a small annual premium was required to provide security to a family in case of the bread-winner's death. Ten years after the Mutual's foundation, when its accumulated funds had risen to £58 862, Fairbairn, in addressing the Society's annual general meeting, was to say, 'If so many thousand pounds thus collected by a comparatively trifling annual self denial relieve even one bitter grief; if [such] forethought tends to smooth the pillow of the dying, such an institution as this should be recommended to everyone who hopes to gather family ties around him.'[1]

Charles Bell, now a family man himself, understood the soundness of the principle of mutual life assurance and in September 1845, when his second son was barely a month old, he took out policy No. 157, thus assuring his life for £1000. Later he was to add a second policy, this time for £400, and so he consolidated an association with what came to be known as 'Old Mutual' that was to endure for the rest of his life.

The following year was a busy one for Bell. His professional responsibilities were increasing and after 15 April 1846, when he was promoted to the office of assistant surveyor-general on the retirement of Fred Hertzog, they became even more burdensome.[2] Meanwhile, events on the Eastern Frontier were giving cause for alarm throughout the Colony. Early in March 1846, a colonial patrol despatched to arrest a Xhosa suspected of stealing an axe from a store in Fort Beaufort[3] had been ambushed near a place called Burnshill. Not only were 125 wagons destroyed and much equipment lost in the skirmish, but the Colony was invaded, so sparking off yet another bitter conflict – the so-called War of the Axe, or Seventh Frontier War. British troops were hurried to the area; Colonial commandos mustered in Cape Town before setting off overland for the Frontier; and Cape Malay volunteers travelled by sea to Port Elizabeth.[4] Also despatched by sea was the Corps for Liberated Africans and Free Blacks raised in Cape Town specially to escort convoys to the war zone.

All this excitement in Cape Town was witnessed by Charles Bell and depicted by him in pen and wash as a record for posterity.

Mutual Life Assurance Society
of the
CAPE OF GOOD HOPE.
PROPOSAL FOR AN ASSURANCE

MUTUAL LIFE ASSURANCE SOCIETY
of the
CAPE OF GOOD HOPE.

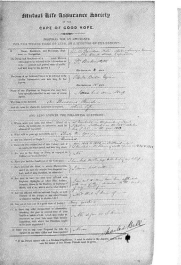

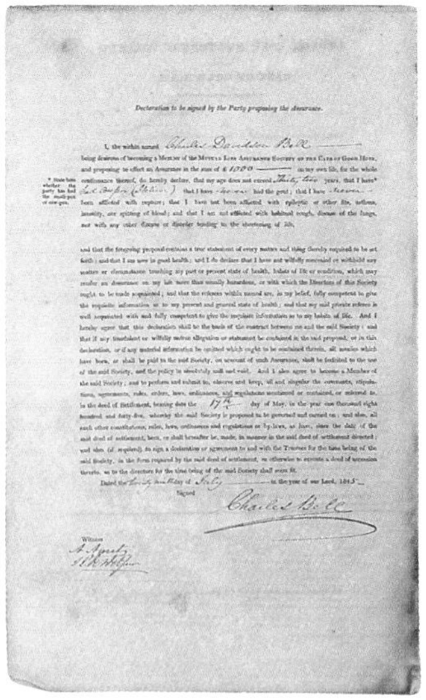

figure 1
Documentation relating to Charles Bell becoming a member of the Mutual Life Assurance Society.
Old Mutual Collection

The first document (left), headed 'Proposal for an Assurance' and in the name of Charles Bell, was completed by Dr Henry Bickersteth, the Mutual's first surgeon. He declared that Bell had been known to him for fifteen years and that, to the best of his belief, he had 'had the Cow Pox' but did not suffer from rheumatism or gout, fits, asthma, insanity, spitting of the blood or various other dangerous complaints.

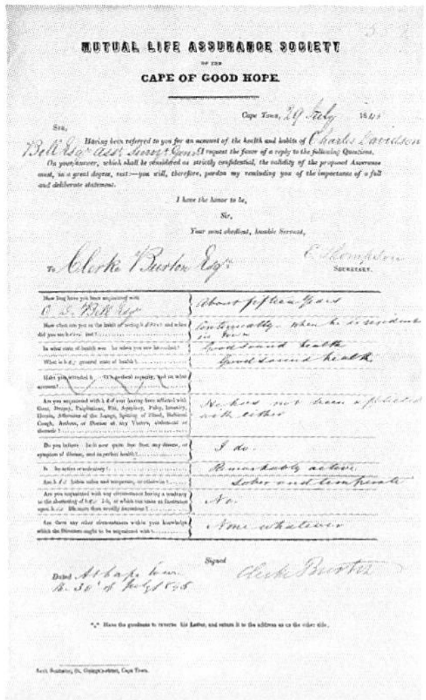

The second document (centre), a questionnaire completed by Clerke Burton, Master of the Supreme Court, testifies to Bell's suitability as a policyholder of the Mutual and is dated 30 July 1845. In Burton's opinion, Bell was 'sober and temperate', while to the question, 'Is he active or sedentary?' he replied, 'Remarkably active'.

The third document is Bell's own declaration, dated 29 July 1845, that he is 'desirous of becoming a member of the Mutual Life Assurance Society of the Cape of Good Hope and proposing to effect an Assurance in the sum of £1000' on his life.

Mutual Life Assurance Society
of the
CAPE OF GOOD HOPE.
POLICY OF ASSURANCE

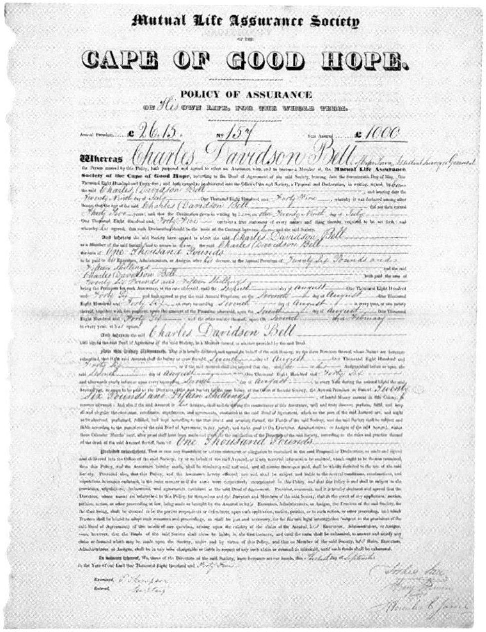

figure 2
Mutual Life Assurance Society policy document.
Old Mutual Collection

By this document Charles Bell insured his life for £1000 with the Mutual Life Assurance Society of the Cape of Good Hope, now known as Old Mutual. Dated 29 July 1845 and numbered 157, the policy was taken out two months after the foundation of the Society. Earlier, Bell had been one of the 166 citizens of the Cape Colony who had signed a request for the establishment of South Africa's first life assurance society. A director from 1850 until 1857, and again from 1859 until 1873, Bell was chairman from 1865 to 1873. Old Mutual, now the Republic's largest life assurance business, issued policy number 10 000 000 in 1995, its 150th anniversary year.

He also produced over fifty monochrome drawings of events that took place on the Eastern Frontier during the war, all of them contained in a sketchbook which he entitled *Rough Sketches of Scenes illustrative of late events in Southern Africa*. These were the days before the existence of official war artists and it is certain that Bell himself was not sent to the Frontier to take up such a post, nor did he witness any of the actual battles or skirmishes that took place during the War of the Axe. The many official letters that he wrote from Cape Town during the twenty months that the war lasted provide evidence of this, as did Piazzi Smyth in his obituary of Bell:

> In 1846, while still in Cape Town, by sheer dint of his knowledge of the eastern country and people, he produced a long series of drawings in black and white, representing events in the Kaffir war then raging under Sir Peregrine Maitland – drawings which astonished and delighted the soldiers who had been engaged in the operations – and being sent home, were taken on one occasion by the Duke of Wellington into his private study, to con over alone, before giving his opinion on the conduct of that war to the House of Lords.[5]

Since numbers of these sketches of events during the war appeared in the *Illustrated London News* – founded in 1842 as a pictorial periodical – it seems possible that Bell might have been commissioned to produce them by the publishers. No proof of this has been discovered, but from some of those that appeared in the journal, it seems clear that Bell sent them to London expecting them to be engraved and published. In the *Illustrated London News* of 25 July 1846, the engravings are described as having been 'derived from the same authentic source as those now presented to the reader – the sketches of a clever Artist in the Colony'. But, as was its custom, the journal did not mention him, or indeed any other artist/correspondent, by name.

One wonders, then, how it was that Bell was able to depict the actual events of the war with such accuracy, for an examination of each picture reveals that it corresponds in detail with the published record. Certainly Bell's experience in the field as a surveyor during the years 1842 to 1844 enabled him to present with authenticity a background of deep wooded ravines and rugged slopes typical of the Amatola Mountains where most of

the action of the Seventh Frontier War took place. The dramatic portrayal of actual events is not so easy to explain, however, though Bell would probably have read in local newspapers accounts of sorties and skirmishes as they occurred. He could also have met returning soldiers and discussed with them details of their experiences in action, or even obtained from them amateur sketches made *in situ*. Bell himself gave credit, as sources, to such artists as the engineer, Lieutenant William Jervois, and the watercolourist, H.W.H.C. Piers. He also acknowledged the work of Captain Robert Granger of the Malay Volunteer Corps and of his old travelling companion, Andrew Geddes Bain. Of interest, too, are the portrayals of Xhosa personalities – both male and female – that Bell included in this sketchbook; among them are the chiefs Maqoma and his half-brother Sandile, both of whom played leading roles in the Seventh Frontier War. It may be that these depictions were executed before the war broke out, and that Bell actually met the subjects of his sketches during the years that he spent in Grahamstown as a surveyor.

In *Rough Sketches of Scenes…* Bell reveals his steady development both as an artist and as a man. By this stage he is able to convey the drama and action of a situation yet, unlike many war artists who were to follow him, he does not idealise or sentimentalise the scenes that he depicts. On the contrary, he emphasises violence or cruelty as it occurs between adversaries, often focusing on what he saw as the barbaric ruthlessness of the Xhosa. In these sketches we see Bell emerging as a mature man, but undoubtedly as a sensitive one.

At the end of August 1846 Charles Bell wrote to his chief, Surveyor-General Colonel Charles Michell, applying for permission to visit Scotland on long leave.[6] He was aware that it was scarcely a propitious moment to make such an application, for the powers-that-be were more than preoccupied with what he called 'the present Caffre War'. Nevertheless, for Bell it was essential to make his application at that moment for Michell himself was about to take eight months' leave. Bell's was a long letter expressed in an extraordinarily convoluted style that conveys the impression that he was writing under considerable strain. This is not surprising, for Michell's impending absence would add to his responsibility at the office while the necessity to complete his war sketches to deadline kept him glued to his drawing board for many long hours after he returned home. Nevertheless, sixteen years had passed since he had last seen his family in Scotland and his urge to visit them all after so long a separation obviously gave him courage to make the request in the strongest possible terms. After explaining that 'self denial during many years' had enabled him to save up sufficient money to travel overseas, he wrote that he 'respectfully [begged] leave to submit that the urgency of private affairs relating to the heart being dependent on

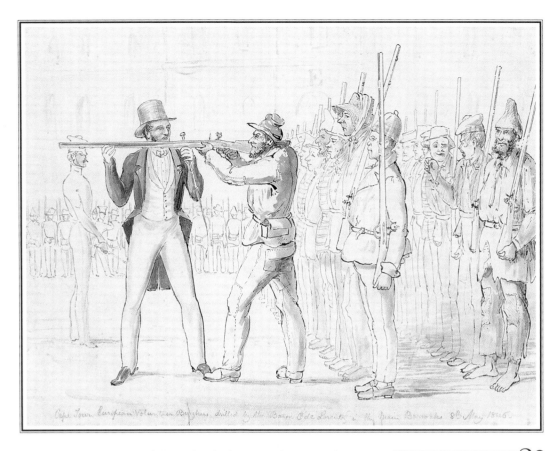

Cape Town European Volunteer Burghers, drilled by the Baron C de Lorentz in the main Barracks 8th May 1846.

the warmth of feeling of the individual, cannot be so easily measured and demonstrated as private affairs relating to pecuniary matters. Nevertheless,' he continued, 'a partial exposure of my circumstances may tend to shew comparatively the importance of my object in my own estimation…'. Having disclosed his 'circumstances' – which appear no more than a great wish to see his ageing parents – Bell goes on to tell Michell that he will have to spend every penny that he owns on his intended visit and that never again will he be able to afford 'a repetition of the indulgence, even if reduced to the last stage of ill health'.

History does not record Michell's immediate reply to this heart-rending letter; probably he did not have time to write to Bell before leaving the office. However, one assumes that it met with a sympathetic response for on 11 February 1847 Charles Bell wrote to his old friend, Thomas Maclear, at the Observatory. 'If I can do anything for you in England,' ran his letter, 'command me from Landsend to John O'Groats – I intend to deposit my Vrouw & kinderen with my Father and my uncle and go scampering about all sorts of places at home and abroad within the limits of steam and a two years leave I may add of my purse, but third class trains and a good pair of legs

figure 3
Levy in Cape Town. Baron C. de Lorentz drills European volunteer burghers. Main barracks. 8 May 1846.
Pen and wash. 18.5 x 24 cm.
Bell Heritage Trust Collection, UCT

When news was received in Cape Town that the Seventh Frontier War – the 'War of the Axe' – had broken out in the Eastern Cape, men of all kinds and classes volunteered for service. Charles Bell, with typical astuteness and humour, depicts the contrast between the sophisticated (if eccentric) superintendent of police, Baron Charles de Lorentz, and the rough and ready burghers whom he is attempting to drill.

may do a great deal – especially for one who can luxuriate under a bush and feast on a carbonatjie.'[7]

By the beginning of April Bell was sorting out his affairs in Cape Town in preparation for an absence of fifteen months. Among other things, he had to be certain that he would remain covered by insurance while away, and for this purpose the Mutual granted him a special licence to 'reside in any part of Europe in time of peace without paying any additional Premium'. He was also permitted to visit the countries on the southern and eastern shores of the Mediterranean but only on the understanding that should he die while there his policy would become void.[8] As far as is known, on this occasion Bell went no further than the British Isles.

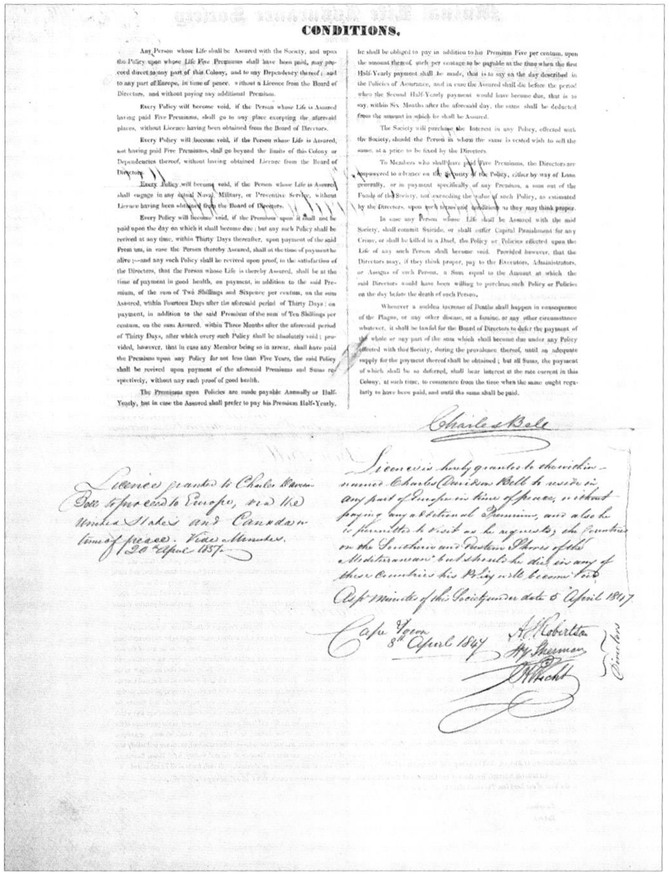

CONDITIONS.

Any Person whose Life shall be Assured with the Society, and upon the Policy upon whose Life Five Premiums shall have been paid, may proceed direct to any part of this Colony, and to any Dependency thereof; and to any part of Europe, in time of peace, without a Licence from the Board of Directors, and without paying any additional Premium.

Every Policy will become void, if the Person whose Life is Assured having paid Five Premiums, shall go to any place excepting the aforesaid places, without Licence having been obtained from the Board of Directors.

Every Policy will become void, if the Person whose Life is Assured, not having paid Five Premiums, shall go beyond the limits of this Colony or Dependencies thereof, without having obtained Licence from the Board of Directors.

Every Policy will become void, if the Person whose Life is Assured shall engage in any actual Naval, Military, or Preventive Service, without Licence having been obtained from the Board of Directors.

Every Policy will become void, if the Premium upon it shall not be paid upon the day on which it shall become due; but any such Policy shall be revived at any time, within Thirty Days thereafter, upon payment of the said Premium, in case the Person thereby Assured, shall at the time of payment be alive;—and any such Policy shall be revived upon proof, to the satisfaction of the Directors, that the Person whose Life is thereby Assured, shall be at the time of payment in good health, on payment, in addition to the said Premium, of the sum of Two Shillings and Sixpence per centum, on the sum Assured, within Fourteen Days after the aforesaid period of Thirty Days; on payment, in addition to the said Premium of the sum of Ten Shillings per centum, on the sum Assured, within Three Months after the aforesaid period of Thirty Days, after which every such Policy shall be absolutely void; provided, however, that in case any Member being so in arrear, shall have paid the Premiums upon any Policy for not less than Five Years, the said Policy shall be revived upon payment of the aforesaid Premiums and Sums respectively, without any such proof of good health.

The Premiums upon Policies are made payable Annually or Half-Yearly, but in case the Assured shall prefer to pay his Premium Half-Yearly, he shall be obliged to pay in addition to his Premium Five per centum, upon the amount thereof, such per centage to be payable at the time when the first Half-Yearly payment shall be made, that is to say on the day described in the Policies of Assurance, and in case the Assured shall die before the period when the Second Half-Yearly payment would have become due, that is to say, within Six Months after the aforesaid day, the same shall be deducted from the amount in which he shall be Assured.

The Society will purchase the Interest in any Policy, effected with the Society, should the Person in whom the same is vested wish to sell the same, at a price to be fixed by the Directors.

To Members who shall have paid Five Premiums, the Directors are empowered to advance on the Security of the Policy, either by way of Loan generally, or in payment specifically of any Premium, a sum out of the Funds of the Society, not exceeding the value of such Policy, as estimated by the Directors, upon such terms and conditions as they may think proper.

In case any Person whose Life shall be Assured with the said Society, shall commit Suicide, or shall suffer Capital Punishment for any Crime, or shall be killed in a Duel, the Policy or Policies effected upon the Life of any such Person shall become void. Provided however, that the Directors may, if they think proper, pay to the Executors, Administrators, or Assigns of such Person, a Sum equal to the Amount at which the said Directors would have been willing to purchase such Policy or Policies on the day before the death of such Person.

Whenever a sudden increase of Deaths shall happen in consequence of the Plague, or any other disease, or a famine, or any other circumstance whatever, it shall be lawful for the Board of Directors to defer the payment of the whole or any part of the sum which shall become due under any Policy effected with this Society, during the prevalence thereof, until an adequate supply for the payment thereof shall be obtained; but all Sums, the payment of which shall be so deferred, shall bear interest at the rate current in this Colony, at such time, to commence from the time when the same ought regularly to have been paid, and until the same shall be paid.

Charles Bell

Licence granted to Charles Davidson Bell to proceed to Europe, via the United States and Canada in time of peace. Vide Minutes 20th April 1857.

Licence is hereby granted to the within named Charles Davidson Bell to reside in any part of Europe in time of peace, without paying any additional Premium, and also to be permitted to visit as he requests, the Countries on the Southern and Eastern Shores of the Mediterranean but should he die in any of these Countries his Policy will become void.

As p^r Minutes of the Society under date 5 April 1847

Cape Town 8th April 1847

A. Robertson
Hy Sherman
[illegible]
Directors

figure 4
Assurance policy conditions.
Old Mutual Collection

The endorsed conditions of assurance on Charles Bell's life policy by which he was granted licence to travel abroad while remaining fully covered. Dated 5 April 1847, shortly before the date he was due to sail for Britain with Martha and his two young sons, the document grants him permission 'to reside in any part of Europe in time of peace without paying any additional Premium'.

Michell returned to his office at the beginning of May and a few days later wrote to Bell thanking him for the 'able manner' with which he had conducted the many and varied duties that had devolved upon him as *locum tenens* – he had taken on Michell's responsibilities as civil engineer and as member of the Central Roads Board as well as those of surveyor-general. 'That you may enjoy health and happiness during your approaching respite from official labours,' he wrote, 'is both my own earnest prayer and that of every member of our department.'[9] Within days, Charles Bell, his wife and his two small sons had set sail from Table Bay on what was to be, in more senses than one, an exceedingly significant holiday.

Naturally, it would have been Bell's first intention to visit his family, including Colonel Bell and Lady Catherine, but unfortunately there is no known record of any of these reunions. What is certain, however, is that he spent a good deal of time with his friend, Piazzi Smyth, who had left Cape Town in October 1845 to take up the post of Astronomer Royal in Edinburgh.[10] Smyth not only was an artist himself, but was extremely interested in devices that could be applied to artistic reproduction. While at the Cape, he had eagerly taken up the recently invented skill of photography and since his return to Edinburgh had applied himself with equal ardour to lithography, a method of printing from the smooth surface of limestone which had been invented at the end of the eighteenth century but remained relatively unknown in Britain until the 1830s. Enthusiasm is contagious, and when Bell called at Smyth's house at No. 1 Hillside Crescent on the evening of 3 November, he was so enthralled by his friend's new hobby that he immediately tried his own hand at it. A lively picture of the occasion has fortunately survived in a letter written by Piazzi Smyth to his printer, W. Walton, the following day.[11] 'As I was packing up last night,' Smyth told him, 'an old Cape friend called, having come here for a few months, which he is going to spend in Edinburgh; his name is Mr Charles Bell, an old friend of Mr Ford's, went on some expeditions of discovery into the interior with him ... Mr Bell is the author of the view of the war in Kaffirland at the Cape, which appeared in the illustrated News some time ago.'

Smyth had recently received some lithotints from Walton, and when Bell saw these he immediately picked up a brush and, in the flickering candlelight, dashed off a sketch of three heads on the edge of one of the stones prepared for drawing. When he saw the pull made from this, Bell was apparently so delighted that he immediately got to work on some more lithographs based on his South African sketches. Smyth told Walton that Bell had 'brought home an immense number more drawings of the Kaffir War, which he wants to lithograph this winter, together with his "Expedition" views'. Bell lost no time in obtaining several stones for himself, ordered a lithographic press from the Edinburgh firm of Schenck & Co. and immediately 'threw off a number of South African subjects'.

Smyth himself kept the proof copy of Bell's first endeavour at lithography made that autumn evening in his house, and also what must have been his first unaided attempt at the craft. This was the title page to his planned *Scraps from my South African Sketch Books*, to which he added the date 1848 and his initials, CB. These two examples, as well as the other lithographs which Bell produced in Edinburgh, Smyth later inserted in a scrapbook which he entitled 'C. Piazzi Smyth's South African Microcosm, or, Sketches Descriptive of the Cape, in all degrees of imperfection and unfinish (sic) from Nature and Various Travellers there but chiefly after Charles Bell Esq. Surveyor General of the Cape of Good Hope Including some of his lithotints. 1835–1846'.[12]

Bell's exuberant pleasure in his first experiment at lithography remains to delight all who see reproductions of the title page to *Scraps from my South African Sketch Books*. Below two (apparently) Khoikhoi figures seated against a mountain background, Bell has written with almost naive ebullience (in crayon): 'Hip, Hip –

Hoorah!!!!' while, more soberly above it appears the inscription 'drawn and printed by C. Bell. No. 1 Hillside Cresct Lith: Press.' At the base of the lithograph, there appears in Smyth's hand, and in Indian ink, 'FIRST ATTEMPT AT LITHOGRAPHY'.

Now there was no stopping Bell in his enthusiasm for this new-found art form. Not only did it appeal to his inventive turn of mind, but the press itself was (in the words of Piazzi Smyth) 'a novel and important accession at that time to its means of graphic multiplication'.[13] Twenty-seven lithographs appear in Smyth's Edinburgh collection; all of these were produced while Bell was on holiday there, giving some idea of the speed at which he worked. Only two known lithographs are dated after his return to the Cape and one other has been tentatively assigned to that period.[14] It is possible that other examples of Bell's lithography have been lost, or it may be that professional demands at the Cape made it impossible for him to maintain the high rate of production he had achieved while on holiday.

Charles Bell remained in Britain with his family for some time after his exciting visit to Piazzi Smyth. At some stage he travelled to London where he managed to retrieve at last the numerous sketches and paintings he had made during the expedition of 1834–1836 and which Andrew Smith had brought to England with him. Eventually, on 29 May 1848, the family sailed from the Downs for the Cape in the barque *Claudine* which was bound for Madras.[15] By the time of their departure Martha was almost three months pregnant with her third child. Her condition, however, did not seem to detract from her attractions for, according to later gossip, seeds of a passionate romance between her and a fellow passenger, an assistant surgeon in the Madras Army named Lestock Wilson Stewart, were sown on the voyage. When the Bells disembarked at Table Bay on 16 August, Stewart apparently continued to India aboard the *Claudine*.

On his arrival home Charles Bell learnt that Colonel Michell, who had been in poor health for some time, had retired to England and that, from 12 July 1848, he had succeeded him as surveyor-general at a salary of £700 a year.[16] By this stage he had taken over ownership of his uncle's house, Canigou, in Rondebosch and it was here that his first daughter, Catherine Mariann, was born on 16 December 1848. She was baptised on 20 February 1849 by the Rev. George Hough in St Paul's Anglican church, of which members of the Ebden family were not only parishioners but benefactors.

For them – indeed for everyone at the Cape – 1849 proved to be a fateful year, for news had been received that the British government approved the plan of Secretary of State Lord Grey to make use of the Colony as a penal settlement. Indeed, plans were already in hand to transport a shipload of convicts to the Cape later in the year. The effect on the local inhabitants was

electrifying; it was intolerable that the name and reputation of their colony should be blemished in this manner, or that it should be used as a dumping ground, comparable to Australia, for unwanted felons – never mind that many of them were Irishmen captured in 'Widow McCormack's potato patch rebellion' of 1848. Over the following months emotions ran high and thousands of people rallied to various mass meetings to protest vociferously against what they saw as a threatened invasion of the sanctity of their homes.

Eventually, when the *Neptune*, a ship carrying 300 ticket-of-leave convicts, sailed into the winter haven of Simon's Bay on 19 September 1849, the colonists' fury knew no bounds. Church bells tolled drearily; alarm bells clanged and tradesmen of all kinds adamantly refused to provide food or services not only to the ship's wretched cargo, but to anyone who so much as exchanged a few words with any of its crew. Drumming up support for the citizens' cause and organising the demonstrations was a body known as the Anti-Convict Association, its leaders John Fairbairn and John Bardwell Ebden. At the time the latter was a member of the Legislative Council but, since it was legally powerless to do anything about the situation, he felt bound to resign from it. For five months the *Neptune* lay outside Simon's Town, its sorry cargo somehow surviving near starvation and

figure 5
Scraps from my South African Sketch Books. 1848.
Lithograph. 21.5 x 27 cm.
Bell Heritage Trust Collection, UCT

As the inscription on the representation of a mountain indicates, this illustration was intended to appear on the title page of an album, Scraps from my South African Sketch Books, *which Charles Bell planned. In a sense it is epoch-making, for it represents Bell's first attempt at lithography. In fact, so overjoyed were Bell and Charles Piazzi Smyth with the result of the experiment, that Bell added the jubilant words 'Hip, Hip – Hoorah!!!!' to his friend's proof copy.*

figure 6
The Great Meeting held in front of the Commercial Hall, Cape Town, 4 July 1849 (Anti-Convict Meeting) by T.W. Bowler. 1850.
Lithograph. 33.2 x 48.6 cm.
Coll: Dr Frank Bradlow

The people of Cape Town had strong feelings about the convict issue, as Thomas Bowler, a contemporary of Charles Bell, shows in his lithograph depicting the great anti-convict meeting. Bell would have been well aware of the issue, as his father-in-law, John Bardwell Ebden, was one of the leaders of the protests against landing convicted felons at the Cape.

enduring both the heat of summer and the constant battering of the prevailing southeast wind. Then, at last, on 21 February 1850 word was received from the Colonial Office that the *Neptune* was to proceed to Van Diemen's Land (today's Tasmania) and the anti-convict lobby knew that it had won the day.

It must have been a traumatic time for the Ebden family, and not only because of the close involvement of John Bardwell in the *Neptune* débâcle. At the end of the previous year, disturbing rumours arose regarding the position of one of the Ebden sons vis-à-vis the Mutual Life Assurance Society of the Cape of Good Hope. John Watts Ebden, then forty years old, was an advocate of the Cape Supreme Court and unmarried; since 1848 he had also been a director of the Mutual. This appointment was considered in business circles to be a highly prestigious one, but gossip

going the rounds of Cape society towards the end of 1849 suggested that the younger John Ebden was not fit to hold it.[17] This was made plain to him when he was summoned to appear at a board meeting on 3 January 1850 and given a letter to read while his fellow directors silently and solemnly looked on. This done, he handed back the letter to the chairman, it was torn up, and Ebden left the meeting. Two days later he was officially informed that his continued presence on the board was considered 'prejudicial to the interests of the Society' and that consequently he was dismissed as a director with immediate effect. Someone of impeccable character had to be found to take Ebden's seat on the board, and the man considered most suitable was none other than his brother-in-law, Charles Bell.

No reason was given then or later for the drastic treatment

meted out to John Watts Ebden, but faded documents in the Cape Archives suggest why this man, destined to become a judge of the Cape Supreme Court, should have provoked the censure of his peers. John Watts Ebden's death notice reveals two important facts: first, that he remained a bachelor until he died, aged 77, in 1888; and secondly, that he was the father of three children all bearing the surname Lewis, who were born just before or after the time of his dismissal from the Mutual's board. A death notice is usually signed by the next of kin present at the time; in his case the signatory is one Louisa Lewis, obviously the mother of the children and their father's close companion. A further indication of Ebden's intimacy with the Lewis family is to be found in his will which makes more than adequate financial provision for them all.

Whatever John Watts Ebden's reason for not 'making an honest woman' of Louisa, the situation was obviously a distressing one and can hardly have given any joy to the proud and self-righteous Ebdens. But there was worse in store for them all. Early in April 1850 Martha Antoinetta Bell received a summons to appear before the judges of the Supreme Court on 13 April 'to show why the bonds of marriage between her and Charles Davidson Bell Esq. [should] not be declared to be dissolved by reason of Adultery committed by the said Martha Antoinetta Bell with one Lestock Wilson Stewart on or about 10 January 1850 and on divers days between the said 10 January 1850 and 5 April 1850'. The defendant's plea and the plaintiff's declaration were filed on 18 and 29 May respectively and the trial began on Thursday 11 June, in the very building where Charles Bell had his office.[18]

As was customary in those days, no account of the divorce proceedings appeared in the newspapers, but one can imagine that with the eloquent and witty William Porter as plaintiff's counsel, the hearing must, if nothing more, have been interesting. It is almost ironic that the Chief Justice, Sir John Wylde, was on the bench when he himself was known to have been party to an equally salacious scandal.[19] Nevertheless, he had the reputation of being wise and impartial in his judgments and the case involving Martha Bell was no exception. The trial lasted for two weeks and every day the loyal Thomas Maclear made his way from the Royal Observatory to town to support his friend Charles Bell in

his time of need. Indeed, it is those good correspondents, Thomas and Mary Maclear, that posterity must thank for their accounts of what must have been Cape Town's *cause célèbre* of the decade. Shortly before the trial began, on 18 May 1850, Maclear wrote to Piazzi Smyth:

> I am wretched respecting poor Bell's position in regard to his good for nothing wife. She has dishonoured him & their children. She has been carrying on a criminal intercourse with a Dr Stewart from India. He – Bell – is living in Cape Town with the children pending the decision of legal proceedings in the supreme court by which he hopes to obtain a divorce from his wife – & damages from the *scamp*! Their relatives are moving Heaven & Earth to prevent a divorce; in other words the *morality* of the affair is secondary in their opinion, they would have him take back a woman who it is asserted prostituted herself in the *fields*, in open daylight!!! Bell's was a love *match*. I have said more on this disgusting subject than I should have said, but for the interest I have (& you have) taken in the prosperity of our friend. He is sadly cut up in health brought on by his misery. They sojourned with you I think when they visited Edinburgh...[20]

Three weeks after the trial was over, on 11 July 1850, Mary Maclear vividly described the entire unhappy affair in a letter to her friend Lady Herschel, who had known both the Bell and Ebden families well while she lived at the Cape in the 1830s.

It appears on their voyage from England acquaintance was made with this Dr Stewart (and even then things were suspicious) he went on to India but the end of last year visited the Cape as an invalid – we first heard of him as one of a party of Indian gentlemen[31] who had taken Mrs Brinks old house near the observatory and given it the name 'Maiden's Hope'. Between Mrs Bell and this Doctor Stewart, meetings were constant at her own house ... Notes of hers miscarried and by mistake were opened in which she made assignments with him – but one night her husband returning home an hour or so before he was expected and entering the back way and suddenly coming into the drawing room found the guilty pair! An investigation into circumstances took place. Mrs Bell proposed quickly to have a divorce effected but her family would not hear of such a thing and although her conduct had long occasioned them the greatest uneasiness they would not or said they would not believe her guilty ... she assumes a very bold front and still avers to her innocence

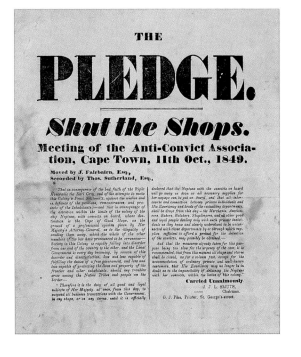

THE

PLEDGE.

Shut the Shops.

Meeting of the Anti-Convict Association, Cape Town, 11th Oct., 1849.

Moved by J. Fairbairn, Esq.,
Seconded by Thos. Sutherland, Esq.,

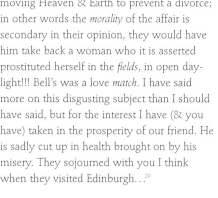

figure 7 **Leaflet distributed during the Anti-Convict Agitation. 1849.**
Coll: University of Cape Town Libraries

The Pledge – a notice that appeared in the South African Commercial Advertiser *and was also distributed as a leaflet to the citizens of Cape Town requiring them to pledge their support to the anti-convict movement. Shops, businesses and individuals were boycotted and punished if they had any dealings at all, no matter how charitable, with the* Neptune, *her crew or her cargo of convicts.*

and 'hopes her enemies may one day be found out and longs to give the Attorney General[22] a little of her mind'! This conduct saves us from all feeling of compassion for her – Penitence and misery would have affected it bitterly.[23]

The trial ended on Saturday 22 June 1850 and on 1 July the Court granted Charles Bell his divorce. Three days later Martha lodged a petition against the judgment but this was dismissed with costs. Counsellor John Watts Ebden, acting for his sister, asked for leave to appeal to the Privy Council in London. So far as is known nothing came of this, no doubt, so Mrs Maclear told Lady Herschel, because such an action could 'only be to vex and protract matters and occasion expense'. Charles Bell obtained custody of all three children – although Martha had sworn never to part from her daughter – and she was ordered to leave Canigou where she had remained doggedly throughout the trial.

figure 8
Gnadenthal. 17th Oct. 1850.
Pencil. 28.5 x 21 cm.
Bell Heritage Trust Collection, UCT

Charles Bell executed this sensitive pencil sketch of a small boy while visiting the mission station at Genadendal on 17 October 1850, the very day on which his former wife, Martha Antoinetta, gave birth to a daughter reputedly fathered by her lover, Lestock Wilson Stewart.

Meanwhile, in a civil action, Bell sued Stewart for £2000 damages, since, he alleged, the doctor 'wrongfully, wickedly and unjustly did debauch and carnally know' Martha, as a result of which he had been 'greatly injured'. Once more the Court found in Bell's favour, though damages were given at only £500 as the judge was of the opinion that Martha had been the seducer.[24]

The sordid story did not end there. On 17 October, when Charles was away in Genadendal,[25] Martha gave birth to a daughter. The child was to be named Charlotte Margaret and her baptism was arranged for the morning of 27 January 1851. The church was to be St Paul's, Rondebosch, and the officiating chaplain was the Rev. John Fry. However, before the service took place, Charles Bell came to hear about it and when he realised that Martha would probably give his name as the child's father, he hastily wrote a letter to Fry in an attempt to stop this from happening. 'It is now too late to obtain legal advice as to the means of preventing this,' he wrote, 'but I will not, if I possibly can avoid it, permit my name to be thus used, and I in the mean time protest against it because this child was not born in the bonds of wedlock; its birth took place nine months after its mother was living in notorious adultery with Lestock Wilson Stewart of the Madras Medical Establishment as proved by sentence of the Supreme Court of this Colony on 1st July 1850 re Bell vs Bell.'[26] In other words, Charles Bell declared that, unlike Stewart, he had not 'carnally known' Martha during the crucial period when conception took place; hence his emphatic denial of paternity.

Situated not more than two kilometres from Canigou along the Camp Ground Road in Rondebosch and almost next door to J.B. Ebden's mansion, Belmont, was the house 'Charlie's Hope'. Perhaps, in this particular context, its name was appropriate but here, at all events, Fry was living in company with a menagerie of animals from which he supplied specimens from time to time to the private zoo of the Earl of Derby in England.[27] To Charlie's Hope the letter was delivered with all speed, its contents filling Fry, naturally, with more than a degree of perplexity. Now it was his turn to write a hasty letter, this time to Robert Gray, first bishop of Cape Town, who had arrived in the Colony only three years before. 'My Lord,' it began, 'Previous to administering the rite of Baptism to Mrs Bell's child this morning, I received the enclosed protest from Charles Bell Esqr declining to have his name entered on the Register of Baptisms in St Paul's Church, Rondebosch. This is a case quite new to me, and I do not know of any precedent to guide me in the matter, I therefore beg to receive your Lordship's instructions as to the course proper to be pursued.'[28]

Up to Protea, later Bishopscourt – known well to Charles Bell some twenty years earlier as the country home of Sir Lowry and

Lady Frances Cole – galloped the messenger bearing Fry's letter. This second journey was somewhat longer than the first and St Paul's fretting chaplain had to wait with some nail-biting for the Bishop's reply. Although it has not survived, it must have arrived in time for Fry to take cognisance of whatever Gray's instructions were regarding the baptism of Charlotte Margaret. Obviously the ceremony did take place on 27 January 1851, for St Paul's register, now held in the South African Library, Cape Town, states as much. However, in the column where the name of the father should appear, Fry evaded the issue of paternity and wrote: 'Daughter of Martha Antoinetta, fifth daughter of John Bardwell Ebden Esq' pronounced to be divorced from Charles Davidson Bell, by sentence of the Supreme Court, dated the 1st of July 1850.'

Interrupted marriage ceremonies occur frequently in literature and sometimes in fact; not so often have interrupted baptisms been recorded. Not that Charlotte Margaret's christening was actually interrupted, but there is no doubt that Charles Bell's last-minute refusal to be cited as the father upset the proceedings. There were almost certainly tears and protests on Martha's part and any celebration held afterwards must have been a miserable affair. At all events, the powerful Ebdens took up the cudgels on Martha's behalf and a letter written ostensibly by her at Belmont was delivered to John Fry at St Paul's a few days later. It read:

> When I brought my child Charlotte Margaret Bell to be baptized by you in St Paul's Church, Rondebosch, on the 27th January 1851, in the sight of God and Man, I little expected that any opposition would be made by her father to have the baptism of his daughter registered in any but the legal and usual manner. After the baptism was over I was surprised at Mr Bell's scandalous and unfeeling letter to you, the accusations of which I pronounce to be false and I do with truth most solemnly assert that my child Charlotte Margaret Bell was procreated in the bonds of wedlock [with] Mr Bell, and that no other person *can* be the father of the child & I shall not rest until steps be taken to establish her legitimacy.[29]

There followed complaints regarding the manner in which the baptism was recorded and threats to refer the matter to the bishop, but no alterations were ever made to the entry in the register, nor was the luckless infant ever formally declared to be legitimate.

The Ebdens, it seems, would not accept that anyone other than Bell was the father of Charlotte Margaret. In a will made jointly with his wife, Antoinetta Adriana, on 14 May 1852,[30] John Bardwell Ebden makes bequests to all Martha's children including 'a fourth child … named Charlotte Margaret Bell which had been procreated by the said Charles Davidson Bell with his said wife before the commencement of the … [divorce] Action which child is left dependent upon her mother and without any support

from her father…'. Sadly, Charlotte did not live to inherit anything from her grandfather for, according to a later will, dated 10 April 1866,[31] she had by then died in some unmentioned place and on some unstated date.

However strongly John Bardwell Ebden may have protested his daughter Martha's innocence, one does wonder whether he eventually became somewhat disillusioned about her. In a codicil to the will of May 1852, dated 25 January 1861, he cancelled his bequest to her of £500 'which sum has actually been paid by the Testator in defending an Action which was instituted against her by her husband Charles Davidson Bell … on which Account the Testator considers himself justified in charging her with expenses paid by him.' Was that justification due to his subsequent discovery of the truth, or had her later behaviour proved unacceptable?

Martha must have married later, for in an affidavit dated 1885

figure 9
Fytje. Bushman girl.
Bot River, 15th Oct. 1850.
Pencil. 28.5 x 21.5 cm.
Bell Heritage Trust Collection, UCT

Bell's sympathetic approach to children, no matter how lowly their status, is revealed in this slight but appealing pencil sketch.

in which J.B. Ebden's sons, Alfred and Harry, were appointed executors of their father's estate, she is mentioned as Martha Antoinetta Moyes. No trace has so far been found of Mr Moyes. There have been claims that Martha left South Africa 'with the gardener',[32] but so far these have not been substantiated; nor is it known whether 'the gardener' was in fact Moyes. The fate of Lestock Wilson Stewart also remains a mystery. Mrs Maclear,

however, concludes her letter of 11 July 1850 to Lady Herschel with a hint that things in Cape Town had become too hot for him. 'Can you conceive of a greater disgrace!' she writes. 'Dr Stewart is reported to have been smuggled off in a ship which sailed for India two days ago.'

And so, it seems, the cad escaped, leaving Martha literally holding the baby.

figure 10
Levy in Cape Town. Liberated African Corps mustered for embarkation. 1846.
Pen, pencil and wash.
17.5 x 24 cm.
Bell Heritage Trust Collection, UCT

'Liberated' Africans were West Africans rescued by British frigates from ships pursuing the slave trade after it had been officially abolished. Once at the Cape, they were obliged to work for fourteen years before being given their freedom. Bell, not surprisingly, sees the incongruity of combining black faces and kapparings with the glengarries and 'trews' favoured by Scottish regiments.

figure 11
First embarkation of Malay volunteers at the South Jetty, Cape Town. 14 May 1846.
Pen and wash. 18.5 x 24.5 cm.
Bell Heritage Trust Collection, UCT

Charles Bell captured, in pen and wash, the 'Malay' contingent rallying to the cause as an imam and their womenfolk wave farewell. The direction in which the flags are flying indicates that a stiff northwest wind was blowing and presages a rough passage to East London, where they would disembark.

Embarkation of part of the Malay Volunteers — Cape Town 14 May 1846.

figure 12 **Fort Beaufort, from a sketch by Lieut. W.F.D. Jervois R.E. 1846.**
Pen and wash. 17.5 x 25.5 cm. Bell Heritage Trust Collection, UCT

Bell's sketch of Fort Beaufort, an important settlement on the Eastern Frontier during the War of the Axe, was taken from an original by fellow land surveyor and authority on defences and fortifications, Sir William Jervois. Some of the sketches made by Bell on the subject of the frontier war appeared as engravings in the Illustrated London News.

Graham's Town, from a sketch by H.W. Piers Esq. Ordnance D.
Pen and wash. 18 x 24 cm. Bell Heritage Trust Collection, UCT

Although Charles Bell was not in the Eastern Cape during the Seventh Frontier War, he produced many sketches of events that occurred at that time. Some of these were based on the works of other, possibly less skilled artists, one of them being H.W.H.C. Piers, who had actually been present at the time. Grahamstown, as Piers saw it, had changed little since the Bells had lived there a few years earlier.

figure 14 **Interior of Nel's camp during attack. 2 June 1846.**
Pen and wash. 17.5 x 24 cm. Bell Heritage Trust Collection, UCT

Bell was certainly not present on this occasion during the War of the Axe but, basing his pen and wash sketch on another artist's work and his own knowledge of the people and the terrain, he conveys the event with fidelity. Encircled by the laager, the women and children load the guns while the men, protected by the wagons, fire at the approaching enemy.

figure 15 **Ox-wagon around fire.**
Watercolour. 16 x 22 cm. Old Mutual Collection

A scene that must have been familiar to Charles Bell – travellers gathered around the fire while the evening meal is being prepared in the traditional potjie. *The man on the left plays the fiddle as the fire crackles, and the lone woman stirs the* bredie. *In the background, beyond the covered wagon, a draught-ox dozes peacefully.*

figure 16
Kafir warrior in the old war dress.
Pen and wash. 24 x 18 cm.
Bell Heritage Trust Collection,
UCT

*His interest in ethnography
aroused during Dr Andrew Smith's
expedition into the southern African
interior (1834–1836), Charles Bell
continued to depict the manners
and customs of South Africa's
indigenous peoples when he was
living in the Eastern Cape some ten
years later. In the bottom right-
hand corner of the sketch he has
signed what are presumed to be his
initials in Taylor's shorthand.*

26. — Kafir Warrior. — in the Old War dress. —

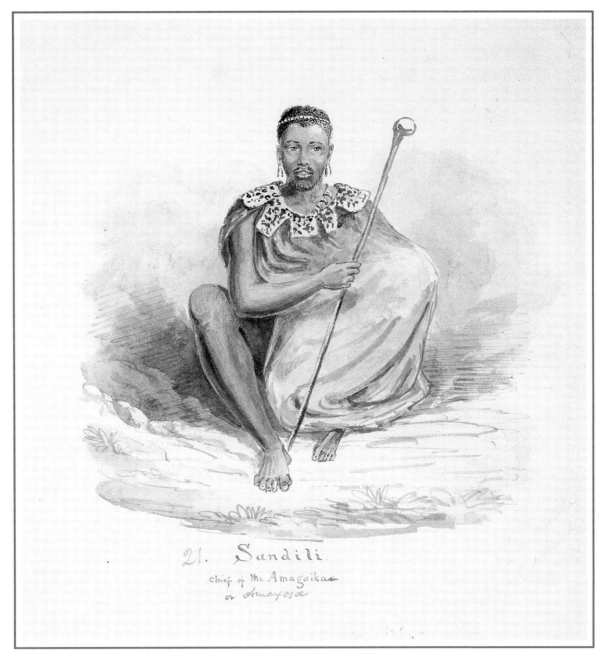

figure 17
Sandili, chief of the Amagaika or Amaxosae.
Pen and wash. 24 x 19 cm.
Bell Heritage Trust Collection, UCT

Sandile (1820–1878) inherited the paramount chieftainship of the Rharhabe branch of the western Xhosa as a child. He endeavoured to withstand the growing pressure of white domination throughout his life, but died while resisting the forces of Great Britain during the Ninth, and last, Frontier War. Bell shows him as a young man, with his withered left foot partially hidden under his blanket.

21. Sandili
chief of the Amagaika
or Amayosa

figure 18
Kaffir Chief Macoma.
c. **1849.**
Watercolour. 16.9 x 21.4 cm.
William Fehr Collection

*In this painting Charles Bell depicts
the Rharhabe chief Maqoma
(1798–1873) as a noble warrior,
though perhaps his disconsolate
bearing is some clue to the
disappointments he experienced in
life. Ngqika's eldest son and
half-brother to Sandile, Maqoma
excelled as a guerilla fighter in
numerous clashes with the British.
After spending twenty-one years in
exile on Robben Island he was
released, only to be found guilty of
incitement to violence shortly afterwards. He was then returned to
Robben Island, where he lived out
the rest of his days.*

Portrait of Queen Sutu_ the Great Wife of the late Chief Gaika of the Amakosæ and mother of the present Chief Sandili_

figure 19
Sutu. Great wife of the late Chief Gaika of the Amakosie.
Pen and wash. 24 x 17.5 cm.
Bell Heritage Trust Collection, UCT

This sketch by Charles Bell shows Suthu, a princess in her own right and widow of Ngqika, paramount chief of the Rharhabe in what later became the Ciskei. On the death of her husband in 1829, Suthu became regent to his successor, her eight-year-old son, Sandile. As Bell depicts her, she was every inch the matriarch.

figure 20

The Schoolmaster reading *De Zuid-Afrikaan*. **1850.**
Watercolour. 10.7 x 17.8 cm.
William Fehr Collection

On his travels as a surveyor, Charles Bell was often welcomed into the homes of simple Cape farmers, many of whom were quite unable to read or write. In this sketch for an oil painting (which was exhibited under the title 'The Boer's Voorhuis') he depicts a familiar scene – the schoolmaster explaining the contents of the Cape's 'High Dutch' newspaper, while the farmer and his family listen with solemn interest.

figure 21
Hottentots.
Lithograph. 36 x 26 cm.
Bell Heritage Trust Collection,
UCT

*Another of Charles Bell's early
lithographs shows a pair of carefree
Khoikhoi as he so often saw them –
the man with his bottle of 'Cape
smoke' and the woman with her
clay pipe. Unusual though, are the
couple's smart clothes and happy
expressions, although it seems that
Nemesis, in the form of the furious
woman behind them, intends their
pleasure to be shortlived.*

Chapter 6

DIVERSITY IN MATURITY

In the 1850s the British Empire was at its zenith. *Symbolic of its power and focus of its national pride was the Crystal Palace, erected in Hyde Park in 1851 to house the Great Industrial Exhibition and to display the marvels of modern technology and scientific achievement to a rapturous public. Not least among those who visited the exhibition was Queen Victoria herself: quite carried away by it all, she was to write in her diary on 29 April — no doubt with a profound sigh of satisfaction — 'We are capable of doing anything'.*

figure 1
Silver medal. 1851.
South African Cultural History Museum

This silver medal, designed by Charles Bell and engraved by T.B. Hopkins, was awarded on instructions from the governor, Sir Harry Smith, as an expression of his high regard for the men fighting under his command during the Eighth Frontier War, particularly those who had helped him make his escape from the enemy. Although Smith had no right to commission the award, the medal is in fact extremely valuable today because of its rarity and the uniqueness of its design. About 22 examples are known to exist.

In many ways Charles Bell was a true product of the age and the nation into which he was born for he, too, could do almost anything. Certainly, it was during this decade of inventiveness and creativity, of exploring new avenues as well as new lands, that he was to find expression for his disparate and exceptional talents. Since boyhood he had been sketching in ink and painting in watercolours; more recently he had begun to show an interest in etching and in lithography. Now – like the Empire – he had reached his prime, and the time had come to venture into other media and new skills; to research and invent and design with all the confidence of a true artist and a mature scientist. His divorce behind him, his reputation remained unscathed by the scandal that had both shocked and intrigued local Victorian society. Indeed, he found himself much in demand to serve on public bodies where, in those days, an unsullied character was a prerequisite. At the same time, his office of surveyor-general carried with it both status and considerable responsibilities. Charles Bell, in fact, had become a man of moral stature much respected throughout the community.

At the Cape at this time the idea of representative government was in the forefront of almost every informed mind. Following the departure, in February 1850, of the *Neptune* and its ill-loved cargo, the clamour for parliamentary representation, and at least a degree of autonomy for the Colony, had grown steadily louder. So determined was the local populace to get its own way that, on 23 October 1850, it dispatched John Fairbairn to England with

a copy of a draft constitution in his pocket and a mandate to persuade the British government to accede to the Colony's demands. For over a year, Capetonians waited impatiently for news of success but they were destined for disappointment. When Fairbairn returned home on 26 November 1851 he had to admit that his request had been received with scant sympathy at the Colonial Office. Indeed, it seemed to his supporters at the Cape that people in high places had failed to take his plea seriously.

Successful though the year 1851 undoubtedly had been in Britain itself, its first days could hardly have been described as auspicious in South Africa. With the new year came the news that on Christmas Eve 1850 yet another frontier war – the eighth, destined to be the longest and bloodiest of them all– had erupted in the Eastern Cape.[1] Once more troops, supported by levies of local volunteers, were hurried from Cape Town to the Eastern Frontier where the governor, Sir Harry Smith, was holed up by the enemy in a small fort in the Amatola Mountains. Eventually, hustled out by about 250 men of the Cape Mounted Rifles – a predominantly Cape Coloured regiment – Smith made his escape and, on returning to his base, decided to honour his rescuers, and any other meritorious members of the levies, by decorating them with a special medal.[2] To Charles Bell, who was commissioned to design it, the task would have been both a privilege and, since it was something completely new to him, a challenge to his creative spirit. The finished product was certainly a work of art;

figure 2
**Dutch Reformed Church,
Cape Town, by T.W. Bowler.
1851.**
Pencil on coloured chalk paper.
12.7 x 21 cm.
Coll: MuseumAfrica

*This work by Thomas Bowler
shows a 'sandwich man' advertising Cape Town's First Exhibition of
Fine Arts outside the Groote Kerk.
Held from 10 February until the
last week of March 1851, the
exhibition was pronounced a great
success. Almost three thousand
people, paying a shilling each,
admired the five hundred exhibits,
many of which were on loan. Bell
was awarded a gold medal for 'the
best historical painting in oil'.*

it was also unique in that it was not only the first medal to be designed and struck entirely in South Africa, but the first to be worn by an honoured few of the country's fighting men. The editor of *The Cape Monitor* of 25 April 1851 reported that he 'had been favoured with an inspection' of the medal, the design of which 'presents on the face, the British Lion, standing proudly, surmounted by a victorious wreath'. In a more recent publication,[3] the author describes the lion as being 'rather eastern look-ing ... bewhiskered and with very curly mane ... with tail curled above his back, standing on a representation of the veld'. Below the lion is the date, 1851. The recipient's name is inscribed on the reverse side, as well as the fact that the medal was presented by Sir Harry Smith 'for gallantry in the field'. Not that everyone approved of the governor's munificent gesture: there were rumbles from the powers-that-be in London that the award of medals was the prerogative of the Queen, but no matter: today the 1851 war medal is among the most rare of its kind and much

sought after by numismatists. Some twenty-two medals are known to be still in existence, and plaster casts made from them show that Bell originally designed at least two obverse and six reverse dies for it.

These were good days for Charles Bell. Not only had he been singled out by Sir Harry Smith for a rare and privileged assign-ment, but he would have been glowing with a sense of achieve-ment after his considerable success in Cape Town's First Exhibition of Fine Arts. Held a month earlier in the new school rooms adjoining the Government Gardens,[4] this event was the outcome of a meeting held in the Public Library on 12 October of the previous year. The purpose of that meeting was 'to consider the propriety of getting together the best pictures, statues, &c, &c, to be exhibited ... together with works of art from artists, students, and amateurs resident in the colony with a view to give an impetus to local talent, as well as to furnish means for reward-ing the labours of the artist, and stimulating him to future and honourable exertions and enterprise'.[5] A committee, which included Charles Bell, William Porter and a promising architect named Gilbert MacDougall, was duly elected and plans for the exhibition immediately drawn up. Originally the show was intended to run from 10 February until 15 March 1851, but it met with such gratifying success that it was extended for a further week. Tickets cost a shilling each (reduced to sixpence during the final few days) and during the six weeks that it was open, no fewer than 2984 people came to admire the exhibits. There were over 500 of them, mostly paintings loaned by their owners, but in addition there were a good many original competitive works in a diversity of classes, including some interesting statuary which was much admired.

The catalogue of exhibits reveals that there was no lack of art collectors in Cape Town in the mid-nineteenth century. Among those who loaned works are the names of prosperous merchants Ewan Christian (he owned a splendid collection of marine scenes), and Bell's former father-in-law, John Bardwell Ebden, who exhibited, besides others, a painting entitled 'A green-grocer reading the ballad of Jim Crow'. Sir John Wylde boldly submitted

figure 3
The Strand-loopers' visit to Van Riebeeck. 1850.
Oil. 46 x 61 cm.
Private Collection, Cape Town

A sketch for this oil painting showing Jan van Riebeeck entertaining 'Strand-loopers' was also on show at the 1851 exhibition. Bell quotes the inspiration for this subject as an extract from Van Riebeeck's journal dated 20 April 1652, two weeks after his arrival at the Cape. 'Saw nothing of any natives from the land of Saldania or anywhere else,' wrote the commander, 'save 4 or 5 of the Strand-loopers, who brought with them nothing but lean bodies and hungry bellies, which we filled with pearl barley and bread.'

a portrait of himself; Colonel Abraham Josias Cloete – much involved at the time with the Eighth Frontier War – provided a variety of landscapes while, from the wealth of its treasures, the South African Public Library selected a portrait of Charles I by Van Dyk and 'Interior with figures' of the school of Teniers. Not surprisingly, Gilbert MacDougall's contributions included a number of architectural plans and elevations, among them those of new buildings 'in the Tudor period of Gothic architecture' designed for the Diocesan College on Woodlands Estate.[6] He also loaned some interesting statuary by a lesser known Italian sculptor called Ambrozzi: one piece was a cast entitled 'Eve at the fountain' while another, purporting to be a bust of Michelangelo, was pronounced by certain philistines visiting the exhibition to bear an uncanny resemblance to Sir Andries Stockenström![7]

Charles Bell submitted no fewer than fifteen paintings of his own and an even greater number of works by other artists from his personal collection. He also exhibited several remarkable life-size clay models – a genre in which he had lately become interested. They were sculpted 'in the round' and depicted a variety of the ethnic types which he had come across during his various ventures into the interior. Later, so it is believed, the figures were presented to the South African Museum but today their whereabouts are unknown, possibly because the clay fragmented easily and the models were broken. One could wish that it were possible to see Bell's statuette, 'Dorothea bathing her feet', which belonged to local master of fox hounds and society wit, Percy Vigors, but this, sadly enough, has disappeared as well.

Eight prizes in all were awarded, of which three were gold medals. The first of these went to Charles Bell for 'the best historical painting in oil'. Entitled 'Arrival of Van Riebeeck 1652', it is one of several works which Bell based on extracts from the journal of Jan van Riebeeck, and has become famous as an illustration in school history books. It shows the Dutch commander with his henchmen, all of them hatted, helmeted and flag-flying, greeting a group of scantily clad Khoikhoi with Devil's Peak in the background. A second historical painting by Bell, also in oils and entitled 'The isle of the Holy Cross', was another exhibit. For over a century it was thought to be a depiction of the occasion in December 1487 when the Portuguese navigator, Bartolomeu Dias, raised a cross, or *padrao*, at Angra Pequena (now Lüderitz Bay) on the southwestern coast of Africa. However, the catalogue of the exhibition indicates that this painting in fact represents a similar event that took place early in 1488 – Dias raising a *padrao* on the islet of St Croix in Algoa Bay. Both these works are recorded as having belonged at one stage to William Porter, but by 1866 they had been acquired by the South African Public Library, where they may still be found.[8]

At this first exhibition, a second gold medal was awarded to Thomas Bowler who, like Bell, had exhibited a large number of paintings. The winning entry, adjudged the best original watercolour, was a seascape entitled 'Departure of Lord Lowther from Table Bay'. Winner of the third gold medal was Gilbert MacDougall whose model of a proposed House of Representatives for the Cape – a popular subject at the time – was described as being 'very carefully executed'. All in all, the exhibition was proclaimed an unqualified success and proved that there were in the Colony 'men amongst us who have proved themselves to be possessed of no ordinary talent',[9] a statement that must have pleased even the four women – Miss Kilgour, Mrs Joseph, Miss Billingsley and a modest lady who gave her name only as 'Miss R' – who were awarded prizes.[10] The names of many of the artists listed in the catalogue have long been forgotten; those of others, such as Charles Bell, Thomas Bowler and Thomas Baines, are now among the ranks of the famous, their nineteenth-century Africana paintings invariably fetching prices that would astonish their creators.

It was during the exhibition that Bell took leave in order to spend some time with his friend, Andrew Geddes Bain, then hard at work constructing the mountain pass later known as Bain's Kloof. Bell was anxious to assist Bain in completing a geological map of South Africa,[11] in which, as a qualified surveyor, he took a professional interest. It may have been during this visit that Bell and Bain discussed the possibility that coal – always much sought after – might exist in the southwestern Cape, a theory expounded half a century earlier by the visiting British official, John Barrow, in his work, *An account of travels into the interior of southern Africa*. Bell, the scientist, clearly dismissed these claims outright. It was far more probable, he maintained, that what Barrow described as a carbonized formation might be the timbers of a ship 'submerged in Historic Times' and held by local legend to be buried in the unprepossessing sands of the Cape Flats. It was a fascinating theory, particularly since the Greek philosopher, Herodotus, had told of how, some six hundred years BC, Phoenician mariners had reached the southern extremity of Africa where they had spent some time ashore. Indeed, the story so intrigued the lieutenant-governor, Charles Henry Darling, when he learnt of it that he had ordered Bell to 'trace [his] authorities, examine the locality [of the wreck] if it could be found, and enquire further'.[12]

Naturally Bell lost no time in obeying Darling's instructions. It seems that he found what he believed to be the wreck without difficulty, although he gave no hint as to how he discovered its location in the bed of the Hardekraaltjie stream which now flows through the present town of Bellville, named after him. He investigated it thoroughly and reported, 'However extraordinary it may seem, I am compelled to believe that this wood is part of a

figure 4
**The isle of the Holy Cross.
1850.**
Oil. 75 x 92 cm.
Coll: South African Library

*The entry in the catalogue to Cape
Town's First Exhibition of Fine Arts
states that the painting represents
the landing of Bartolomeu Dias on
'a small rocky Islet in Algoa Bay,
which he named Santa Croiz, and
on which he erected a Cross and
administered the Sacrament'. The
albatross gracefully poised above
the sailors at work places the event
in the cool oceans of the southern
hemisphere.*

large vessel upwards of seventy feet in length wrecked when the
sea washed up to some of the sea beaches on Lion's Head – and
now raised hundreds of feet in height above the present high
water mark and left at a distance of at least 10 miles from the
sea.' The wood was embedded in stiff clay about ten or twelve
feet deep, with 'ribs and knees' protruding to half that height.
Bell was anxious to continue the examination but that, of course,
would involve some expense. A mere £20 would be sufficient
(so he told the secretary to government to whom he was obliged
to report), and as 'the ancient vessel' lay on government-owned
land, he suggested (respectfully) that the government might
agree to provide it. His request was duly passed on to Henry
Darling who hastily scrawled his endorsement across the corner
of a page. 'Inform Mr Bell,' he wrote, 'that I am obliged by the
trouble he has already taken in this matter and, considering the
Enquiry one of great interest, I readily place the sum mentioned
at his disposal.'[13]

No trace has so far been found of any expenditure of public
money on such a project in the mid-nineteenth century, nor is it
known whether or not Charles
Bell ever continued his investigation. Yet, unscientific though
such a theory undoubtedly is, it
continues to capture the imagination. Rising through the
swirling mists of antiquity is the
vision of intrepid ancient
mariners navigating their fragile
craft to the very edge of the
unexplored extremity of the
continent, only to be cut off in
the midst of their adventure by
foundering somewhere in a
50-kilometre stretch of ocean
separating Table Mountain from
the Hottentots Holland range.
Bell, and others who may have
sought the mythical vessel in the
past, might not have been
successful but legends die hard,
especially if they involve a mystery. As recently as the 1980s,
post-graduate students at the
University of Cape Town's
Department of Archaeology
embarked on an intensive
programme of research into
what could have been the
remains of a prehistoric ship rumoured to be buried inconve-
niently on a police-owned rugby ground in the vicinity of the
Maitland cemeteries. The results, achieved by learned academics
aided by state-of-the-art technology and sponsored by Old
Mutual, were uniformly disappointing for there was no evidence
that any ancient vessel had ever found its grave in those
windswept sands.[14]

By the early 1850s, Charles Bell was not only a respected
Justice of the Peace[15] but, by a Proclamation of 7 January 1852,
he had also been appointed to the Central Board of Public
Roads.[16] This involved him in creating links between places widely separated in a wildly rugged land and, in doing so, of making
the rough places plain. Possibly more interesting to posterity,
however, is Bell's selection in 1852 as one of three officials serving on a board of enquiry briefed to report on 'the desirability or
otherwise of the institution of prepayment of postage [in the
Cape Colony] by means of stamps'. Barely a decade had passed
since the British government had accepted Rowland Hill's enterprising plan for postal reform which reduced costs and increased

efficiency by the simple process of sticking stamps (at a minimal cost) to letters and parcels. It was a system that the surveyor-general, Colonel Charles Michell, had investigated while on a visit to England at the end of 1846 and on which he reported to the governor, Sir Henry Pottinger, on his return in April of the following year. Bell would have been intrigued by the idea of using pre-paid postage stamps, especially as creating a design for those to be used by the Cape of Good Hope would involve the sort of meticulous resourcefulness in which he excelled. He must surely have been instrumental in drawing up the enquiry board's interim report presented to the government on 25 August 1852, for a passage in it reads: 'In order to obviate errors in sorting letters so stamped, we would suggest the adoption of a device of size and shape so different from those of the English Postage Stamps as to catch the eye at a glance, and we would propose a Triangle, with a figure of "HOPE" in the centre with the words, "POSTAGE, FOUR PENCE, CAPE OF GOOD HOPE" on the surrounding border … as represented in the accompanying sketch by the Surveyor-General.'[17] Attached to the report were two designs by Bell. The first was a triangle as suggested, but the figure of Hope in the centre was shown reclining against an anchor.[18] Around the border were the words 'Postage Four Pence Cape of Good Hope'. The second design was five-sided: the head of Queen Victoria appeared in the centre with words identical to those on the triangular stamp within the border.

The authorities lost no time in making up their minds: the triangle, for a number of reasons, was their choice. 'Various other designs such as that hereunto annexed marked No. 2, might be suggested,' they stated, 'but we are disposed to recommend the triangle as most convenient, economical and distinctive.'[19] Within a week, a communication to the Secretary of State for the Colonies was dispatched to London and with it went a letter addressed to Messrs Perkins, Bacon & Co., contractors to the British government who had produced most of the earliest stamps to be issued. Enclosed with this letter was a sheet of paper headed, in Bell's handwriting, 'COPY Sketches of proposed shapes of POSTAGE STAMPS for the colony of the Cape of Good Hope sig[d] Charles Bell S.G.'.[20] Perkins, Bacon were instructed to obtain the necessary dies and to print with all speed fifty thousand one-penny stamps in red and one hundred thousand four-penny stamps in blue, both of them following the triangular

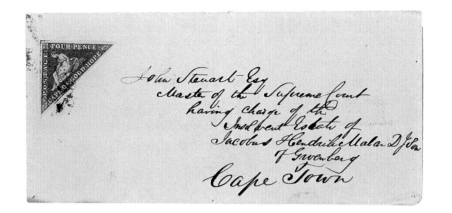

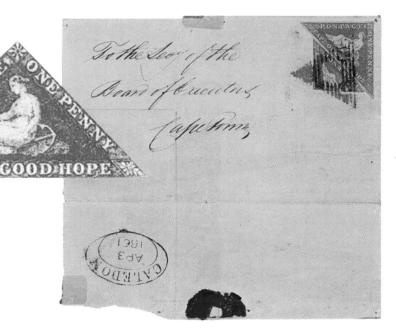

figure 5
Cape triangular stamps.
South African Cultural History Museum

Charles Bell's triangular design for the new pre-paid postage stamp was intended to be 'so different from those of the English Postage Stamps as to catch the eye at a glance', and it was approved above other designs on the grounds of being 'most convenient, economical and distinctive'. Both the red one-penny and the blue four-penny stamps bore a figure of Hope in the centre, and the words 'CAPE OF GOOD HOPE', 'POSTAGE' and 'ONE PENNY' or 'FOUR PENCE' around the border.

design as closely as possible. The Colonial Office also placed a standing order for an additional five thousand penny and ten thousand four-penny stamps to be supplied monthly.[21] The printers made some slight 'adjustments' to Bell's original, most notable being that the figure of Hope was arranged in 'a more restful position instead of being placed bolt upright on a higher seat'.[22] The stamps were produced in record time and the complete order was dispatched to the Cape on 11 May 1853.

By the time the consignment reached Cape Town, preparations were complete for the introduction, on 1 September 1853, of pre-paid postage by means of stamps which could be obtained from approved holders of retail shop licences. Unlike modern stamps, the triangulars were not perforated and they could be severed

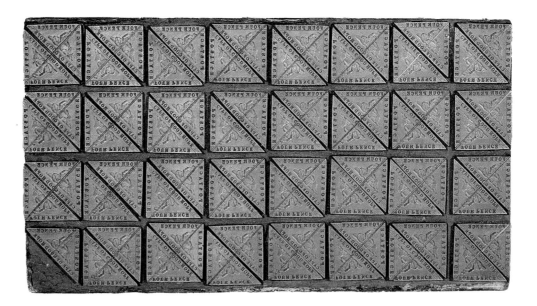

figure 6
Cape triangular stamp plates.
South African Cultural History Museum

When local stocks of the Cape triangular stamps were unexpectedly depleted in 1861, Cape printer Saul Solomon produced an emergency supply with the aid of engraver C.J. Roberts. These plates were used to print the somewhat crudely engraved local stamps, which have since become extremely valuable.

from one another only by cutting them with scissors.[23] Since those days philatelists have regarded the classic simplicity of the Cape triangular to be comparable with that of the world's first stamp, the famous British 'penny black' which still represents the very acme of postage stamp design. After a long period during which stamps became 'busier' and more elaborate, design returned at last to the clean lines of the 1840s and 1850s with the introduction of the current British definitive series first issued in 1967.[24]

Perkins, Bacon continued to provide the Cape with its stamps until 1861 when the Cape printers, Saul Solomon & Co., aided by the engraver, C.J. Roberts, responded to an unexpected shortage by producing an emergency supply of 125 102 red penny stamps and 113 256 four-penny blues. These somewhat crudely engraved, so-called 'woodblock' provisional stamps, particularly those with errors of colour, are extremely rare and valuable today. (The errors of colour resulted when a printer placed a four-penny stereotype in a one-penny plate and vice versa. This meant that one stamp of each plate was printed in the incorrect colour.) The basic design persisted until 1864 and although other variations on the triangular theme have been produced from time to time, none of these has ever compared with Bell's original in either artistry or rarity. In fact, today the 'Cape triangular' is one of the stamps most sought after and highly prized by philatelists throughout the world. No doubt Charles Bell would be astonished to hear what present day collectors are prepared to pay for the stamps he designed in 1852.[25]

Certainly, for Charles Bell that year had been a busy one. His directorship of the Mutual Life Assurance Society was of increasing interest to him, as was his association with local Freemasonry

– it was in 1852 that he became Master of the Hope Lodge.[26] As the year drew to a close he found himself once more involved in an art exhibition – Cape Town's second – which opened on 23 November. The old Dessinian Library, housed in the consistory of the Groote Kerk, provided the venue and thirteen prominent citizens were appointed to the committee. Among them, once more, were both Charles Bell and William Porter,[27] but the unfortunate Gilbert MacDougall had died earlier that year aged only 37. This was a sad loss for Cape Town for MacDougall was a man of considerable enterprise who, as early as 2 April 1851, had proposed that the city should have its own building 'designed in the classical style' for 'an annual exposition of works of Art … lectures, concerts and the sale and disposal of paintings'.[28] New on the committee was Abraham de Smidt, a young artist of promise who was one of Bell's colleagues in the Survey Department.

One of the exhibitors with a future inextricably linked with Bell's was listed as 'Master' Daniel Krynauw, eleven-year-old son of Anthony David Krynauw of the house 'Krynauwshof' in the Gardens and scion of an old and respected Cape family. Bell himself exhibited six paintings, one of which was described as 'a sketchy, or rather unfinished, portrait of the Secretary to the Government', while another was a full length portrait of Sir Harry Smith.[29] All in all, however, the second exhibition was something of a disappointment after the success of the first. For one thing there were fewer exhibits – only 325 – and during a run of almost three months no more than 835 visitors attended it. Expenses were high and, with takings amounting to a mere £61, the organisers were left with a deficit of the same amount.

Naturally there were no funds for prizes and as a result artistic enthusiasm at the Cape was considerably dampened.

Nevertheless, there were those who enjoyed the show immensely, among them one of Bowler's pupils, a young lady called Emma Rutherfoord, who happened, also, to be an admirer of Charles Bell's. 'You cannot think what a pretty exhibition we have this year,' she enthused in a letter to her sister, Mary Reeves, newly married and living in India. 'It is much prettier than the last … It is in the Consistory of the Dutch Church, arranged in three rooms with folding doors opening into one another which have been removed … There are some lovely little statuettes and a little Gipsy Girl's head done by Palardo which I much admired, indeed there are several new pictures and some very good ones I believe.'[30] This time some credit was given to female artists, fourteen of whom exhibited. Miss Kilgour, a prize-winner in 1851, was singled out for her commendable paintings entitled 'At Green Point' and 'Off Portsmouth'. 'Considering these works to be the productions of a young lady,' condescended a reporter in the *South African Commercial Advertiser* of 19 January 1853, 'they show a great deal of talent and painstaking.'

By the time Charles Bell reached his fortieth year he found himself increasingly appointed to serve on committees and commissions. Some of these must have been tedious in the extreme but Bell, whose irrepressible sense of the absurd was so evident in his early sketches, could see the humour in the most improbable situations. One of these arose during the hearing of a commission appointed in November 1853 to enquire into accusations made against the surgeon-superintendent of the General Infirmary on Robben Island.[31] At this bleak spot Bell arrived on 7 December, with two fellow members of the board of enquiry – William Hope (later auditor-general) and the magistrate at Piketberg, a Captain Hill.

Altogether it was an extraordinary, if not bizarre, scenario. Here were three middle-aged, highly respectable civil servants stepping ashore on an island, roughly oval in shape, just less than 3,5 kilometres long and more or less half as wide, virtually flat, virtually waterless, and since time immemorial, constantly buffeted by howling winds and restless, tempestuous seas. Cape Town itself was less than ten kilometres southwards, but so isolated was – and is – Robben Island that, once confined there, only the most foolhardy of men would even think of attempting to escape from it. This, of course, led to its choice as a place of incarceration for malefactors in the earliest days of white occupation at the Cape and, in a much later period, bestowed on it a most sinister role in South African history.[32] Robben Island has fulfilled many functions, but in December 1853, when the commissioners arrived, it provided a habitation for lepers, lunatics, paupers and the chronic sick.[33] To care for these unfortunates a substantial staff was also present, among them the

figure 7 **Anglican church on Robben Island by W.S.W.** Watercolour. 25 x 40 cm. Coll: South African Library

This watercolour of the first church on Robben Island was painted by W.S.W., a mental patient at the infirmary on the island, who died in 1882. While visiting Robben Island to conduct a commission of enquiry, Charles Bell would have been particularly interested to see this church since it was designed by his uncle, John Bell, and built by convict labour in 1841.

figure 8
Convict.
Watercolour. 16 x 10.8 cm.
Coll: MuseumAfrica

From the early days of white settlement until the end of the twentieth century, Robben Island was used sporadically as a penal colony. The background of this painting suggests that Bell sketched the man in chains while on the island, but this would have been earlier than his visit there in 1853. By then all convicts had been removed to work on the roads of the mainland and Robben Island had become a station for lepers, paupers and the chronically sick.

personnel on the island were satisfied with the situation: further and even more damaging accusations were made against the doctor and Charles Bell and his two companions set off bent on discovering the truth. The surgeon-superintendent, so said his accusers, was barbarous in his treatment of the insane; he restrained the intransigent by means of ropes, chains and hand-cuffs. He prescribed his 'house medicine' consisting of salts and a tartar emetic 'without reference to constitution or malady'.[36] He fed wine to the 'difficult' inmates and was frequently so drunk himself that he could barely stagger. And, possibly worst of all in the eyes of his denouncers, he was frequently guilty of 'lewd behaviour to females'.

The commissioners deliberately arrived without warning and, on investigating the quarters in which the lepers, lunatics and the chronic sick were living, were pleasantly surprised to find the infirmary spick and span. This evidence of efficiency, so decided Hope, Hill and Bell, could only be the result of the surgeon-superintendent's 'constant and rigid attention to duty, and the enforcements of his commands'. What the commission had to decide was whether that rigidity had degenerated into cruelty to the patients and prisoners. They also had to find out whether Dr Birtwhistle's private life, as well as his official conduct, was 'such as to be subversive of the morality of the residents and detrimental to the religious efforts of the chaplain'.

The enquiry occupied the commissioners for ten days, during which they found themselves stirring up a veritable hornets' nest of gossip and intrigue. There was no lack of evidence against the doctor, and all the island's inhabitants, from the chaplain to the hospital laundress, were only too anxious to provide it. After listening carefully – and not without a sense of the absurdity of it all – to all the complainants, Bell dismissed every single claim, describing the allegations as 'monstrous'. He found that Birtwhistle's supposed drunken staggering was the result of a kick on the knee inflicted by one of the lunatics in a fit of frenzy, and as for 'an insinuation ... of adulterous intercourse or undue familiarity with Mrs Jenkins [the butcher's wife] this [was] really too bad', as would be obvious to anyone who set eyes on the lady in person. 'She is not fair,' said Bell with somewhat unkind candour, 'and is something beyond fat and forty. She is the wife of a strong, healthy, good-looking husband, the mother of a bearded man, also of a pretty daughter on the verge of girlhood, and a numerous group of other offspring.' Recalling the hilariously funny caricatures of Cape Town's inhabitants tossed off by Bell in his youth, one cannot help wishing he had bequeathed to posterity similar sketches of Mrs Jenkins, and indeed of all the other players in the Robben Island drama.

As the result of the enquiry, Dr John Birtwhistle was once more severely admonished, but still his accusers refused to

surgeon-superintendent, a certain Dr John Birtwhistle, who had been appointed some five years earlier. Even this unfortunate man's name, and that of the hospital matron Sophia Biggles – who happened to be his in-house companion – have a Dickensian ring about them. Certainly, conditions on the island left much to be desired and rumours were rife as to the sordid goings-on among the various classes of inmates.[34]

A commission of enquiry held in March 1853 resulted in no more than a strong reprimand for Dr Birtwhistle – against whom numerous 'wild assertions and improbable charges' had been made.[35] However, neither the inhabitants of Cape Town nor the

be silenced. In the end they had their way for, following a demand in parliament from Sir Andries Stockenström supported by other colonial spokesmen in August 1855, Robben Island's surgeon-superintendent was summarily, ignominiously and permanently dismissed.[37]

Unfortunately for Charles Bell, his duties as a commissioner on Robben Island made it impossible for him to attend the official opening of Bain's Kloof Pass on 12 December 1853. Bell had known Andrew Geddes Bain since the days of Smith's expedition in the 1830s, and for four years he had watched as his friend directed work on the mountain road that was to bear his name. Its engineering had proved a mammoth task for, completed, the road was 30 kilometres long and included a 16-kilometre tunnel which had been blasted out of the mountainside with gunpowder. Unfortunately, animals drawing vehicles over the pass balked at entering the impenetrable darkness of the tunnel, and when part of the roof collapsed, it was abandoned.[38] To Bell, the official opening of the road would have been a significant occasion for he had been commissioned to design the splendid silver epergne presented to Bain by public subscription in celebration of his achievement. This elaborate piece of plate, almost 60 centimetres high, is adorned with various figures and objects representing Bain's profession and interests. Below matching candlesticks flanking an intricate bowl, a seated figure of Minerva, goddess of handicrafts and wisdom, holds a torch in one hand and a mirror in the other. At her feet there are compasses, a triangle, a globe and a book, while the base of the epergne itself is embellished with three fossil skulls and several small palaeontological specimens. The piece was made in London by the silversmith Hunt and Roskell and in elaboration of design and proficiency of workmanship would do credit to the most skilled of Victorian craftsmen. In his part in creating this epergne, Charles Bell had shown himself master of yet another branch of the arts.

figure 9 **Silver epergne. 1853.**

An example of Charles Bell's skill as a designer of silverware is this elaborate epergne commissioned to honour the geologist and road-maker, Andrew Geddes Bain, after the opening of the Bain's Kloof Pass in 1853. Seated at the centre above a globe, a book, compasses and a triangle is the goddess Minerva, a mirror in one hand and a torch in the other. On the three feet of the piece are models of fossil skulls and primitive sea creatures, including ammonites, crinoids and nautiloids.

CHAPTER 7

A MAN OF GOOD REPORT

The year 1854 proved an exciting one for the Cape of Good Hope. For one thing, representative government, so long and so passionately desired in the Colony, was becoming a reality at last. On 21 April 1853 the vessel Lady Jocelyn — a fine new steamer equipped with a full three-masted rig — had arrived in Table Bay bringing with her from London the final draft of the new constitution. In October that year the old legislative council, inaugurated in 1834, was dissolved and preparations began for the convening of a new parliament consisting of the governor, an elective legislative council presided over by the chief justice, and an elective House of Assembly. Matters reached a welcome climax on 1 July 1854 when the members of both Houses — they numbered 61 in all — assembled in the state-room of Government House to witness the formal opening of Parliament by Lieutenant-Governor Charles Henry Darling.[1] A new era in the history of South Africa had begun.

Politics was not the only matter of interest to the colonists at this time: the unsettled financial state of the Cape was also of considerable concern. During the early years of the decade, the Colony had experienced a spurt of exceptional prosperity, the consequent mood of confidence resulting in the appearance, between 1850 and 1852, of three new commercial banks and of prospectuses for several others.[2] However, by the beginning of 1854 both revenue and exports were showing a depressing decline and, perhaps encouraged by news of the recent discovery of gold in Australia, Cape Town businessmen began to turn their minds to the possibility of exploiting the copper that had long been known to exist in Namaqualand.[3] Indeed, long before any white man settled at the Cape, passing European mariners had bartered with the indigenous inhabitants for their copper trinkets; and in 1685 Governor Simon van der Stel, at the head of a cavalcade of men and wagons, had headed northwards from *'het vlek van die Kaap'*[4] to seek the mineral – successfully – in the rocky wastes south of the Orange River.

Prospecting in the area had continued sporadically ever since, but it was only after the acquisition of mineral rights by Philips & King, a Cape Town firm of merchants and shipping agents, and the publication, on 13 September 1853, of a proclamation concerning the mining of non-auriferous metals in Namaqualand, that operations began in earnest, particularly on the farms Spektakel, Springbok and Concordia.[5] Excitement in Cape Town escalated after a report entitled *Papers and correspondence on*

Namaqualand[6] was published in 1854, in which Andrew Geddes Bain wrote enthusiastically about the prospects of the area. 'I have little doubt,' ran his report, 'that all the country from the Oliphants River to the Orange River abounds in mineral wealth, and only wants to be thoroughly explored to develop its riches.'[7]

The effect of such confident words on the people of Cape Town – and, soon afterwards, of the world – was electric, and this was no surprise since no lodestone is more powerful than the promise of instant wealth. Everyone, in the words of newspaper editor R.W. Murray, seemed immediately possessed by a 'mad fever' and men of every walk of life abandoned the security of home and hearth to sink shafts and empty their own pockets in the copperfields of Namaqualand. He wrote:

> Every day of the week, Sundays not excepted ... vehicles of all sorts – spring vans and Cape carts well horsed – nothing short of a cart and a span of four – wagons and eight or ten horses, the vehicles crammed full of passengers, prospectors, managing directors, captains of mines, speculators, all well packed up with judiciously-selected supplies of the necessaries of life, and many of the luxuries, all bound for the Namaqualand mines ... All sorts and conditions of men set up as mining experts – tinkers, tailors, soldiers and sailors. Men in business and professional men shut up their shops and closed their offices and went off to see for themselves ... New companies sprung (sic) up more suddenly than mushrooms – scrip flew round with a swiftness that no bird could have kept up with.[8]

Not surprisingly, there were disputes regarding land claims, since the inhabitants of what had become mining areas virtually overnight found themselves and their homes threatened by the hurly-burly of copper mania. The obvious and most objective person to investigate the situation was the surveyor-general, Charles Bell – not that he was above being influenced by the excitement, especially as he clearly had tremendous faith in the opinion of his friend, Andrew Geddes Bain, whose report he had read.[9]

Bell set off from Cape Town on his second commission in Namaqualand in August 1854. It was spring and although the countryside must have been at its colourful best when he arrived, four months of increasing heat and discomfort lay ahead of him. During this time, he was 'exposed to every variety of weather [and] severe physical exertion'; besides, the combined problems of supplying 'mere animal wants [with a] means of locomotion', were not exactly favourable to the 'intellectual effort and office work' required of him. Nevertheless, he produced a detailed report which has proved one of the most important documents for which he was responsible.[10] His brief, in the first place, was to investigate all areas under dispute as well as any centres claimed or pointed out to him, so that licences could be issued. He also had to enquire into the claims of 'Aborigines and other natives' and into the 'physical character and productions, geology, climate, food and water, lines of communications and ports' of the entire territory.

Obviously it would be no small task, for Bell knew from experience that Namaqualand consisted of '9000 square miles, half of it a dreary waste of heavy sand and half of it a howling wilderness of lofty rugged mountain chains and peaks, with extensive tracts where no blade of grass or drop of water, however bitter, can be found'. Nevertheless, Bain's report had inspired him with 'highly excited ideas of inexhaustible wealth' so at least he approached the project in an optimistic frame of mind. Nor did he experience anything to dampen his expectations at the mining areas of Springbok, Concordia and even at unprepossessing Spektakel. He was both surprised and impressed by 'the fair and gentlemanlike manner' with which the conflicting claims were presented to him by the applicants – indeed by the conduct of all concerned, no matter what sharp practices they may have indulged in previously.

Although Bell was familiar with the ruggedness of the countryside in these parts, it was only when he travelled further towards the Orange River that he realised how utterly desolate were the northern reaches of Namaqualand. Nevertheless, though not a qualified geologist, he recognised the potential of the brilliantly beautiful gemstones that were there for the taking. He brought back 54 different kinds and would have collected more but he

was over-burdened as it was and, anyway, he had other things to think of. 'I had to husband my strength,' he wrote in his report, 'and save my horse for my more immediate work for which I was better qualified. I had tools and books to carry...' But Namaqualand, he concluded, was a most interesting field for any geologist 'desirous of examining the "hypogene" formations'. Besides, the climate, 'though not very agreeable' was, on the whole, good and food was readily available, while 'the vegetable productions of the whole country [were] curious in a scientific point of view and most interesting to a botanist'. Like other

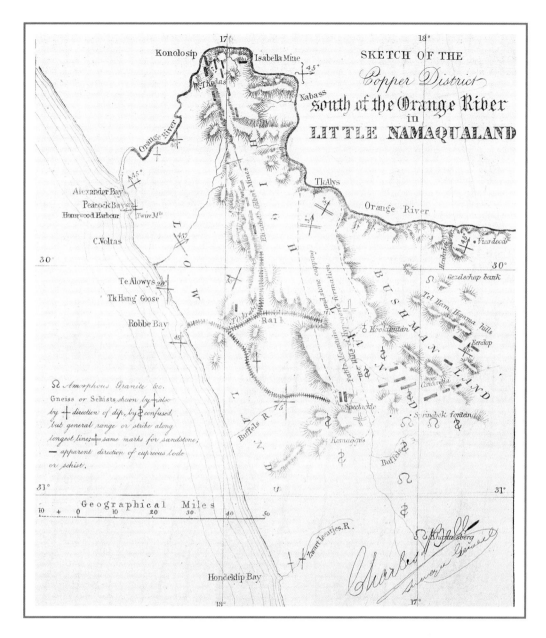

*Charles Bell's map of Little Namaqualand, the copper district south of the Orange River. To modern readers,
possibly the most interesting aspect of a report that was both detailed and perceptive is his advice regarding land
tenure in respect of the indigenous people of the area. Long before any land claims court came into existence, he
dealt with the matter sympathetically and recommended that justice should be meted out to people whose land
had been removed from them by self-seeking colonists.*

travellers before him,[11] he was fascinated by the grasses of the
region known as Bushmanland and thought them worth
harvesting as fodder. He wrote: 'I have seen tracts of country in
Bushmanland, far as the eye can reach, covered with waving seed
grass, like cornfields…' Bell commented on much else – on the
obstacle presented by the 'barrier of mountains' to internal
communications, on the lack of outspans, on the need for dams,
and he investigated the possibility of a tram or railway system
to carry copper to the coast.

Of all the facets of Charles Bell's report on Namaqualand in
1854, possibly that concerning the claims of 'Aborigines and
other natives' and his relations with these peoples, is the most
enlightening to the modern reader. During Andrew Smith's
expedition of 1834–1836, he had gained considerable experience
of 'aboriginal tenure of land' as it had existed in South Africa
before any white man arrived to claim a share. 'Individual
property in land was unknown,' observed Bell. 'That Little
Namaqualand was also thus possessed and occupied in prehistoric times, by the Bushmen and Nama Hottentots, I have every
reason to conclude.'

At first it was not easy to approach this subject with the local
inhabitants, who watched his activities with suspicion and
observed his every move from a distance 'with gloomy looks'.
Eventually he managed to gain the confidence of 'one of the
most respectable Bastards of Kookfontein', who explained that
the people regarded him as the eye and ear of the Cape government and consequently were very worried about what they
called 'the oppression'. To reassure them that they had no cause
for anxiety – in fact, the government had inserted a clause in
every lease protecting them from loss and damage – and to hear
their complaints, Bell called a meeting of all the local chief men at
Kookfontein on 13 September 1854.[12] About twenty attended, all
of them immaculately dressed in the European fashion of the
day, frock coats and top hats being much in favour. The exploitation of copper in the area concerned them not at all, except that
the diggers allowed their cattle to trample over their lands. What
distressed the chiefs was that they had asked the government
for certain lands to be reserved for their use but they still had
nothing to show, 'neither beacon nor chart', by which they might
prove their right of possession or to use as a warning to
trespassers. Their claims to the land rested on no documents or
title deeds, but only on its occupation by chiefs of their tribes
since time immemorial. They hoped to obtain grants but this
would entail an official survey and an expense which they could
not afford. This preliminary assembly gave Bell much food for
thought and he consequently made arrangements to hold a
second meeting on 30 November at a place called T'kamaggas
for, so said the people, 'their fathers had always lived there'.

On this occasion, Bell interviewed several of the chief men separately as he suspected that some were traditional and bitter enemies. He met the 'so-called Bushman chieftain, T'Kamghaap' by flickering firelight. This man's people, Bell discovered, were not as primitive as he had imagined: they wore European clothing and they owned a small flock of goats. In fact, they had taken a long step beyond the 'pure Bushman' and were strong enough to maintain their position 'if not crushed under the present high pressure of progress of improvement in Namaqualand'. All T'Kamghaap claimed was a short strip of land along the Orange River 'from T'Kodas to Nabass' – both of them places occupied by his forefathers. Not so modest were the demands made by the Nama chief, Paul Lynx. He and his people merely wanted to be left in undisturbed possession of their land – but it was vast in area and included the strip claimed by T'Kamghaap. It was indeed unfortunate that between Paul Lynx's Nama and T'Kamghaap's Bushmen an age-long and apparently irreconcilable strife existed.

And so the interviews continued until, eventually, Bell called all the delegates together and addressed them:

> You all see that I do not ride at ease in my cart, merely looking through my telescope at the mountains and the people and listening to what the managers of the mines and missionaries … may say of you: but I scramble over your hills, I talk to you, and sit by your fires . . . making acquaintance of your wives and children – for he who would speak as a man must first learn as a child. I have seen that in this land there is grass where there is no water, and water where there is no grass. I have seen that there are numberless places where water could be found in the ground, or where dams could be made to preserve the rain.

Bell asked the chiefs to express their opinions regarding the development of the land and its people for, he said, it appeared to him that copper was one of the Creator's gifts to man and that their country, although poor in other respects, was rich in this metal. He told them that 'in many portions of the earth, otherwise rich, nations had need of it, and would gladly send food and clothing, and tools and money to Namaqualand in exchange for it'. He spoke of the skill and labour of miners and of the money invested in

copper production, and he asked the chiefs whether they were capable of producing and smelting the copper themselves. To this, so said Bell, the answer was usually, 'No, no: take the copper, we can't raise it, and don't want it'.[13]

At the end of four months of hard labour in a harsh land, Bell had many recommendations to make. While fulfilling the requirements of the investigation to the letter, he had also made a serious effort to get to know people from every section of the community, to assess their aspirations and to make suggestions, where appropriate, regarding their moral upliftment and education. Reserve and develop all copper mines, he advised; allocate land by fixing boundaries; protect the mission stations from intrusion by the neighbouring mines 'on the grounds that men lately rescued from heathenism ought not to be exposed to risk of moral contagion through the examples of the miners'. It was important that the 'Aborigines and other natives' should be encouraged to build their own houses 'for the sake of education and decency'. His Victorian sense of propriety was shocked to see that married and unmarried people and children were 'promiscuously' huddled together at night in their mat huts, and

figure 3
Near Cape Town.
Photograph.
Bell Heritage Trust Collection,
UCT

Camped in the veld, apparently near Cape Town, a party of land surveyors and their handlangers *(assistants) pose with their theodolites. It may be that Charles Bell is the bearded – and commanding – figure, hand on hip, in the right foreground.*

he recommended 'bringing more civilised habits' to them and allocating land for churches and schools.

Charles Bell's report became available to the general public early in 1855 and was received with much interest; in fact, his information on Namaqualand and the diagrams he made of its geology, as well as copies of three of his sketches of mining methods, were included in a booklet dealing with the Cape at the Colony's stand at the Paris exhibition held later that year. In April, he was required to appear before a commission which met in Cape Town to report, among other things, on the feasibility of establishing a railway linking the mining areas to the ports in the region.[14] Experience of the terrain and the needs of the mining companies had shown Bell that, while a railway to the workings near the Orange River was not practical, undoubtedly a steam transport service was an absolute necessity in the central and southern areas of Namaqualand if the mines there proved 'half as productive as seems to be expected'. Unfortunately this was not to be the case and most of Bell's recommendations never came to fruition, for within a few months the 'copper bubble' had burst. During the past months, reports from the mines had become increasingly depressing and the newspapers were full of dire warnings. Companies, once so full of promise, collapsed; scrip that had changed hands at high premiums became virtually worthless, and day after day broken men filed disconsolately through the insolvency court.[15] Alas, the collapse of the copper industry meant that the hopes and dreams of many a prospector were shattered for ever.

Charles Bell, fortunately, was no speculator – unlike his friend, the highly respectable attorney-general, William Porter, who, caught up in the general euphoria, lost 'thousands of pounds'.[16] For Bell, 'looking very well, grown very stout and [wearing] a quantity of moustache etc.',[17] it was back to the civil service treadmill – but not for long, for in September he received instructions to proceed on another journey of inspection and report on his findings. This time he was required to investigate the land claims of a group of the Mfengu people – then known as the Fingoes – living at a place called Clarkson in the Tsitsikamma region between Plettenberg Bay and Humansdorp. The word 'Mfengu' is derived from *ukufenguza*, meaning 'to wander about seeking advice',[18] and is an indication of the unsettled history of these people. During the frontier wars they often served as allies of the British, for which service they were rewarded with tracts of country – hence their settlement in the Tsitsikamma in 1837 on land where both soil and situation were to prove 'utterly worthless'.[19] In time, this unhappy band sank into impoverishment, and many abandoned all they had to make the dreary journey back to the Eastern Cape.

It was the state of affairs among the remnants of these Mfengu people, as well as their land claims, that Bell was required to investigate. In September 1855 he wrote to the colonial secretary Rawson W. Rawson informing him of his 'readiness to proceed' on his assignment, for which he had equipped himself with a cart, tents, four draught and saddle horses complete with driver and leader.[20] On his way to the Tsitsikamma, he proposed to inspect several other areas in which the government was concerned and, on his return, to vary his route and take in the Knysna forests which he had never yet visited. 'As during the last five years,' he reminded his superior, 'I have not had above three days leave at once nor above twenty days of leave altogether, I

figure 4 **At work in Namaqualand.**
Photograph. Bell Heritage Trust Collection, UCT

This photograph shows three surveyors apparently engaged in discussion in a tent.
It is known that Charles Bell was a pioneer in the field of photography at the Cape, and it may be
that he took the photograph himself or that he is the bearded man on the left.

figure 5 **Country Hottentots, travelling.**
Watercolour. 14 x 21.5 cm. Bell Heritage Trust Collection, UCT

Accompanied by dogs of no known breed, barefoot 'father' leads the way, prized rifle over his shoulder and knobkerrie
in his hand, while 'mother' humps the baby on her back and the small boy follows. To Charles Bell, acquainted as he
was with the wide spaces of Namaqualand, this would have been a familiar sight.

figure 6 **Hottentot hut. On tree, nest of republican birds. Possibly 1835.**
Watercolour. 13.5 x 21.5 cm. Bell Heritage Trust Collection, UCT

*'Nest of republican birds' – so runs Charles Bell's somewhat mystifying caption to this painting. The 'republican birds'
are probably sociable weavers whose communal grass nests are a common feature of the western arid parts of southern
Africa. The woman with the umbrella has just emerged from a* matjieshuis, *a dwelling typical of parts of
Namaqualand, to welcome the visiting family.*

trust I may be now permitted, for the benefit … of my health, should I have the opportunity without material hindrance to my work. All allowances will of course be deducted for days thus spent as also for such extra time as may be required for detours to visit new localities where the extra expense is incommensurate with the probable benefit to be desired by Government from my extended local knowledge.'[21] Such honesty among civil servants, it seems, was taken for granted in Bell's day.

Bell had not been long back at the Cape after completing this project – and, presumably, his brief holiday – when he was again required to present himself at a government commission of enquiry. Under discussion was the alienation of the Rondebosch Camp Ground, an area some 95 morgen 410 square roods[22] in extent on the fringe of the Cape Flats.[23] Canigou – the house Bell had acquired from his uncle, Colonel John Bell – stood on land adjoining the Camp Ground; and it was somewhere on the Camp Ground itself that Martha Bell had been discovered in a compromising position with her lover, Lestock Wilson Stewart.[24] Charles Bell, both as surveyor-general and as informed landowner, was obviously the ideal person to provide the commission of enquiry with information regarding the Camp Ground, which, on 31 January 1854, had been granted by the government to 'the English Church'. The question put to Charles Bell now was what rights did the people living in Rondebosch have in relation to the Camp Ground? Wagons, he said in answer, frequently outspanned there; cattle grazed there and people were able (once they had obtained permission from the authorities) to help themselves to sand and stone for building purposes. The Camp Ground might belong to the bishop, but there was no doubt that the people still regarded it as commonage.

Over the following years there were other government investigations in which Bell acted either as commissioner or as witness. At the end of 1856, for example, he was instructed to travel to the Eastern Cape and there meet several groups of settlers on their arrival. These were former soldiers of the British German Legion, a corps raised for service in the Crimea but no longer required now that peace had been concluded with the Russians. Between the end of December and the following February 2362 men and 556 women and children arrived by sea – and a very rum lot Charles Bell thought they were.[25] Far from being smart and disciplined soldiers, most of the men seemed 'low and desperate characters', no more than sweepings of the slums of the great continental towns.

Needless to say, within a very short time the entire scheme had proved a disaster. The situation in which the settlers were expected to build their homes was dangerously close to the, understandably, suspicious Xhosa. The shortage of women – only 360 of the men were accompanied by their wives – was bound to lead to trouble. Besides, the tempting promises of the British government did not materialise. The settlers had scant shelter; the land they were allocated cost £5 an acre instead of the two shillings they had been led to expect; their clothes and boots wore out and they could not afford to replace them. Altogether, from the surveyor-general's point of view, this could only be described as one of his less happy assignments. Nevertheless, he completed it with his customary conscientiousness and, no doubt, returned to Cape Town with all speed.

figure 7
Hottentot family.
Watercolour. 22.8 x 15.2 cm.
Private Collection, Cape Town

A rare worked-up watercolour of one of Charles Bell's favourite subjects. There was usually a strong element of caricature in Bell's depictions of indigenous people, especially the Hottentots. In this painting he shows a degree of sympathy with his subjects, thus imbuing the family as a whole with an air of simple dignity.

figure 8 **Table Mountain and Devil's Hill, from the Camp Ground, on the edge of the Cape Flats.**
Watercolour. 13 x 20.5 cm. Bell Heritage Trust Collection, UCT

To Charles Bell, living at Canigou on the Camp Ground, this view westwards would have been an unfailing source of wonder as its moods and shades changed with the hour and the season. Here, delicately wreathed with the mists of autumn, the mountain is enhanced by the space – now lost to suburbia – that surrounds it.

figure 9 **Common travelling horse waggon.**
Watercolour. 14 x 21.5 cm. Bell Heritage Trust Collection, UCT

*With what appear to be the peaks of the Simonsberg, near Stellenbosch, overlooking them, six pairs of horses step out smartly as they head inland from
Cape Town. No doubt this scene reminded Charles Bell of a similar wagon in which he and Dr Andrew Smith's party covered the first stage of the journey of
exploration into the southern African interior.*

Chapter 8

'A MULTIFARIOUS LIFE'

Charles Piazzi Smyth, in his obituary of Charles Bell, referred to his friend's 'extraordinary exertions' and his 'most multifarious life',[1] and certainly, Bell's interests extended far beyond his professional duties. The 1850s and 1860s were probably the busiest years of his life; possibly they were also the most creative. Long-standing pursuits were developed and extended during this period; new ones were eagerly taken up and, at the same time, his business interests widened. In every sphere, Charles Bell, now in his forties, seemed possessed by what his son-in-law, Dumaresq Williamson Manning, called a 'restless activity'[2] in which there was neither time nor space for idleness.

figure 1
Banknotes, Cape Commercial Bank.
Coll: National Cultural History Museum

During the 1850s Bell became increasingly involved in local commerce and was appointed director of at least three business houses. He turned his talents to designing banknotes and share certificates, to each of which he applied his originality and artistic skills. A £5 banknote (bottom) issued by the Cape Commercial Bank – of which he was a director – bears the printed words 'Charles Bell delt. 1854'. It is assumed that he was responsible for all notes issued by the bank, including the accompanying ones from the Pretoria and Stellenbosch branches.

Having designed the first postage stamps issued in the Colony to the satisfaction – indeed, the admiration – of the public generally, Bell was next required to turn his attention to banknotes. In 1854 he was responsible for those of the newly established Cape Commercial Bank of which he had been appointed a director, and we see his hand, too, in the elegant decorative border surrounding the certificates issued to its shareholders. Five years later, when there was still strong competition between the numerous banks that had sprung up in the Colony and banknotes rivalled one another for originality of design, he was to produce similar creative work for the Queenstown Bank.[3]

Clearly, Bell's integrity and leadership qualities were such that the financial institutions then making an appearance in Cape Town saw him as an asset to their boards of directors, and in 1856, when the General Estate and Orphan Chamber was founded, he was appointed its chairman. This privately owned trust company, like others of its kind, had assumed the financial responsibilities of the old *weeskamers* (orphanages) established in the early days of Dutch rule, for it took care of the funds of orphans while, at the same time, providing a reliable source of income for investors.[4] To Charles Bell, his association with the new Chamber was an opportunity to combine and demonstrate two skills – wood-carving and heraldry – which were at this time absorbing his mind. The result was a rectangular plaque in which stylised foliage falls as mantling round a circular medallion. Several classical figures, in relief, are grouped together in the medallion, and below it there is a carving of the arms of the City of Cape Town – an early example of Bell's habit of including coats of arms, where appropriate, in his art works. The words 'General Estate and Orphan Chamber, Heerengracht, Cape Town, Cape of Good Hope' are inscribed in scrolls above and below the medallion with the date, 1856, appearing at the top edge of the carving. It might be imagined that Bell would have presented the plaque to the Chamber as soon as he had finished working on it, but, according to a small brass plate attached to the lower edge of the frame, it was only in 1915 that Bell's son, Alexander, donated it to the institution as a gift.

On 12 May 1856, Bell wrote to the colonial secretary, Rawson W. Rawson, asking him to grant him eighteen months' leave in order to visit Great Britain for the benefit of his health. 'For the last four or five years,' he wrote, 'I have suffered from my head whenever I apply myself to lengthened investigation or intricate questions, and of late the liability to headache and confusion of mind has increased. In other respects, I never was in more perfect health or more fit for hardships or privation, and, I might add, for bodily exertion.' His ailment, he claimed, was the result of 'some slight injuries arising from accident and overwork' during his visit to Namaqualand in 1854. Certainly, he had taken ill while on the copperfields; in fact, on 30 November 1854, he had written to Rawson telling him that he had been 'so depressed … physically and mentally' that for 'upwards of two days' he could do nothing but sleep. Hardly had he recovered, when he was afflicted with rheumatism that was so severe that he had to be lifted in and out of bed. Fortunately mustard plasters and other nostrums soon restored him, but it seems the old complaints returned once he was back in Cape Town. With long leave in mind, he had set all his affairs in the office in order and, so he told Rawson in 1856, he sincerely believed that his colleagues in the civil service might benefit if he were allowed to let his head rest for a while.[5]

But Charles Bell's appeals were in vain and his request was turned down. The problem, it seems, was the anticipated arrival of the German settlers, and it was almost a year later, a week after he had completed his investigation into their affairs, that he approached the

colonial secretary for a second time.[6] On this occasion he wrote: 'I respectfully draw attention to an application for leave of absence to England forwarded to you nearly twelve months ago – to which I received no written reply having been verbally informed that no leave could be granted except in the case of illness or urgent private affairs.' Again he gave ill health as his reason for requiring leave: a complete change of scene and rest from work were what he needed, for, he admitted, 'I am losing my capability of thinking rightly and steadily'. Also, he found he was becoming unreasonably irritable, which was not to be wondered at since he had 'endured many things within the last ten years that could hardly fail to leave their stamp on the hardest brain'. Was this, one wonders, a reference to the heartbreak inflicted upon him by Martha's infidelity and the consequent trauma of their divorce? He could produce 'no certificate of bodily illness', he said, nor could he blame his

state of health on the rough life to which a land surveyor is occasionally exposed – but, he reminded his superior (as he had done on a previous occasion), in all his years in the Survey Office he had never taken advantage of the six weeks' annual leave due to civil servants, nor had he any wish to share the fate of others who had declined this privilege 'until it was too late'.

This time Bell's appeals were successful and in a letter of 28 April 1857 he expressed his gratitude to the governor for sanctioning his leave. Arrangements were made immediately for his departure and soon afterwards he sailed from Table Bay in the vessel, *L'Impératrice Eugénie*, accompanied by his children. It was to be Bell's first visit to the land of his birth for ten years, and while he must have looked forward to seeing his ageing parents again, not to mention his uncle – a Knight Commander of the Order of the Bath[7] and a widower for the past two years – perhaps he was also a little sad at the prospect of a long separation from his friends at the Cape. Among these he now counted the Krynauw family, with whom he had become increasingly intimate. Despite a considerable difference in age, young Daniel, who had exhibited in Cape Town's First Exhibition of Fine Arts as an eleven-year-old in 1852, had become a firm friend. So, too, had his older sister, Helena, and it may be that it was partly to take stock of his relationship with this charming young lady that Charles Bell had decided to travel so far from the Cape and to remain away for so long.

Be that as it may, he would not be returning to Cape Town until the end of 1858, and was therefore obliged to retire from the board of the Mutual Life Assurance Society since its founding document required the resignation of any director who was absent from meetings for three consecutive months or longer.

Nevertheless, Bell's time abroad was well spent: he revived his friendship with Piazzi Smyth and pursued his many hobbies untrammelled by official responsibilities. One of his interests at this time was the art of photography to which he had probably been introduced by Smyth at least a decade earlier. The latter, no

doubt encouraged by Sir John Herschel's pioneering work in this field, was producing photographs at the Cape as early as 1842, despite a frustrating lack of equipment and materials.[8] Bell, with his insatiable fascination for all things new and ingenious, was taking his own photographs by the mid-1850s, as evidenced by an album of his work in the Bell Heritage Trust Collection at the University of Cape Town. Two photographs in this album, believed to have been taken by Bell, show work in progress on the original seven-foot-gauge railway line to the new Table Bay harbour which was under construction in the 1850s.[9] Other photographs were clearly taken even earlier, for they show events that almost certainly occurred during Bell's visit to Namaqualand in 1854.

Historically, these photographs are both fascinating and valuable; technically and artistically, they reveal astonishing skill. However, the photograph almost certainly originating from the 1850s which is of particular interest was taken not by, but of, Bell, seemingly during his 1857–1858 visit to Scotland. It shows an amiable-looking man – Bell – standing beside a camera on a

figure 4 **Members of the Cape Volunteer Cavalry.**
Photograph by J. Kirkman. Coll: Museum Africa

With a cannon in the background and his steed at his side, William Porter, in the uniform of the corps he founded, the Cape Volunteer Cavalry, assumes an impressive stance surrounded by fellow officers and men. Having a photograph taken in the mid-nineteenth century was, clearly, a serious affair.

figure 5 **Members of the Cape Volunteer Cavalry. *c*.1860.**
Watercolour. 10.9 x 14.5 cm. Coll: MuseumAfrica

The same group, as depicted in colour by Charles Bell. It was a popular custom in the early days of photography for artists to copy in colour or even paint over an original photograph. In this instance, it must be admitted, there is little resemblance between the facial features of the men in the photograph and those of their equivalents in the painting.

tripod. Beside him is his elder son, John, at the time in his early teens. A photograph, obviously printed from the same negative, was found in a second album, this one presented to the History of Science Section of the National Museums of Scotland in 1942. It had belonged to Dr John Adamson (1809–1870), a well-known pioneer of early Scottish photography who was distantly related to Charles Bell and who may well have photographed him and the boy during the Bells' visit.[10] The photograph is one of very few likenesses – either photographic or hand-drawn – of Bell at this stage in his life and, in addition to its purely scientific interest, it gives a pleasing glimpse into the private life and personality of the man himself.

When Charles Bell returned to Cape Town with his family towards the end of 1858, he was welcomed back onto the board of the Mutual. By this time the city's[11] Third Exhibition of Fine Arts was in full swing. It had been formally opened on 6 October by the Dean of Cape Town, the Very Reverend Henry Douglas, who subjected his audience to a dissertation on art which, when published in a booklet to commemorate the event, occupied no fewer than thirty-four octavo pages. The venue for the exhibition was a large room in the government offices which was usually occupied by the Legislative Council but subsequently known as the Record Room.[12] Never, according to a rapturous article in *The Cape Argus* of 11 November, had the Legislature 'been devoted to a nobler or holier purpose' for there could be 'no greater treat than to be admitted to an exhibition of pictures'. Bell had been appointed to the committee but escaped (no doubt gratefully) the various problems that beset the preparations. This time he exhibited no new works, though the oils 'Arrival of Van Riebeeck 1652' and 'The isle of the Holy Cross' – loaned by William Porter – were on show once more, as was the statuette of Dorothea. Some 500 exhibits in all were offered to an eager

figure 6 **Charles Bell and his son, John.** *c.* **1857.**
Bell Heritage Trust Collection, UCT

This study of Charles Bell – unusually beardless – with a camera and his elder son, John, was taken during his visit to Scotland with his children in 1857. The photograph is held in the Bell Heritage Trust Collection, but there is also a copy in Edinburgh in an album that belonged to the Scottish pioneer photographer, Dr John Adamson, whose brother-in-law, Oswald H. Bell, was related to Charles Bell.

public, 2500 of whom paid the entrance price of one shilling before the doors finally closed on 24 January 1859. Among the artists whose works were on view were such famous painters as Van Dyk, Turner and Landseer, and, closer to home, Thomas Bowler. An increasingly sophisticated Cape Town, it seems, was slowly learning to appreciate the visual arts.

By 1859, Bell had been employed by the Colonial government for almost thirty years, during which time the notoriously insalubrious old building in which he had his offices had become steadily more crowded and unhealthy. Built at the end of the eighteenth century to lodge up to 600 slaves owned by the Dutch East India Company, it underwent numerous alterations and renovations over the years until, at the beginning of the nineteenth century, it was declared unsuitable for its original purpose and the slaves were moved out. The building was then converted into government offices and the Supreme Court, the Master's Office, the Receiver of Revenue and other public services moved in, though the accommodation provided was scarcely conducive to the efficient conduct of the Colony's affairs.[13] Cluttered with dusty papers, shoddily built, insufferably hot in summer, draughty in winter and overwhelmed by the stench emanating from the filthy canal in the street below, it was a source of constant wretchedness to those who endeavoured to work in it. Bell found the conditions insufferable and wrote innumerable letters to the colonial secretary in an attempt to improve matters. In March 1859 he was obliged to request that a grating should be fitted to the windows of his office 'to prevent the North West winds from blowing through it the Effluvia of the sewers … which have rendered it almost impossible to retain our rooms. The end of the offices have again been abandoned this afternoon'.[14]

Despite discomforts, the surveyor-general's department

continued to attract new employees, including Daniel Krynauw who had joined it as an 'unfixed clerk' at the beginning of 1859. It was clear that this young man was fulfilling his early promise as an artist and Bell could confidently recommend his permanent appointment on the strength of his 'ability and willingness in general work' as well as his capabilities as a draughtsman. 'Above all,' wrote Bell to the colonial secretary, 'he makes use of his opportunities of learning the duties of the department and will soon be self-taught without taxing the time of those about him.'[15] Bell was quite correct in his assessment of Krynauw: in July 1859 Daniel was appointed fourth clerk in the surveyor-general's office and took his work seriously enough to take leave that year, in order to prepare for the approaching examinations 'which [would] increase his efficiency'.[16] In the light of subsequent

figure 7
Mutual Life Assurance Society emblem.
Old Mutual Collection

The original emblem of the Mutual Life Assurance Society of the Cape of Good Hope, as designed by its chairman, Charles Davidson Bell, in about 1870. The decorative surround is typical of Bell's style and the three interlocked anchors, symbolic of the Cape's maritime association and the stability of the Society, were his creation. Although the design of the emblem has undergone many transformations, the concept of unshakeable strength of the triple anchors remains unchanged.

figure 8
First draft for Mutual Life Assurance Society emblem.
Pencil. 25 x 19.5 cm.
Old Mutual Collection

Inscribed with the name of the Society and with the words Ne careant cari tumulo nunc cere, *Bell's original design for the Mutual's emblem is similar to that of the Cape triangular stamps, featuring the figure of Hope resting on an anchor and scattering seeds on a fertile earth. It is not known why this design was rejected, but certainly the emblem embodying the three anchors has more immediate impact.*

events, one is hardly surprised at Bell's enthusiastic support of Daniel Krynauw, for on 7 July 1859, after the required period of courtship, Charles Bell was to marry his young protégé's sister, Helena Gertruida Johanna.

Of course, there had been certain snags to be overcome. Before the marriage could take place, Bell was obliged to obtain a special licence proving that he had been granted a divorce from Martha Antoinetta and was therefore free to marry again.[17] Then, Helena's father, Anthony David, might have had certain understandable objections. To become the wife of a widower was one thing; for a girl as young as Helena to marry a divorcé (particularly in Victorian times) was quite another, even though Charles had undoubtedly been 'the innocent party'. There was

the considerable age difference (twenty-six years), and then, too, there were three children to take on, two of them already in their teens. However, all went well and over the following twenty years the marriage was to prove entirely successful. The ceremony took place at the Groote Kerk in Cape Town and was solemnised by the Rev. Abraham Faure, a highly regarded theologian and leading figure in many branches of Cape society. It is probable that Faure knew the Krynauws well, for they both belonged to old Cape families of high standing in the town, and the Krynauws were members of Faure's Groote Kerk congregation. Anthony Krynauw was a prosperous merchant and director of such financial institutions as the Board of Executors, the Executeurs Kamer and the South African Bank.[18] He lived with his family in a handsome house named 'Krynauwshof' a stone's throw from Hope Mill, and it was possibly there that he first met Charles when the young man was lodging with Colonel John and Lady Catherine Bell.

Bell decided to commemorate his marriage to Helena in a most unusual manner. His tribute to the union of the Bell and Krynauw families took the form of an oval tray engraved with about forty heraldic devices representing the coats of arms of both his forebears and those of Helena. He designed the devices himself, and either engraved them personally or commissioned someone else to do so. The tray, measuring 807 millimetres long, 560 millimetres wide and 46 millimetres deep, has in its centre an engraved panel surrounding the Bell and Krynauw arms which are combined into a single shield – or, in heraldic terms, 'marshalled'. Above it is a helmet suitable to the degree of the husband: superimposed is a stag's head – his crest – while on either side there is mantling in which a scroll bearing the Bell motto, *Fulget virtus* ('Moral excellence radiates light') is incorporated. The arms of the husband's parents – Bell and Davidson – are engraved separately on one side of the central panel, while those of the wife's parents – Krynauw and Gie – are on the other. Bordering the tray there are eighteen coats of arms relevant to the male forebears of the couple, alternating with eighteen lozenges (one of which is left blank) representing the arms of the female ancestors.[19]

figure 9 **Probably John Alexander Bell.**
Pencil. 24.5 x 20 cm. Bell Heritage Trust Collection, UCT

Bell's affinity for children is clear from the sensitive manner in which he sketched them. This young boy may be Bell's eldest son, John Alexander, who was born in Grahamstown on 25 January 1843. John became an examining officer in Her Majesty's Customs at Port Elizabeth. He died suddenly while on a visit to England in 1878, leaving his widow and four young children in extremely straitened circumstances.

figure 10 **Probably Helena Krynauw. 1853.**
Pen and wash. 23 x 18 cm. Bell Heritage Trust Collection, UCT

After the dissolution of his first marriage in 1850, Charles Bell became increasingly friendly with the family of David Krynauw, a distinguished member of an old Cape family. On 7 July 1859 Bell married Krynauw's daughter, Helena, and although he was twenty-six years her senior, the marriage was to prove a happy one. If the young woman portrayed here is indeed Helena, she would have been in her teens at the time.

figure 11 **Probably Catherine Mariann Bell.**
Pencil. 26.5 x 21 cm. Bell Heritage Trust Collection, UCT

This little girl may be Bell's eldest daughter and the sister of John Alexander, whose profile resembles her own. Catherine Mariann was born to Martha Antoinetta Bell at Canigou, Rondebosch, in 1849 and died at her father's Green Point home in July 1863. She is buried in St Paul's churchyard, Rondebosch, where the grave she shares with two infant siblings is surrounded by a fence incorporating the Bell family arms.

figure 12 **Brass tray.**
Coll: MuseumAfrica

Charles Bell designed a brass tray to celebrate his marriage to Helena Krynauw on 7 July 1859. Engraved with the armorial bearings of several generations of the Bell and Krynauw families, the tray is 807 millimetres long and 506 millimetres wide. In the central panel five heraldic representations surround the marshalled arms of Bell and Krynauw and incorporate the Bell motto: Fulget virtus. The Bell family's arms are on the left (sinister) of the tray and the Krynauw family's are on the right (dexter).

'A MULTIFARIOUS LIFE' 115

figure 13 **Krynauwshof, by Daniel Krynauw. 1856.**
Watercolour. 20 x 29 cm. Bell Heritage Trust Collection, UCT

Krynauwshof was the family home of Bell's second wife, Helena, whose father, Anthony David Krynauw, was a merchant of substance and a respected member of the Groote Kerk congregation. Krynauwshof was situated in the Gardens not far from Hope Mill, and it is possible that Bell knew the family when he lived there in his youth. The Krynauws were an artistic family: this painting of their home was executed by Helena's brother, Daniel.

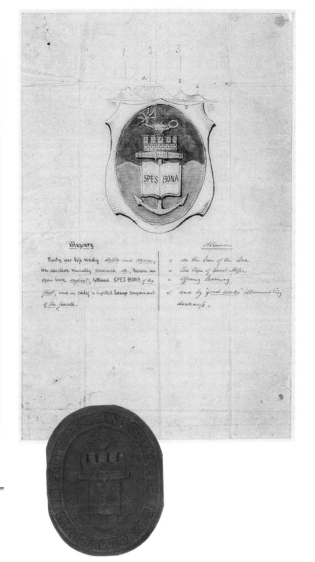

figure 14
Letter to Langham Dale, superintendent-general for education at the Cape of Good Hope. 1859.
University of Cape Town Archive

On 7 November 1859 Charles Bell wrote to Langham Dale about the design of the seal of the South African College, sending with his letter a clay model of the seal.

figure 15
Silver spade.
South African Cultural History Museum

The silver spade used by the governor, Sir George Grey, in March 1859 to turn the first sod of the Cape's original railway line to Wellington. It is not known who designed this fine piece, but there is a decided 'family likeness' between the spade and other silverware for which Charles Bell was responsible. Besides, the inscription was executed by C.J. Roberts, engraver of Bell's Cape triangular stamps, and the silversmith was Paolo Gaffodio, who worked on the silver trigger used by Prince Alfred to initiate work on the harbour breakwater in 1860 (see page 120).

It is not certain exactly when Charles Bell undertook the daunting task of designing the tray, but he probably spent considerable time on it during the years following his marriage to Helena. The finished product is a splendid work of art and indicates that Bell's knowledge of the complexities of heraldry had reached an advanced stage by the late 1850s, and that his skill as a designer was formidable. Indeed, such was his reputation that he was commissioned to design a coat of arms for the South African College in whose foundation, thirty years earlier, his uncle, Colonel John Bell, had played a significant part. Bell provided a die and clay model of the seal which could be used on prizes or certificates and sent it, on 7 November 1859, to Professor Langham Dale, newly appointed superintendent-general of education, together with the appropriate heraldic description. For some unknown reason, the seal appears to have been laid to one side and remained completely forgotten until 1888, when it was discovered by chance and put to its intended use. Still in use today, the coat of arms is familiar to anyone associated with the University of Cape Town or with the South African College School.[20]

The year 1859 was certainly an extremely eventful one for Charles Bell. Even before it began, he had unexpectedly found himself entrusted with the supervision of the railway at that time being planned to link Cape Town to Wellington 58 miles inland. Originally, the Cape civil engineer, George Pilkington,[21] had been responsible for surveying the railway and laying it out, but he had unfortunately died in 1858, leaving the task unfinished. The responsibility of completing the line now fell on the shoulders of the surveyor-general who, in the words of Charles Piazzi Smyth, 'was the only one amongst them who could lay out railway curves, build bridges, raise embankments, bore tunnels, inspect locomotives and, in a word, save them'.[22]

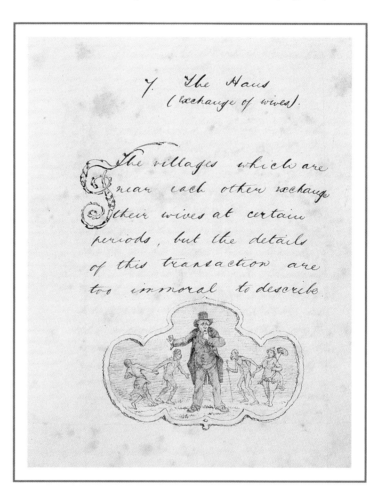

On 31 March 1859 the governor, Sir George Grey, inaugurated work on the line by turning the first sod with a spade specially provided, and on 22 March two years later the colonial secretary, Rawson W. Rawson, declared the railway open as far as the twelfth milestone from Cape Town.[23] This landmark stood at the intersection of the roads from Cape Town and the village of D'Urbanville (originally known as Pampoenkraal) and it was therefore decided to call the new railway station D'Urban Road. However, to honour the surveyor-general, who had played a large part in the construction of the line, the town that was to be established alongside it was officially named Bellville.[24] Charles Bell would certainly be surprised to see the huge industrial and suburban sprawl that has developed from what was no more than a hamlet when it was given his name almost 150 years ago.

It was fortunate for Helena that she belonged to an artistic family for her husband's pre-occupation with paint and brush, graver, pen and pencil during the early days of their marriage, might otherwise have tried her patience to the utmost. As it was, she must have shared Charles's feelings of excitement and honour when, in 1859, Sir George Grey commissioned him to embellish three books from his remarkable library.[25] Since taking over the governorship of the Cape in 1854, Sir George had shown himself particularly interested in the languages, manners and customs of the local indigenous people, so it is not surprising to find a considerable number of works on ethnography and philology in the collection. Two of those that Bell was required to illustrate were books of this nature: one, hand-written, was *The Gospel of St Matthew in the Hottentot language*,[26] translated from English by the well-known Methodist missionary and Nama linguist, Henry Tindall. With a wooden spine and frames inlaid with a simple floral design, this remarkable book has tin covers which Bell etched with the title and appropriate illustrations, most of them depicting Nama figures apparently reading the scriptures. A pencil inscription on the fly-leaf reads: 'Etched in tin by Mr C. Bell, Surveyor general, Cape of Good Hope, who was intimately acquainted with the native tribes for whom the gospel was translated and whoes (sic) likeness he has faithfully depicted.'

Interestingly enough, a small coloured medallion showing a nativity scene and a brilliant painting of butterflies and a spray of ericas adorn the end papers. The artist in both cases is George French Angas,[27] who may have met Bell when he arrived at the Cape early in 1847. Angas had accompanied Sir George Grey on his expedition into the interior of South Australia in 1845,[28] and it is likely that the governor gave these two watercolours to Bell, with the request that they should be incorporated into his binding.

The second manuscript is inscribed on the title page: *An Account of the Korana with a description of their Customs drawn up for His Excellency Sir George Grey, K.C.B., by the Revd C.F. Wuras and illustrated by C.D. Bell.*[29] Illustrated in pen and ink, this work indicates that, as a caricaturist, the artist was as adept as ever. The subject may be serious but the illustrations are almost invariably humorous: Bell's animals are quaint – a serpent is teased by a bird; lions and rhinos are creatures of amusement, not of terror – and men and women are downright funny. Headings and initial letters are embellished; and group scenes show how familiar Bell was with the customs and behaviour of the people he drew.

Very different is the third volume entrusted to Bell for illustration. Bound in scarlet leather, gilt-edged and printed on fine hand-made paper, this book, entitled *Epigrammata*,[30] is treasured

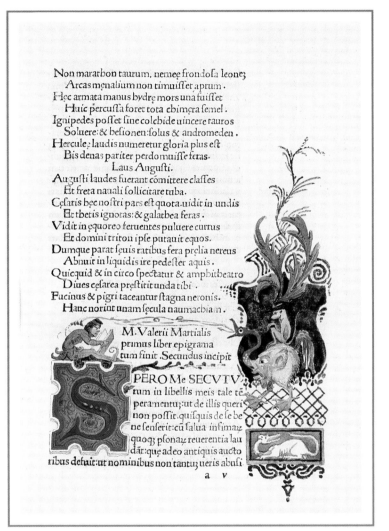

among the 119 priceless works in the Grey Collection for it dates back as far as 1475 when mechanical printing was in its infancy. The author is the Roman writer, Marcus Valerius Martialis, known as the father of the Latin epigram, who was born at much the same time as Jesus Christ was crucified in another part of Caesar's empire. Not surprisingly, the work – divided into a number of 'books' – is an exercise in wit and satire which Martialis converts into a canvas crowded with human oddities of every kind, among them fops and fortune-hunters, busybodies, orators, philosophers, poisoners, jugglers and acrobats.[31] The margins are wide and initial letters have been deliberately omitted to allow the illuminator space in which to display his art, thus presenting Charles Bell with an opportunity to venture into yet another genre. The result is a marvellous conglomerate of monsters and eccentrics, of mermaids and mermen, dragons and goblins, many of them entwined in foliage and adorned with flowers.

Bell started off by using gold leaf and although the passing years have dulled the sheen, the twirls and tendrils of the embellishments, not to mention the elongated noses and enormous ears of the grotesque figures, continue to charm and to amuse. The first page is a decorative delight, but as the work moves on Bell appears to have run out of time and possibly of inspiration because the illuminations become progressively simpler. Nevertheless, here is Bell at his most ebullient – and this is no surprise, for the work was undertaken at the time of his marriage to Helena when his personal life was once more all happiness and joy. It was 1860; a new decade was beginning, and there was still much in store for Charles Bell.

figure 18
Epigrammata.
Coll: South African Library

Bell's light-hearted and often satirical illustrations add to the witty character of Epigrammata, *a work by Marcus Valerius Martialis which is among the 119 priceless volumes in the Grey Collection of the South African Library. Originally published in Venice by Johannes de Colonia and Johannes Manthem in 1475, this volume was bound in red Victorian grained leather, possibly goatskin, in about 1850.*

Chapter 9

YEARS OF RESPONSIBILITY

On Monday 17 September 1860 Cape Town was en fête, for Prince Alfred — Queen Victoria's 'own sailor son' as effusive journalists of the day referred to him — had come to town. Never mind that it rained intermittently throughout the day or that a stiff northwester was whipping a hundred flags into a frenzy. Over fifteen thousand citizens of every creed and colour had begun crowding the whole extent of the waterfront early in the morning and not even a hurricane would be allowed to dampen their exuberance. The prince, a midshipman aged fourteen, had arrived to inaugurate the construction of Table Bay's harbour, and Cape Town's frenetic response to the occasion was an expression of loyalty never before known in the Colony.

figure 1 (left)
Silver trigger. 1860.
Watercolour. 12.5 x 11 cm.
Bell Heritage Trust Collection, UCT

figure 2 (right)
Silver trigger. 1860
Photograph by Frederick York.
Coll: MuseumAfrica

A watercolour by Charles Bell and a photograph by Frederick York show the massive silver trigger designed by Bell for Prince Alfred to use when he tipped into the sea the load of stones forming the foundation of Cape Town harbour's breakwater on 17 September 1860. At the base of the trigger dolphins are flanked by Neptune and a triton whose threats to a dismasted ship are foiled by shields bearing the colonial arms and those of Sir George Grey. The silversmith was Paolo Gaffodio and the engraver Thomas Hopkins.

There is no known record that Charles Bell and Helena attended the festivities, but it is extremely probable that they were there – even if it meant leaving at home their baby daughter, Helena Isabella, born at Krynauwshof on 31 May. Charles would have been anxious to watch the proceedings for he had been responsible for designing the elaborate silver trigger which the prince was to use to release a load of rocks from the wagon on which they were piled, and so allow them to tumble into the sea at the point where the breakwater was to be constructed. All went as planned, and later the governor, Sir George Grey, solemnly presented the silver trigger to Prince Alfred as a keepsake. The trigger itself, a magnificent piece of work, was in the Clarence House collection until 1901, when it was sold at a 'grand auction' for thirty guineas, but at least the watercolour design which Bell created for it remains and may be seen by anyone who visits the treasures of the Bell Heritage Trust Collection held at the University of Cape Town.

Fortunately, too, we have a detailed description of the trigger, which appeared in *The Cape Argus* of Thursday, 13 September 1860:

It consists of 40 oz. of massive silver, and is the finest piece of workmanship of the kind ever produced in the colony. The design by Mr Bell, the Surveyor-General, shows a base of dolphins exquisitely carved, surrounded on either side by Neptune and a Triton, emblematic of the Waves and Wind threatening a dismasted ship, which is protected from the Fury by the colonial arms and the arms of Sir Geo. Grey beautifully engraved on their respective shields. Above are the Royal Arms, on which are quartered those of His Royal Highness as Duke of Saxony. Still higher is a coil of massive silver decorated with a reef-knot, oak leaves etc. The execution of the work has been admirably effected by Mr Gaffodio,[1] under the direction and aid of Mr Bell.

The inauguration of the breakwater was only one of a host of entertainments organised for the young prince during a hectic visit lasting from his arrival in Simon's Bay in HMS *Euryalis* on 24 July 1860 until he set sail for home on 19 September. During those two months he made an extensive tour of the country, travelling as far afield as Natal. He met everyone of importance, including several well-known African chiefs; joined an astonishing hunt in the Orange Free State – modern-day environmentalists would have been horrified at its brutality; attended balls and receptions; planted trees and opened public buildings. An account of all this was published in one of the most fascinating books to appear in South Africa during the nineteenth century. Written by an anony-

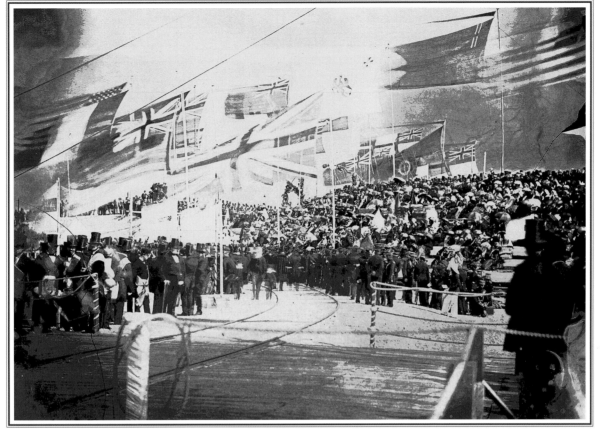

figure 3
Inauguration of Cape Town's breakwater, 17 September 1860.
Photograph by Frederick York.
Coll: MuseumAfrica

Frederick York's photograph of the ceremony at which Prince Alfred inaugurated the Table Bay breakwater depicts a scene that was also perpetuated in paintings by both Thomas Baines and Thomas Bowler. York, who arrived at the Cape in January 1855, was officially commissioned to take photographs of this occasion and to accompany the young prince on his tour of the hinterland. Some of his photographs are tipped into the book The Progress of Prince Alfred… *and show the documentary value of what was at the time a new medium.*

mous – and ecstatic – author, it was entitled *The progress of Prince Alfred through South Africa*, and claimed to be 'purely colonial' in every respect. The publisher, and probably the author, was Saul Solomon, a genius trapped in the body of a dwarf and, incidentally, Bell's successor as chairman of the Mutual. The book, produced in the year following the prince's visit, was bound in bright blue cloth tooled in gold and is the first South African volume in which 'tipped-in' photographs have been used as illustrations. Some of these were taken by the Cape Town photographer, Frederick York, who accompanied the prince during his tour of the Colony, while others are of paintings by Thomas Bowler and Thomas Baines.

In addition to these photographs, nine illustrations in the form of wood engravings by Charles Bell were printed with the text, each one of them a demonstration of Bell's versatility and skill. This was especially remarkable as it appears that not only was Bell entirely self-taught in the art of wood engraving, but also he had to 'make do' both with local wood – possibly olive – and whatever tools were available.[2] His efforts did not pass unappreciated: in the introduction to the book, the publisher gave Bell

credit 'for the valuable help he … rendered in the admirable designs of his pencil and the spirited results of his amateur graver'.[3] Bell probably engraved the woodblocks himself – it was rare for an artist also to be an engraver – and was almost certainly also responsible for the book's splendid cover block.[4] The design is an elaborate one which includes several heraldic devices. Pride of place above the title is given to the prince's coat of arms, which is supported by the traditional British lion and unicorn above oak leaves and acorns. Below the title there are festoons of vine leaves and bunches of grapes symbolic of the wine-producing Cape. Inside, the corners of the pages are embellished with delicate little vignettes in which English roses, Scottish thistles and crowns are intertwined. Once again, one is left wondering how it was that the surveyor-general – whose bulky official reports and correspondence must have demanded his attention during many hours of his daily life – had time to create a work such as this that incorporates such exquisite and painstaking artistry.

Seven years later – in 1867 – Prince Alfred was to return to lay the foundation stone of the graving dock in Table Bay harbour.

For the practical performance of this function the prince, now a twenty-one-year-old captain in the Royal Navy, was handed a silver trowel which Charles Bell had decorated with birds, flowers and an appropriate inscription. It seems that this work of art, like the silver trigger, was taken home to England by the prince, no doubt with the effusive blessings of Capetonians, but at the same time depriving the Colony of a second masterpiece in this genre.

By 1860 Bell was including heraldic devices and coats of arms in his artworks as often as the opportunity arose, and as the decade progressed so his fascination with this intriguing subject increased. Probably inspired by the Krynauw family which had originated in Germany, he explored the arms and armorial devices of long-established Cape colonials of Dutch, German and French descent, which, until then, had been little known to, or appreciated by, those entitled to them. Heraldic rules on the Continent differ from those governing the holding of arms in Great Britain, for in such countries as Holland and Switzerland anyone has the right to adopt a family coat of arms without interference from the

authorities.[5] From old seals and signet rings, tombstones, funeral hatchments and the like, Bell began to collect the coats of arms of local families of Dutch, French and German descent, and to sketch them and to blazon them in proper heraldic terminology. Eventually he decided to compile an exhaustive work on the subject, and on 10 September 1861 an advertisement to this effect appeared in the *Cape of Good Hope Government Gazette*. Emanating from the steam printing office of Saul Solomon & Co., it appealed to 'South African Families of European descent' to provide 'Arms and Armorial devices … claimed, or used by their forebears, chiefly during the XVII and XVIII Centuries' for inclusion in the work in preparation. The book would be undertaken, the advertisement assured its readers, 'without an idea of pecuniary profit to the author or compiler or publishers', and the style in which it would be produced ('if published at all'), would entirely depend on the descendants of the old colonists themselves. It would give the arms of each family in full, 'with crests, coronets, supporters &c.' such as could be seen on 'old seals, monuments or paintings'. Provided there was

response from four hundred families or more, the cost to each subscriber would not exceed £1. Then followed a list of almost two hundred families whose shields had already been collected, sketched and described by Charles Bell.

Despite Bell's enthusiasm and the encouragement of Saul Solomon, the book was never published, probably because of lack of response and possibly because the early 1860s could not have been a uniformly happy period at the Cape. At this time, few people were untouched by the prevailing atmosphere of gloom, for the Colony was in the grip of a serious financial depression for which there appeared to be no end in sight. Domestically, though, Bell must have been content enough: late in 1860, while retaining Canigou as their summer residence – a popular custom among Capetonians wishing to escape the heat and wind of the city – he and Helena had moved into their new home, 'Belton', in Somerset Road, Green Point. This, like the neighbouring suburb of Sea Point, had developed into a fashionable area over recent years. Many professional men and prosperous merchants made their homes in Green and Sea Point, enjoying the fresh sea air and sweeping view over the bay with its constant comings and goings of ships.[6] It was at Belton that the Bells' two sons were born – Alexander on 15 September 1861

and Anthony, or Tony, on 9 February 1863. But later in that year – on 16 July – and also at Belton, fourteen-year-old Catherine, daughter of Bell's first marriage, died of some unstated illness, thus casting a profound shadow over her father's life. He signed the death notice, declaring that Catherine's only possessions were 'books, trinkets, wearing apparel and some shares in the Cape Commercial Bank – total value £40'. He had wished, he stated, to present the shares to his daughter when she came of age, but this was not to be.[7]

Catherine was buried in the Somerset Road cemetery almost opposite Belton, but her remains were later removed to the Bell's family plot in St Paul's graveyard, Rondebosch. And there the little girl lies to this day, her grave surrounded by a cast-iron fence. Beside her lie two infant siblings: David Duncan Traill and Catherine Susan. Obviously this Catherine was named after her elder sister, but she was destined for an even shorter life, for when she died she was only four months old. By the time of her birth in May 1865, twenty-six-year-old Helena Bell had, in typical Victorian manner, given birth to five babies within six years of her marriage to Charles in July 1859. And in true and tragic Victorian manner, two of these children were to die in infancy.[8] Catherine Mariann's name is the only one that appears

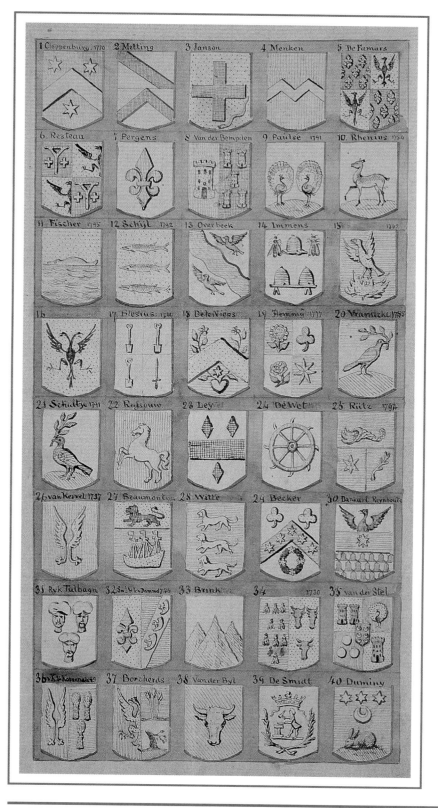

on the grave, where a small plaque records simply that she was the 'beloved daughter of Charles Davidson Bell'. Of her mother, Martha Antoinetta, there is no mention.

The family coat of arms incorporating three church bells is wrought into the iron fence surrounding the children's grave, an indication that, despite his sorrows, Bell had not lost his interest in heraldry. Over the years he continued to work on the collection of Cape shields, describing and sketching them in minute and fascinating detail. It was a formidable task and Bell's life was not long enough to allow for its completion. Fortunately, however, Daniel Krynauw had proved an apt and inspired disciple, and it was he who continued the work after his brother-in-law had left the Cape. Known today as the Bell–Krynauw Collection and held by the South African Library, it is still regarded as providing the most accurate source of information on the bearings of the old families of the Cape.[9]

This catalogue of armorial bearings was certainly not Bell's only heraldically-inspired work. If the Krynauw coat of arms was of interest to him, naturally the bearings and history of his own family held an even greater fascination and before long he began to turn his attention to investigating his own genealogical background in Scotland. The result was a small but priceless book entitled *Memorial of the Clan of the Bells, more particularly the Bells of Kirkonnel & Bells of Blackethouse, Chiefs of the Name* which, according to the title page, was 'printed privately and only for a few friends' by Saul Solomon & Co. of Cape Town in 1864. The name of the author and illustrator appears nowhere in the book, but there is no doubt that Charles Bell was the person responsible, for at the foot of the title page, within a circle, the initials CDB are clearly shown. In every respect this book is a remarkable work: not only does it investigate in detail every known branch and sept of the Bell family from the Middle Ages onwards as well as every anecdote and every legend – no mean feat when the author was half a world away from most of his sources of information – but its illustrations and embellishments are further examples of the masterly manner in which Bell handled the difficult and, at that time, fashionable art-cum-craft of wood engraving. In the text, he did not claim 'any prominent leading position for the name', nor did he discover any members of the family who had 'risen to the rank of Nobles in the Land'.[10] But there was at least one bishop among the Clan of the Bells, and others among its members had distinguished themselves over the centuries in a variety of professions and occupations varying from parliamentarians to academics, from surgeons to soldiers.

In the year that the *Memorial of the Clan of the Bells…* was published Cape Town found itself bereft, by death, of one of its finest and most public-spirited citizens. This was John Fairbairn, born in Scotland in 1794, father of the South African press, supporter of civil rights, promoter of education, and founder, in 1845, of the Mutual Life Assurance Society of the Cape of Good Hope. In almost twenty years he had seen this organisation develop from the smallest of beginnings into one of the most respected and successful financial institutions ever to be established in the Colony. Under his leadership, its capital had grown from the modest premiums paid by a handful of courageous policyholders to accumulated funds of over £187 000. Led by Fairbairn, the Society had outgrown the small office it had shared with a fire insurance company and, in July 1864, moved into its own dignified, three-storey building in Darling Street. But now, unexpectedly, the Mutual was without a chairman and it would take a brave man indeed to take over where Fairbairn had left off.

On 7 October the directors met in their new boardroom to elect his successor and, perhaps predictably, their choice fell on another Scot, a well-known and respected bookseller named Archibald Shaw Robertson who had held the reins while Fairbairn was away in England between 1850 and 1853. However, Robertson's period in office was shortlived: early in the following year he announced that he had decided to return to Scotland and the directors had to look around for someone to take his place. Now, it seems, there was no question as to who the new chairman would be. With his indisputable integrity, his wide experience in so many spheres, his qualities of leadership and his remarkable gifts, Charles Bell was the uncontested

choice. On Monday 3 July 1865 he chaired his first – and the Society's twentieth – annual general meeting at which he paid a moving tribute to his friend, John Fairbairn.

Nevertheless, Charles Bell was not a well man at this time. The fine work involved in the accurate and precise depiction of coats of arms, and also the application required for delicate wood engraving, had inevitably affected his eyes and he was beginning to pay the price for long hours of unrelieved mental and ocular concentration, often by candlelight. According to Piazzi Smyth, Bell 'had always been very short of sight, however keen',[11] and it may be that eye-strain had led to the severe and debilitating headaches from which he was suffering. In a letter to Thomas Maclear written as early as 17 March 1864, he had complained of 'hives of bees' in his brain, and four days later wrote that his head was 'whizzing still'.[12] His condition continued to deteriorate over the following two years, and on 30 April 1866 he collapsed while giving evidence before a commission investigating the law of inheritance in the western districts.[13]

It may be that his ill health had been aggravated by intense personal distress caused by the news that his son, John, now a married man, intended to have his baby son baptised as a Roman Catholic since this was the faith of his wife, Margaret. To Bell, steeped in the Calvinist tenets of the Church of Scotland, this was anathema and his fury knew no bounds. On 23 March 1866 he wrote to John, then employed as a customs official in Port Elizabeth, accusing him of 'apostasy from – or [an] act of contempt of the faith of [his] Fathers', and declared that his son could never again be more to him than an ordinary acquaintance. His letter, which was nothing short of a vicious diatribe, closed with the words: 'I trust that Folly, Deceit and Worse on the part of your own children may never be such as to cause you the bitter disappointment and care and grief which I have undergone since 1848.'[14] Even while making

figure 10
Tomb of Richard Bell, Bishop of Carlisle.
Wood carving. 48 x 32 cm.
Bell Heritage Trust Collection, UCT

In his Memorial of the Clan of the Bells…, *which examines the lineage of people of that name, Bell includes an engraving that he made from a rubbing of the tombstone of Bishop Richard Bell which he found in Carlisle Cathedral. He writes: 'Nothing seems to be known of his descent from or connection with any of the principal branches of the clan.'*

allowances for Bell's ill health at the time, it is difficult not to criticise him for blind intolerance. If such ungovernable rage was his reaction when John's behaviour merely displeased him, perhaps one can spare some sympathy for the erring Martha after all.

And this was not all, for during this period Charles Bell was involved in another distressing episode in which the darker side of his nature was only too apparent. He was, in the middle sixties, chairman not only of the Mutual but of another highly respectable financial institution, the Cape Commercial Bank, founded in 1854.[15] Also serving on this board was a Cape Town attorney named Jan Hendrik Hofmeyr,[16] whose behaviour incensed Bell to such an extent that he felt obliged to dismiss him both as a director and as the bank's legal adviser. There followed a long series of irate letters between the two men, both of them clearly well known to the populace of Cape Town. Hofmeyr, in a letter dated 29 March 1866, refers to his dismissal 'for no special act of misconduct, but generally because I had

become obnoxious to the Board', and challenges Bell 'in terms of the Circular, dated Downing-street, 17th December, 1864' to prove his right 'to sit as a Director of the Cape Commercial Bank, or any other institution of a like nature'. 'Any other institution', referred to the Mutual and to the Umzinto Sugar Company on whose board Bell had apparently served until a short time before.

With hindsight, the quarrel seems to have been a petty one, and both correspondents reveal themselves to be extremely waspish. However, since no details are given of Hofmeyr's apparently reprehensible conduct, it is impossible to take sides. Bell nevertheless must have felt constrained to make the entire unpleasant correspondence known to the shareholders of both the bank and the Mutual, for he published and distributed it in the form of two pamphlets.[17]

By August of 1866 Bell was under such intolerable strain that he applied to the colonial secretary, Richard Southey,[18] for leave to visit England. 'I am too ill to continue in charge of this Office,'

he wrote. 'If the rest and quiet of the voyage restores me so far as to promise me recovery I shall be at my post here within three months.'[19] His request was sympathetically received, and within a week a letter reached him from Southey's office granting him the necessary permission.[20] His illness aside, a visit to Scotland would enable him to spend some time with his parents, both now in their late eighties, and of whom he had seen little enough since he left home as a sixteen-year-old boy. It seems that Helena and the children did not accompany him on this brief visit – at least their names do not appear in the list of passengers who returned with him. A good deal of the three months' leave allowed to Bell would have been spent at sea, and the presence on board ship of three lively children would hardly have contributed to the rest that he was anticipating.

It seems that Bell certainly did benefit from the holiday and that he was in high spirits by the time he set sail for home on board the s.s. *Celt*. Evidence of his good humour is provided by a delightful journal entitled *The Illustrated Celtic Record*, for which the ship's passengers wrote articles and poems and which was later printed in Cape Town by Van der Sandt de Villiers. According to Alan C.G. Lloyd, a former

figure 12 **A well-known advocate on his steed outside the old Supreme Court.** *c.* **1860.**
Pen and watercolour. 17.8 x 25.3 cm. William Fehr Collection

Protected by a dilapidated umbrella and mounted on his emaciated horse, the obviously eccentric lawyer – here lampooned by Charles Bell – ambles along Adderley Street, Cape Town, accompanied by the jeers of youthful onlookers. The identity of the subject is uncertain, but it may have been Jan Hendrik Hofmeyr, a Cape Town advocate with whom Bell had a bitter quarrel.

figure 13
Title page of *The Illustrated Celtic Record.* 1866.
Bell Heritage Trust Collection, UCT

The Illustrated Celtic Record, a journal of the voyage of the s.s. Celt in which Bell made his voyage home from Britain in 1866, reveals Bell at his most high-spirited. Though small in format, it gave him ample scope for both witty writing and amusing illustrations.

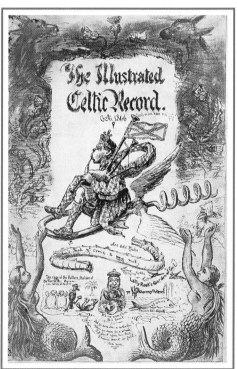

director of the South African Library, this spirited little book 'holds pride of place' among journals which, at one time, were often produced during sea voyages, for it contains numerous amusing illustrations as well as witty doggerel verse contributed by Charles Bell. The subjects of both prose and poems, as well as the relaxed circumstances in which the journal was compiled, gave Bell scope for sketching sea monsters and the other grotesqueries in which his unique humour delighted. The original *Celtic Record*, which unfortunately cannot be traced, would almost certainly have been hand-written and illustrated, whereas in the few printed copies that survive photographs of Bell's fantastic sketches have been tipped in at appropriate places.[21]

Meanwhile, Cape Town's Fourth Exhibition of Fine Arts, with Bell once more on the committee, had opened in the Mutual's new hall on 31 October 1866. Bell, still overseas, was not present to hear the inaugural address by Mr Justice Hendrik Cloete, who had recently retired from the Cape Bench, but as the doors remained open until mid-December he would have made a point of visiting the exhibition on his return from England.[22] Only four of his works were on show, two of which were the perennially popular 'Arrival of Van Riebeeck' and 'The isle of the Holy Cross'. Altogether, although fewer works were shown on this occasion, the exhibition was considered a success and a great improvement on its predecessors.[23] In fact, *Die Volksblad* of 1 November described it as 'a treat

figure 14 **Charles Davidson Bell by John Horsburgh.**
Oil. 75.5 x 62.4 cm. Coll: MuseumAfrica

A portrait of Charles Bell in maturity by the Scottish line engraver, John Horsburgh, who may have been a friend of Bell's. Horsburgh was noted for his portrait of Robert Burns and also for that of Sir Walter Scott, for whose collected works he engraved the vignettes.

which, in a colony like ours, can only be afforded at rare intervals'.

Treats, indeed, were much appreciated in 1866, for there were still no signs of relief from the economic slump that had held the Cape in its thrall for almost a decade. However, in time to come South Africans were able to look back on the summer that spanned 1866 and 1867 as a time when a glimmer of hope did at last – and literally – begin to sparkle on the financial horizon. At first, few took seriously the discovery, in the sands of the northern Cape, of a pebble that shimmered magically in the bright sunshine,[24] but when others, even brighter and better, were found during the following months and positively identified as diamonds, the country's industrial future was sealed. Daily, as in the copper mania of the mid-1850s, Cape Town was to witness fortune hunters in their thousands setting off on hazardous journeys of discovery.

On such staid civil servants as Charles Bell, though, the diamond rush had little personal influence. In fact, now that the beneficial effects of his brief holiday were wearing off, Bell began to feel that conditions in the Cape Civil Service, and specifically his position in it, were intolerable. It is possible, too, that what Piazzi Smyth called Bell's 'pent-up passionate admiration for his native land'[25] had been aroused by seeing Scotland again and he had been seized with a longing to return there permanently. Whatever his reasons, in June 1867 Bell applied to resign as surveyor-general, although he was only in his fifty-fourth year. 'I am desirous of retiring from a Service,' he wrote to the Colonial Secretary, 'into which under present conditions I would not have entered in 1832, and from a position such as I would not have accepted in 1848.'[26]

Once more, all was to no avail: Bell's request was refused and he was obliged to return to the treadmill of the survey department. With considerable reluctance he battled on, even though his health continued to deteriorate and there were times when he was not strong enough to undertake fieldwork. One of these occasions involved a commission he had appointed 'to survey the summit [of Table Mountain], connect the Geodetic Station fixed by Sir Thomas Maclear, Astronomer Royal, on the highest point ... with the property surveys around the base, and to examine the water sources and streams with the object of conducting the water to Cape Town and its suburbs'. Seven men, including Abraham de Smidt, now Bell's second in command, and Daniel Krynauw, were appointed to undertake the survey but Bell declined to join them. 'I would gladly volunteer to be of the party,' he said, 'but doubt my health and strength being equal to the effort.' As things turned out, it was as well that Bell remained at home, for the little group of surveyors was subjected to every possible variety of violent and dangerous weather while on the mountain. One good thing to emerge from the expedition was a collection of amusing sketches produced by Daniel Krynauw. The clever likenesses he had drawn of his companions and his merry sense

figure 15 **Helena Bell by John Horsburgh.**
Oil. 76.4 x 63.5 cm. Coll: MuseumAfrica

Helena Gertruida Johanna Bell, daughter of Anthony David Krynauw, was born in Cape Town in 1839. This portrait conveys the elegance and strength of character of Charles Bell's second wife, to whom he was married for twenty-two years. 'Cape Dutch' by descent, language and religion, she died on 10 September 1881 in Crail, Scotland.

of the absurd once more showed how lightly the mantle of his brother-in-law was falling on his shoulders.[27]

In August 1871, Cape Town saw the official incorporation of the South African Fine Arts Association under the chairmanship of Richard Southey. For years – ever since the first exhibition was mooted in 1851 – supporters of the arts had struggled to establish a permanent association of local artists, but it was only at a meeting held on 21 April 1871 that a committee was formed to bring it to realisation. Most of Cape Town's most distinguished citizens – including, of course, Charles Bell – were on that committee; the governor, Sir Henry Barkly, was elected the association's first president; James Fairbairn (son of John) was the honorary secretary while Daniel Krynauw was appointed treasurer. The rules were simple and the main aim of the association was to promote the arts in the Cape Colony by the formation of a permanent art library, by holding occasional exhibitions, by establishing art unions and by offering prizes.[28]

The first exhibition was held on 4 December 1871 but Bell did not exhibit. However, when the second exhibition was held on 21 August of the following year he was invited to deliver the opening speech. As was the custom of the day, it was a lengthy and high-minded one in which Bell, among other things, gave his listeners some idea of the judges' criteria in awarding prizes and of the association's objectives in holding exhibitions.

The occasion presented an opportunity for two respected academics – Sir Langham Dale and Dr James Cameron, professor of English at the South African College – to thank Bell publicly for his valuable contribution to the fostering of the visual arts at the Cape. For, said Dale, 'amidst the cares of official life he has cultivated a taste for fine arts, and not only holds a high place, but has been ready to give others the benefit of his knowledge'.

But 1872 – an auspicious year in the history of the Cape – was not yet over. To the profound relief of the entire community, the long and tedious economic depression had come to an end at last and the Cape was revelling in boom times such as it had never before experienced. On 22 November the colonists were to see the passing of the Constitution Ordinance Amendment Act,[29] which signified the introduction of responsible government, and in December they would be

witness to the appointment of the Colony's first prime minister, John Charles Molteno, familiarly known as 'the Lion of Beaufort'.[30] At last the Cape had achieved the self-rule for which it had struggled for so long. But the new political order meant changes in the civil service, one of which involved the disbanding of the office of the surveyor-general and its merging with the Department of Crown Lands and Public Works. To the authorities, this was a signal that Bell's wish to retire should be acceded to, and on 29 November he received a letter from the colonial secretary to that effect.[31] He would be granted a pension commensurate with his forty years in the government's employ, and the secretary of state for the colonies would decide whether he would also be allowed an additional amount for special services. Charles Bell's official retirement began on 1 December 1872; his days as a civil servant were over.

figure 16
Wood engraving.

A rural scene, probably in a remote part of Namaqualand, where matjieshuise *such as these were the usual form of dwelling.*

Chapter 10

RETURN TO SCOTLAND

In 1873 Charles Bell, his wife and three youngest children left the Cape of Good Hope to settle permanently in Scotland. No one knows what thoughts passed through their minds as they steamed northwards out of Table Bay, but they must surely have experienced pangs of regret to see the lovely triptych of mountains, backdrop to their lives for so long, dipping slowly below the horizon and out of sight. How, their friends might have asked, would Helena, Cape born and bred, take to living under the grey skies of Edinburgh? Would Charles regret leaving behind the life he had created for himself over the past forty years, and in particular his two elder sons, now grown men?

At least it was certain that the name of Charles Bell would not be easily forgotten at the Cape which had benefitted so richly both from his professional contribution and by the expression of his many and varied talents. It would have satisfied him to know that the reorganised Survey Office remained in good hands, for his former colleague and good friend, Abraham de Smidt – himself an artist of acknowledged merit – had been put in charge of it. It was gratifying, too, to feel that the South African Fine Arts Association would continue its important enterprises and that the various societies and businesses in which he had been interested would live on. No doubt Bell looked forward with pleasurable anticipation to living close to his aged parents and uncle, but the moment when Table Mountain finally faded out of sight must have been a poignant one indeed.

When the Bells arrived in Britain, their first duty call was on Sir John Bell at his home at 55 Cadogan Place in London. John Bell, now ninety-one years old, had been promoted to full

general in June 1860[1] and, since he was the longest-serving officer holding this rank at the time, he was known by the courtesy title of 'Father of the British Army'.[2] Lady Catherine had died in 1855 and Charles Bell, conscious of his uncle's deep affection for him, was prepared to stay with him as long as he was needed. In fact, over a year was to pass before Bell could safely leave the old man and move his family to their new home in Edinburgh. Sir John Bell lived on until 20 November 1876, and when he died at home after suffering a stroke, he was ninety-four years old. His had been a good life in every possible sense.

For the Bells the year 1876 was a melancholy one, for it saw not only the death of Sir John but also the passing of both Charles's parents. His father, Alexander, had reached the venerable age of ninety when he died and his wife, Isabella, five years his junior, survived him by only five days. Whatever feelings Charles Bell might have had about leaving the Cape, at least he had known the comfort of sharing his parents' last years. Throughout

figure 1
Charles and Helena Bell.
Photograph.
Bell Heritage Trust Collection, UCT

This photograph of Charles and Helena Bell was taken in Edinburgh after they had settled in Scotland. The age difference between them of twenty-six years appears not to have affected their relationship, and it seems almost ironic that Helena should have been the first to die.

his life, the fishing town of Crail where he had spent his childhood and where his parents had their home had never ceased to lure him and, in these years of retirement, it gave him joy to live near enough to take his family there for a prolonged visit every summer.[3]

Not surprisingly, Charles Bell's return to the land of his birth aroused in him an active interest in Scotland's rich historical heritage. He became a member of various academic societies, including the Royal Society of Edinburgh and the Scottish Meteorological Society. He was elected to the Society of Antiquaries of Scotland in 1875 and, according to the obituary written by Piazzi Smyth, began to study 'antiquities and history with a devotion that nothing could abate'. In Crail kirkyard he discovered an old runic cross 'doing duty as a paving stone', duly removed it and installed it with fitting honour in a niche within the church itself.[4] He developed an interest in the traditional ballads of Scotland, finding them worthy of illustration in his own inimitable style – though, alas, no specimens of this particular work have so far been located.[5]

figure 2 (left)
Queen Mary's harp.
78.7 cm high; 45.7 cm deep.
Society of Antiquaries of Scotland.

Charles Bell discovered Queen Mary's harp, forgotten and neglected, in a shooting lodge on the Dalguise estate in Scotland. Queen Mary is believed to have taken it with her on a hunting expedition in Perthshire and to have presented it, while there, to a family which retained it for three centuries.

figure 3 (right)
Lamont harp.
96.5 cm high; 47 cm deep.
Society of Antiquaries of Scotland.

Bell discovered the Lamont harp with Queen Mary's harp in Scotland in the 1870s. It was owned by the Lamont family as early as 1464, but Bell believed that it dated back to an older period. He writes: 'It is a plain substantial instrument made more for use than ornament, rather fitted for the wandering minstrel than for noble or royal hands.'

He was fascinated by historic Celtic harps and managed to discover two antique and neglected instruments, together with a pair of brass-studded leather bucklers known as targets and 'a chestful of old broadswords, shirts of chain mail and other antiques', stored, forgotten, in a garret in the Scottish Highlands. This was at Steuartfield, home of John Steuart of Dalguise, retired Master of the Supreme Court at the Cape and almost certainly well known to Bell. The larger of the harps (it measured 38 inches in height) was known as 'the Clarshach Lumanach' or Lamont harp since it had been owned by a family of that name as long ago as 1464. It was 'a plain substantial instrument', wrote Charles Bell, and 'made more for use than ornament, rather fitted for the wandering minstrel than for noble or royal hands'. Much more elaborate than this harp was the second and smaller instrument, which, it seems, was actually played by 'royal hands', though there is no knowing how skilled they were. Measuring 31 inches from top to base and 18 inches at its broadest point, it was known as Queen Mary's harp since it was brought to the highlands of Perthshire by that unhappy monarch when she visited on a hunting excursion in 1563. This harp must have appealed particularly to Bell for it was decorated with elaborate carvings including 'fine foliagenous scroll work', incised interlacing geometrical patterns and figures of various heraldic beasts of a type so dear to his heart.[6] With the blessing of the Steuart family, Bell handed over the harps to the Society of Antiquaries of Scotland in whose safe keeping they have been carefully preserved for over a century.[7]

But these precious objects are not the only relics of Charles Bell's last years in Scotland. Among the holdings of the Bell Heritage Trust Collection there is a small leather-bound album, given to him by Piazzi Smyth, which contains numerous drawings providing a lively insight into his life at this time. Most of them are pencil sketches dated between 1873 and 1876; many are depictions of scenes in the Scottish countryside. There are architectural drawings of buildings and – judging from the annotations – illustrations of what must have been a holiday in Wales. There are pictures of family outings and there are amusing caricatures with captions indicating that Bell certainly had not lost his whimsical sense of humour. The album also lists various expenses incurred by the Bells – plumbers' accounts and the cost of several pieces of furniture. Then there is a record of the rate of growth of the three youngest children over the period August 1873 to December 1876 and what appears to be some sort of secret code in which Bell was obviously dabbling – a reminder,

no doubt, of his early interest in Taylor's system of shorthand.

But Charles Bell did not forget the Cape of Good Hope. After almost six years in Scotland he and Helena returned to the Colony on a prolonged visit, making the popular holiday resort of Kalk Bay their temporary home.[8] However, their arrival at the Cape was not a happy one for they were greeted with the news that, while they were at sea, Charles's son John, now the father of four young children, had died while on a visit to England. Somehow, during the years that had passed since 1866, the bitter rift that had wrenched father and son apart had been healed, for letters written by Charles Bell to his grieving daughter-in-law reveal the warmth and affection that existed between them. For example, in his letter to Margaret dated 8 March 1882, Bell

visit to the Cape. He had, after all, already lost three of his eight children.

Despite his grief, it was important that he should turn his mind to other things, for one of his intentions in visiting the Cape was to attend yet another exhibition of the South African Fine Arts Association. It was due to open in Cape Town on 20 January 1879 and once more Bell had been invited to act as a judge. On this occasion the committee aimed at encouraging local art students and amateurs, and when the prizes were announced, no fewer than twenty-three were awarded to colonial entries.[10] However, when the time came to decide on the winners, Charles Bell had to admit that his eyesight had deteriorated to a point where he felt forced to withdraw as a judge.

figure 7
The Blue Stone, Crail. 1873.
Pencil. 12.5 x 16.5 cm.
Bell Heritage Trust Collection,
UCT

Sketched after Bell's return to Scotland, this lively scene of the village children tumbling out of school proves that he never lost what Piazzi Smyth called his 'appreciation of the ridiculous'. Legend has it that the large 'blue stone' beneath the tree was hurled by the devil against Crail church all the way from the Isle of May. Inhabitants of the town used to kiss the stone before leaving on a journey as a pledge that they would return.

To a man whose pleasures and pastimes lay in the visual arts, whose imaginative energy was always directed towards the creation of beautiful things, this was nothing less than a tragedy.

However, for the moment, he could see well enough to get about. The exhibition – and the holiday – were over within a few months and on 25 March 1879 Helena and Charles Bell, accompanied by their friends Abraham and Gertrude de Smidt, left Cape Town on board the *Conway Castle* bound for Plymouth. Besides the two men's shared interests, Helena Bell and Gertrude de Smidt would have had much in common so the voyage was probably a pleasant one. On arrival in England, the two couples parted, the De Smidts to embark on a whirligig of a holiday in Europe, and Charles and Helena on a mission to

writes: 'You are indeed making a hard fight against the world in spite of scanty means and delicate health. It must be a great effort to keep one boy at College and two daughters at boarding schools. I wish I could do more to help you...'[9] Reassuring as it was for Charles to know that there had been forgiveness on both sides, John's death must have cast a deep shadow over his

Dartmouth to visit John's grave.[11] Neither of them would ever see Cape Town again.

On 10 September 1881 Helena Bell, aged only forty-two, died unexpectedly in the Bells' old house at Crail and was buried in the family grave beside her parents-in-law. Her husband, grief-stricken by her death, was all the more depressed at this time by

The Burial Ground
of the Macgregors
at Inch Cailloch 17/6/75-

figure 8 **The burial ground of the MacGregors. 1875.**
Pencil. 12.5 x 16.5 cm. Bell Heritage Trust Collection, UCT

Bell's retirement to Scotland represented more than simply the termination of his working life. The drawings he made during this last phase introduce a new expressive quality that represents both the relaxation of the scientific spirit and the sense of Bell's emotional involvement in the scene depicted. This late view of the burial ground of the MacGregors is suffused with both a sense of nostalgia and the romance of Scotland.

figure 9
**Mission school
(Hottentot) for the Xtian
house. 1878.**
Watercolour. 25 x 17.5 cm.
Bell Heritage Trust Collection,
UCT

*This scene must have been
painted from memory as it was
executed while Charles Bell
was in Scotland. From the
apparent diligence of the pupils,
the kindly expression of the
schoolmaster and the application
of the old woman struggling to
write, it seems that Bell had
acquired a gentler attitude to
those classes of people whom
he had lampooned when he
was younger.*

written on 8 March 1882 from his home at
No. 4 Glencairn Crescent in Edinburgh, Bell
tells her, 'I can hardly see what I am writing,
and I have gout in my right hand which does
not improve my penmanship – so I shall say no
more now – except that I linger on – have
gained flesh but that for the last week again my
worst symptoms have increased.'

A month later, on Good Friday, 7 April 1882,
Charles Davidson Bell died, aged 68, at home in
Edinburgh. *The St Andrew's Citizen* of 15 April,
under the heading 'Death of a distinguished
native of the east of Fife', recorded that 'his
remains were conveyed by rail for interment in
Crail Churchyard', and that his two young
sons, Alick and Tony, a nephew and a cousin,
were the chief mourners. It is not known when
the news of his death reached the Cape, but on
24 June *The Cape Argus* reprinted an obituary
that had appeared in the parish magazine of
St Bernard's church, Edinburgh. After paying
tribute to Bell's work as the Cape's surveyor-
general, the article continued: 'We cannot close
this paragraph without recording our deep
sense of the loss sustained by the removal of
one who endeared himself to all, and whose
Christian character shone the brighter in sorrow
and illness.'

All this was true enough; but somewhere in
the grey and ancient city of Edinburgh there
was at least one friend who knew better than to
express his opinion of Charles Bell in pious
platitudes; who had known him as he really
was, seen him under the brazen blue skies of
Africa, remembered him in the exuberance of
his youth and in the fulfilment of his middle
years. That friend, Charles Piazzi Smyth,
Scotland's Astronomer Royal and himself an
ageing man, had first encountered Charles Bell
soon after he returned from the expedition to
the Tropic of Capricorn and had seen his paintings of the wilderness of Africa with wide-eyed
astonishment. 'He had been the artist of the
expedition,' Smyth informed the Royal Society
of Scotland soon after Bell's death, 'and such an artist as showed
him to possess the soul of a true genius, if there be anyone in the
world of whom that can be properly said'.

True genius Charles Bell certainly was. When he was barely

the sudden loss of the sight of one eye. 'It was that eye,' wrote
Piazzi Smyth in his obituary, 'whose surrounding muscular con-
tractions had enabled him to keep a strong concave lens in place
through fifty years of excellent work, which had now suddenly
broken down.' In a letter to his daughter-in-law, Margaret,

twenty years old Sir Thomas Maclear had recognised his 'extra-ordinary talents [and] energetic courage' and had predicted, with accuracy, that he would make a success of anything he undertook. Charles Bell's paintings and sketches, his minutely detailed wood engravings, his lithographs, his etchings, the photographs that he took, the silver and brass that he crafted, the shields that he blazoned – all these and more bear testimony to his tremendous and varied output, his astonishing vigour, the originality of his creative imagination and the wide range of his gifts. It is sad indeed that much of his work was inadvertently destroyed by fire and that other fine pieces have mysteriously disappeared. Among these was a walking-stick described by his son-in-law, Dumeresq Manning, as having 'a handle … which was a monkey whose paw could be seen through the almost lattice-like carving stealing the eggs from the nest of a bird'. Gone, too, are the ceilings and doors of Canigou that Bell adorned with his carvings, as well as the stained glass windows designed and fired under his direction especially for that house.[12]

But Charles Bell was more than an artist. In addition to pursuing his chosen career of land surveying, he would turn his enquiring mind to anything that could stimulate his inventive spirit or capture his imagination. Meteorology, archaeology, palaeontology, philately, heraldry, numismatics – all these and more were among his many interests. Nor was merely studying them enough to occupy his active brain; invariably he set his nimble hands to putting into practice what he learnt, to fashioning materially what his mind had devised. Manning remembered that Bell 'had dabbled in patents': the primary features of the Westinghouse brake, so he claimed, 'were evolved from his fertile brain' while another, less successful invention – a tarred catamaran – had almost cost him his life when it capsized in the waves off Sea Point.

Charles Bell never made a personal fortune but, if need be, he could turn his versatile mind to business and to comprehending the financial affairs of the community. He was director of more than one institution, and in a gallery of famous men who have led Old Mutual to become the most prosperous life assurance corporation in South Africa and a role-player in the global economy, his portrait holds a proud place.

There is no doubt that Bell was a God-fearing man but he

figure 10
Crail Town Hall by James Mcmaster. 1880.
Coll: Crail Museum Trust

Charles Bell would have seen Crail Town Hall and its surroundings much like this,
on a wet afternoon, when he returned to his birthplace at the end of his life.

certainly was no saint. A Victorian in the best sense of the word, his moral standards were exceedingly high, so perhaps it is understandable that he was hot tempered on occasion and could be given to intolerance and prejudice – as well his immediate family must have been aware. And perhaps it may seem strange that in a society where prominent men almost unfailingly sought prestige in parliament, Bell showed little interest in politics, though the affairs and welfare of his fellow men, irrespective of race or creed, concerned him greatly. Indeed, in this respect he was a man ahead of his times. This is clear from his far-sighted approach to the land claims of the indigenous inhabitants of Namaqualand – a concern that has a special significance to South Africans in the closing years of the twentieth century. Well over a century before the present land claims court was established with the intention of returning property to its original owners, Bell, in his report of 1855, deplored the manner in which the people of Namaqualand had been deprived of territory traditionally theirs, and he recommended a system of its just re-allocation to those with a legitimate right to it.

This visit to Namaqualand was an occasion – and there were many of them – when Bell took life and his professional responsibilities very seriously. Nevertheless, to the end of his days, that seriousness was tempered by the perceptive and prankish sense of humour which had manifested itself in his exuberant youth. And it is this humour, this sense of fun, this awareness of the absurd and the grotesque and the comic, that sparkles throughout his life and his works like a bright thread in a tapestry already multicoloured. Even in his

sad, last days in Scotland when his health and his eyesight were failing, Bell continued to scribble caricatures that are still delightfully amusing.

People of vast and varied learning – as Charles Bell most certainly was – are known as 'polymaths', and they are rare indeed. For such a man to spend the best years of his 'multifarious life' living and working at the Cape of Good Hope – remote backwater as it was in those days – was, for the entire Colony, an uncommon privilege. But that privilege did not end with Bell's death: from him and his descendants the people of the country of his adoption have inherited a rich bequest – a diversity of treasures that are unique and beautiful, informative and brimful of humour. Those treasures, those priceless paintings and engravings and lithographs; those wood carvings and coats of arms; those postage stamps and photographs, are held in inalienable custody by the John and Charles Bell Heritage Trust in the Manuscripts of the University of Cape Town Libraries. Here, since the Trust came into being in 1978, they have been seen by those fortunate enough to visit or work at the University and they have also, from time to time, been on exhibition. Nevertheless, until the dying years of the twentieth century, Charles Davidson Bell has remained relatively unknown – and certainly little appreciated – both as an artist and as a contributor to the social history of the Cape. Now, more than a century after his death, the publication of this book has set this omission to rights and at last the works of Charles Davidson Bell, together with his fascinating life story, have been made available and accessible to an infinitely wider world. May he receive the recognition that he deserves.

figure 11 **Bell tombstone.**
Photograph. Coll: Dr Frank Bradlow

The simple inscriptions on the Bell family tombstone in Crail kirkyard throw little light on the life, background and achievements of Charles Davidson Bell.

The ART
OF CHARLES BELL:
An Appraisal

by Michael Godby

The ART OF CHARLES BELL:
An Appraisal

Charles Bell *is one of the most significant — and interesting — of all nineteenth-century South African artists. Although, after an early date, his art always came second to an important career in the colonial civil service, it is remarkable not only for its versatility in a range of different media — from woodcuts to oil painting — but also for its extraordinary breadth of subject matter. In comparison with the work of his near contemporaries, Thomas Bowler and Thomas Baines, which is mainly in the genre of landscape, Bell's oeuvre encompasses such different kinds as landscapes — of various types — portraits, ethnographical studies and caricatures. Through these genres, Bell provides a fascinating window onto a world that has vanished, offering views of street life in Cape Town, for example, or an early visual account of social life in the interior.*

figure 1

Caricatures by Sir John Bell.
Ink. 5.5 x 15.5 cm.
Bell Heritage Trust Collection,
UCT

Colonel John Bell, Charles Bell's uncle, enjoyed a distinguished military career in the Napoleonic Wars before being appointed colonial secretary at the Cape in 1828. He had taken responsibility for Charles's education even before his nephew had left Scotland, and it was probably he who introduced him to the amateur art of drawing in landscape and caricature when Charles joined his household at the Cape in 1832. This drawing may depict John Bell's comrades in arms in the Peninsular Campaign: the figure on the right bears some resemblance to Arthur Wellesley, later Duke of Wellington.

However, Bell was a man of his time, and the way he saw and represented these and other subjects reflected the values of his time. For this reason, this essay will examine Bell's art not as an objective record but rather as a construction of reality – of events, certainly, but even landscape spaces – that was particular to Bell's place in history. In my analysis, therefore, the style of the artist is seen not so much as his capability in the formal terms of line, colour, composition, etc., for their own sake, but rather as the constituent parts of a language that expressed the relationship of the artist to his environment. In this essay, in other words, the emphasis will move from the criteria of description and appreciation (of traditional treatments of South African artists) to an analysis of Bell's work as a language that reflects the historical conditions of his time.

In a letter to Frank Bradlow at the time the Bell Collection was entrusted to the University of Cape Town, Jack Manning recalled how Charles Manning, his step-brother and grandson of Charles Bell, had told him that there had been at one time three principal collections of Bell papers: two were destroyed in fires and the third was the one he was proposing to return from England to South

Africa.[1] There is no way of knowing what was in the lost collections, nor whether they contained any artworks at all, but the loss of anything up to two-thirds of his work suggests that present-day knowledge of Bell as an artist lies somewhere on the scale between incomplete and substantially distorted. Assessment of all aspects of this important South African artist should be tempered by this simple fact.

Although Manning omitted to mention the large collection of drawings that entered MuseumAfrica in 1965, and several other works that were known at the time in public and private collections, his idea that the bulk of Bell's work was to be found in no more than three collections, even if not entirely true, draws attention to a peculiar fact regarding Bell's art. It would not be possible to suggest of Thomas Bowler or Thomas Baines, or any other professional artist of this period, that their work was to be found in a mere handful of collections. A large portion of Bell's art, including the MuseumAfrica collection, passed to his children for the simple reason that he did not sell it. Bell's amateur status that is revealed in this observation is significant because it affected every aspect of his art at every point of his career.

It is clear from his biography that, from the time of his arrival in Cape Town in 1832, Charles Bell enjoyed the society of the most powerful and privileged people at the Cape. He made his 'second home' with his uncle, Colonel John Bell, who had been colonial secretary since 1828, and Lady Catherine Bell, daughter of the Earl of Malmesbury and god-daughter of Catherine the Great of Russia. Catherine, moreover, was sister to Lady Frances, the wife of Sir Lowry Cole, the governor of the Cape. John Bell was a distinguished draughtsman, both of picturesque scenes and personal caricatures, and it was probably under his guidance that Charles began to draw. In this privileged milieu, however, talent with a pencil was more of a polite accomplishment than a means of communication, let alone employment. Thus Bell's early work bears the hallmarks – of subject matter, style and apparent audience – of the amateur dilettante.

The surviving drawings by Bell that can certainly be dated to the few years before the Andrew Smith expedition of 1834 fall into two broad categories: landscape and social commentary. These are the categories exploited by John Bell and they also provided the framework for another prolific amateur artist who was visiting the Cape at this time, Sir Charles D'Oyly. D'Oyly appears to have quickly entered the prestigious circle in which Bell moved, for he drew Bell's portrait in 1833 (see page 16); and it is possible that the two artists worked together in Cape Town and its suburbs. In any event, it is likely that the aristocratic D'Oyly made a strong impression on the young man, not least on his understanding of the function of art: this influence would seem to be apparent in the album of drawings of the Cape scene that Bell presented to Lady Frances Cole in 1833 and that is now in the Brenthurst Library. The drawings – caricatures of the obese and indolent 'Boer', picturesque scenes of washing clothes in the streams of Table Mountain (see page 24), and farcical views of a Green Point race meeting held in

a mud-bath (see page 19) – while rarely repeating D'Oyly's actual motifs, invariably reflect his urbane spirit. Not all of these drawings are satirical but, like D'Oyly's, they seem to delight in the provincial character of Cape Town society. Thus, unlike George Cruikshank, the London caricaturist upon whose work they ultimately depend, both D'Oyly and Bell celebrated the exotic nature of their subject matter as an essential part of its humour.

The sense of Bell's foreignness in the country of his adoption is apparent also in his early representations of the Cape landscape. It is probable that some of his work in this genre is lost, but his earliest surviving album is a record of his travels in 1832 around the Cape Peninsula. The set of pen and ink drawings is of the same kind and same date as collections made by Charles D'Oyly, on his way to the baths at Caledon, and Frederick Knyvett, travelling by road from Port Elizabeth to Cape Town. The purpose of all these drawings, obviously, was to record, as factually as possible, the distinctive features of the countryside through which the traveller was passing. The style, therefore, is

figure 2
The Boer.
Ink and wash. 10.8 x 16.7 cm.
Coll: The Brenthurst Library

Charles Bell's first essays in art were in the genres of landscape and caricature that were favoured by both his uncle, John Bell, and the aristocratic Sir Charles D'Oyly, who visited the Cape in 1833. Bell used varieties in the genre of caricature throughout his life to define his relationship to various groups in society. In this drawing, he is giving visual form to the conventional view of Dutch-speaking farmers in the Cape Colony.

The landscape drawings that Bell made on the Andrew Smith expedition of 1834–1836 are, of course, intended to be factual records of the interior. But his brief to portray the character of the landscape appears to have encouraged him to introduce certain elements for expressive purposes. In this drawing, for example, both the balanced structuring of space between the tree, the hillside and the distant horizon, and the arcadian cowherd group clearly derive from the classical tradition of European landscape associated with the name of Claude Lorraine.

linear, outlining the contours of mountains, buildings and other physical forms; and the point of view, very often, is high enough to allow the artist to describe the extent of the foreground plane and whatever it might contain. The drawings might include some indication of the traveller's presence – directly, in the inclusion of his self-image or, indirectly, in conveying a sense of his emotional state by the arrangement of the landscape forms – but for the most part there is little room for feeling in these purpose-fully factual drawings. In fact, Bell supplemented the graphic record of his travels with words, in long hand and in Taylor's shorthand, indicating colour and other forms, and symbols denoting such information as wind direction: one drawing even combines a view of Devil's Peak from the Liesbeek River with a little relief map of the Peninsula.

figure 3 **Devils Peak from Liesbeek River. 1832.**
Pen and ink. 18 x 49 cm. Bell Heritage Trust Collection, UCT

Soon after his arrival at the Cape, Bell made a journey around the Peninsula that he recorded in an album of pencil drawings. The style of these drawings, with its precise delineation of contours and planes, is clearly intended to document the topography of the region. This suggests that Bell used the medium of landscape to familiarise himself with his new surroundings. The factual quality in these drawings is apparent in this double page which shows two different methods for capturing geographical information.

These notations and Bell's precise use of line render his drawings rather more scientific than those of Knyvett and D'Oyly. In fact, the desire to observe and record that is expressed in them may be likened to the scientific projects that flourished at the Cape at this time. The South African Museum was fast becoming established under the direction of Andrew Smith; and, after an unfortunate start, the Royal Observatory took on a new lease under the guidance of the astronomer, Thomas Maclear. The Bell family became closely involved with both the Maclear family and Sir John Herschel who, with his wife Margaret, stayed at the Cape for four years from 1834 to record the stars of the southern hemisphere. Closer to Charles Bell's own age, however, was Charles Piazzi Smyth, who arrived in Cape Town in 1835 to take up the appointment of assistant astronomer.[2] Smyth was also a gifted amateur artist and, in the ten years he worked at the Cape, he established a life-long friendship with Bell. Bell's relationship with this group of scientists cannot have contrasted more strongly with that of the man who was soon to become South Africa's most successful artist, Thomas Bowler. Bowler travelled to the Cape with the Maclears in steerage, and he started work at the Observatory as a servant.[3] When he brought about his own dismissal for truculence, Bowler committed himself to 'make a living', in Maclear's words, from his art. Perhaps significantly, Bell appears to have had very little contact with Bowler until they were brought together as signatories of the Mutual Life Assurance Society in 1845 and, again, as members of the committee of the Fine Arts Exhibition in 1851.

It was obviously Bell's talent for landscape and figure drawing, as well as his reputation for seemingly boundless energy, that recommended him to Dr Andrew Smith for inclusion as second draughtsman in the expedition into the interior in 1834. Interestingly, Bell's amateur status as an artist is tacitly acknowledged

in a letter in which Thomas Maclear describes George Ford, the principal draughtsman of the expedition, as 'a person who supports himself by drawing and portrait painting at the Cape': Bell, meanwhile, is described as 'fit for anything'.[4] However, if it was his experience in landscape and figure drawing that won Bell his place in the expedition, his work in those genres under Andrew Smith's direction was to change radically from his previous practice.

Paradoxically, given the scientific nature of the project, the landscapes Bell made in the course of the Smith expedition appear very much less factual than his recordings of the topography of the Cape Peninsula in his early Cape sketchbook of 1832. The reason for this, of course, lies in the brief Bell was given to depict the landscape. The 'Instructions Addressed to the Director' by the Committee of Management (representing the shareholders of the expedition) required Smith to make 'a faithful record of its route, which can only be done by the aid of astronomical observations made with due regularity and precaution'.[5] This was the task for which John Burrow was trained by Thomas Maclear: at regular intervals, Burrow was to determine the elements of latitude, longitude and elevation, take barometer and thermometer readings, and check magnetic variation and index the errors of the sextants. Similarly, Smith was required to extend geographical knowledge of the interior by charting his route, surveying such features as river basins and mountain ranges through which the expedition passed, and collect whatever information he could of the geological structure of the subcontinent. In other words, scientific means were employed to extract scientific information from the landscape. Bell's task was to complement these findings by capturing the character of the landscape.

Piazzi Smyth, who saw Bell's drawings when they were exhibited in Cape Town at the end of the expedition, wrote many years later in his obituary of his friend, that his landscapes were unadulterated 'by any methods of drawing taught at home on English trees and hedges and shady lanes; for C.D. Bell had taught himself in South Africa on exactly what nature presented to him there … with the very atmosphere also before one to look into'.[6] To judge from an anonymous reviewer's response to

figure 5
Scenery of the Kashan Mountains: the poort of the Urie River. 1835.
Watercolour. 14 x 24.2 cm.
Coll: MuseumAfrica

The composition of this drawing of the Urie River valley in the Kashan Mountains (Magaliesberg) is obviously highly dramatic. The low viewing point makes the mountains seem extraordinarily high; and Bell's decision to place two vultures near the centre was clearly intended to provide a powerful accent to the scene. Many of the landscape drawings Bell made on the expedition use similar features to overlay the factual account of the scene with the sense of the experience of actually being there.

Thomas Bowler's 'Five Views of Natal' in 1845 as 'unfettered by mere rules of composition and recollections of admired, rich representations of European scenery', it was a point of pride in art criticism at the Cape at this time to praise topographical works as direct transcriptions of local scenery.[7] Certainly, Bell's landscapes give a lively account of different terrains in the interior, but it is hardly possible that these paintings were made without the assistance of imported European conventions. For example, the arcadian scene of cowherds and grazing cattle in the foreground of an extensive bush landscape in Bell's 'Sketch on the Border of the Kalahari Desert, 1835' is constructed with the typical repoussoir movement into depth of a classical European landscape in the manner of Claude Lorraine: a twisted tree framing the left

foreground is balanced by a topographical feature set further back on the right, which leads the eye gradually to explore the space in the far distance. Of course, it is possible that Bell did not actually invent these features, but his decision to frame his view of the Kalahari with such accents indicates that he was making use of a convention for the representation of landscape that has certain connotations. On one level, the imposition of a sense of classical balance on the landscape creates a definite idyllic quality in the scene. On another, Bell's use of European pictorial conventions to provide the structure of measurable space from a single controlling viewpoint has clear symbolic significance. Perspective, in this sense, acts as a pictorial equivalent of the scientific measurements being taken by Andrew Smith and John Burrow.

Some landscapes in the expedition series are more obviously conventional than others. Bell's view of the 'Kashan (Magaliesberg) Mountains', for example, is clearly rhetorical in its organisation. Here Bell has used a very low viewpoint to contrast the flatness of the riverbed with the mountain precipices that rise to the very top of the picture format. Twisted trees characterise the vegetation and two vultures on improbably thin branches near the centre of the composition complement the sublime quality of the scene. Such a drawing, of course, communicates simultaneously the acquisition of new geographical knowledge and the thrill involved in obtaining it. Other drawings reflect the presence of the travellers more directly. Bell's 'Sketch on the Modder River' depicts the dense riverine vegetation with two Africans on the near side of the river and the expedition wagons visible in the background. Over and above its topographical purpose, this drawing communicates something of the experience of being in the African wilderness. The landscape features of immense vistas and dense vegetation have a primordial quality about them, while the recumbent forms of the two Africans in the huge spatial expanse provides a virtually edenic accent to the scene.

Charles Bell's other duty, as second draughtsman to the expedition, while George Ford recorded the bountiful animal life for Andrew Smith's *Zoology of Southern Africa* and Smith himself and John Burrow prepared geographical charts and surveys, was to document the appearance and ethnology of the several African peoples encountered by the expedition. To extrapolate from the 'Instructions' of the sponsors to Andrew Smith, Bell was required to contribute to 'an exact portrait of their life as respects their condition, arts, and policy, their language, their appearance, population, origin, and relation to other tribes, or in general whatever tends to elucidate their disposition or resources as sharers or agents in commerce, or their preparation to receive Christianity'. However, the instructions to ascertain their 'religious traditions or practices, if they have any', and to examine their 'social and political arrangements and common traditions, songs, or amusements', etc., in order to determine the state of their intellect, suggest that this part of the scientific project was not entirely objective. In fact, the expedition set off with the prejudice, amongst others, that 'the impression of European skill and power' would have a powerful effect 'on the excited superstition of the savage'. An appropriate image of such supposed African fascination with European 'skill and power' is Bell's frontispiece to his 'Scraps from the Sketch Books of a Wanderer in Southern Africa': this drawing may have been made sometime after the expedition, but its theme is reflected in the account in Smith's *Journal* of a certain Calipi's astonishment at seeing drawings made by Bell and Ford.[8]

That Bell indeed shared the common European prejudice of the time that Africans were an inferior people is evident in his

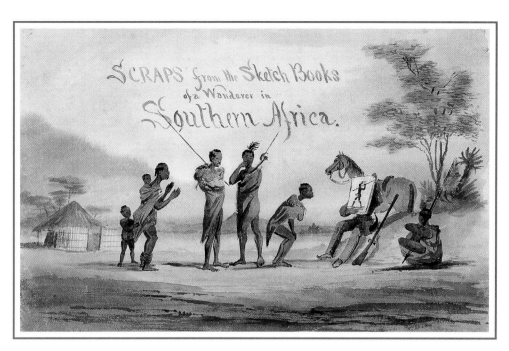

figure 7
Scraps from the Sketch Books of a Wanderer in Southern Africa.
Watercolour. 14 x 21.5 cm.
Bell Heritage Trust Collection, UCT

This title page to a compilation of sketches Bell put together some time after the Andrew Smith expedition may refer to a specific incident recounted in Smith's Journal, *but it was clearly designed to contrast the skill of the European (as subject, artist and likely viewer) with the supposed primitive superstition of African people. Most of Bell's representations of indigenous people overlay the physical description of the subject with a similarly strong indication to the spectator how to interpret it.*

figure 8 **Medicine man blowing counter charm towards the enemy. 1834.**
Watercolour (monochrome). 26.7 x 18.5 cm. Coll: MuseumAfrica

Bell's visual account of social life in the interior is an invaluable ethnographic document, but it is hardly possible that it is without any of the colonial prejudices of the time. This drawing represents what may well be a factual account of the activities of a Barolong medicine man. But Bell's choice of this subject and the manifestly caricatural style in the dancing figures were surely calculated to reinforce existing colonial perceptions of Africans as barbaric and superstitious.

tant source of evidence on social life in the interior at that time. Not surprisingly, Bell's selection of subject matter corresponds closely to the 'Instructions', and thus the programme, of the sponsors. And many drawings reveal a patent satirical intention in their style that is directly at odds with any scientific purpose. Writing at the time of the exhibition in Cape Town, Piazzi Smyth linked Bell's humour to common prejudice in a telling use of the conjunction: '... his pencil has a peculiar twist for the ludicrous *&* he has hit off the manners and customs of the natives to a t' (my emphasis).[10]

A drawing such as 'Medicine man blowing counter charm towards the Enemy' may be analysed in terms of this prejudice. While the style of rendering the medicine man himself, and many other subjects in the collection, is more or less factual, consideration of what he is doing certainly invited ridicule from the Christian rationalist who was Bell's presumed spectator. Moreover, the rendering of the dancing figure in the same drawing clearly exceeds the style of realism and takes on the 'peculiar twist' of caricature. Taken together, the two figures communicate effectively the very idea of primitive superstition.

The medicine man sketch shows that Bell had at his command different styles for the representation of the human subject. Seemingly under the influence of John Bell and Charles D'Oyly in his early essays in figure drawing, Bell had developed a style of satirical caricature that connotes a sense of superiority and detachment. Significantly, this style had been noticed in the early days of the expedition, for Andrew Geddes Bain, who travelled for a time with the party, wrote that Bell's 'graphic and Cruikshankian labours ... were the subject of daily admiration to us all'.[11] For Bain to describe Bell's work indiscriminately in these terms suggests that there may have been other, perhaps 'unofficial', drawings of camp life that did not survive with the commissioned expedition studies. Be that as it may: Bell clearly used caricature as one method of communicating his sense of racial superiority over his African subjects.

From this it is clear that Bell's style reveals bias even in a supposedly scientific project. Paradoxically, the same bias is apparent in renderings of the African subject that seem at first sight to be heroic and idealising. Bell, like Thomas Baines and other painters of African people, occasionally invoked the paradigm of the 'noble savage' by self-consciously composing his image in the style of classical sculpture or otherwise inferring a quality of antique simplicity. In representations of this type in an African context, needless to say, the perception of nobility was utterly dependent on the understanding of the primitive status of the subject. Although the 'noble savage' idiom was based largely on antique sculpture, the painter could complement this view of the African subject by setting it within appropriately primordial

extraordinary treatment of the daughter of the Sotho king, Moshoeshoe, that he cheerfully recounted in a letter of 25 December 1834 to his sister Christina in Scotland.[9] Bell reported that when the unnamed young woman visited him at the wagons he 'painted her cheeks green, her brow red & tipped her nose with gold leaf'; and he concluded that he 'had not the least ambition to become the son in law even of the Bassuto King for all his cattle & herds & tribes of naked savages'. This prejudice is apparent in the ethnographic drawings he made on the expedition, notwithstanding the fact that they also constitute an impor-

treatments of landscape, such as the arcadian and wilderness types we have seen.

Bell's representation of the Matabele warrior in the image of the 'noble savage' appears in at least two drawings, one of which is dated 1841, i.e. five years after the expedition had returned to Cape Town. Bell's willingness to repeat, even copy paintings, sometimes years after his original version, coupled with the generic treatment of landscape background and the patent lack of direct observation of the figure, all confirm that this image is a stereotype – or a visual cliché distilling the conventional wisdom regarding the subject in the Colony at the time. In the ten years between the return of the expedition and his album recording the outbreak of the War of the Axe, Bell made a quantity of pencil and watercolour drawings of picturesque scenes showing the appearance and activities of indigenous people at the Cape (see pages 21 to 29). While those drawings that record social activities, in Greenmarket Square and elsewhere, are generally freshly observed and anecdotal, those that focus on individual types tend towards stereotypical treatment. Because Bell is perhaps best known today by this sort of work, it is worth exploring the phenomenon in some detail.

In a letter written to Christina in 1837, Charles Bell sketched himself in four very different personae – as rugged explorer, urbane equestrian, suave socialite and industrious civil servant. In the light of this evident enjoyment of a complex, multiple identity, it is surprising that Bell's depictions of people of other races are consistently one-dimensional at this time. Significantly, he seems to have ceased drawing caricatures, in the manner of his uncle and Charles D'Oyly, of British society at the Cape. And his rendering of other groups also abandoned his 'peculiar twist' of caricature for the generalised image of the stereotype. The distinction is a fine one, but rather important. Whereas caricature is communicated in the exaggeration of some or other feature that is observed in each particular subject, the stereotype, as visual cliché, is simply a vehicle for prejudice. Thus, in Bell's view – and that of many other colonists – of the people with whom he shared his urban environment, those he called 'Hottentots' were invariably lazy, belligerent, dishevelled and drunk, while those he called 'Malays' were well dressed, dignified, industrious and devout. Similarly, in the hinterland, the 'Boer' was ignorant, indolent and fat, and rural 'Hottentots' were simply picturesque with their pipe-smoking women and ox-riding habit. Needless to say, while Bell insisted that certain behaviour typified any given subject, he also maintained a very restricted image of its physical form. In the same way that his 'Boer' was invariably fat, so he took every opportunity to exaggerate the appearance of steatopygia in his 'Hottentot' and 'Bushman' subjects.

A number of Bell's designs of this kind were reproduced,

sometimes several times, by himself, John White (fl. 1840–1852: the now accepted identity of the artist previously known only from his signature 'J.W.'), or other artists. There was clearly a demand for such 'types', as well as stereotypical Cape scenes such as ox-wagons and views of Table Bay. The evidence of George Duff, who also specialised in these 'native types', suggests that these drawings were sold through stationers' shops, especially to visitors to Cape Town: Duff petitioned the government for financial assistance in the off-season 'until by the arrival of fresh ships the demand for drawings of natives, etc., which [he is] in the habit of executing for the shops may increase'.[12]

Bell and certain other artists of his time made images of 'native types' that they sold through print shops, mostly to visitors to Cape Town. Several of these stereotyped images survive in many examples, including some that are clearly copies by one artist of another's work. In the generation immediately preceding the commercial exploitation of photography, these drawings anticipated the function of picture postcards as pictorial souvenirs of a visit. The drawings, therefore, represent conventional wisdom in the Cape Colony on each racial 'type' rather than direct observation of the subject. Bell's depiction of so-called 'Hottentots' is obviously caricatural in terms of both activity and physical features. And his facetious intent is apparent in the detail of the notice advertising a meeting of the Temperance Society.

Copyright in such images was not readily enforceable and it is recorded that 'J.W.' himself did not authorise the use of 42 of his designs in *Sketches of Various Classes and Tribes Inhabiting the Cape of Good Hope* that was published anonymously in London in 1851.[13] Moreover, perhaps out of professional considerations, it seems that Bell was reluctant to sign much of his work of this kind. For all these reasons, it is not now possible to reconstruct Bell's position in this trade – in particular, his relationship with John White and whether or not he profited from the sale of such work.

Nor is it possible to tell what function these images served other than to reinforce and circulate existing prejudices. But it is interesting to speculate why they appear to have constituted such an important part of Bell's work at this particular stage of his career. In 1840 Bell was appointed second assistant surveyor-general at the Cape, in retrospect, if not at the time, the first real step of his life-long career. In 1841 he married Martha, the fifth daughter of the prosperous and powerful John Bardwell Ebden. And, in the same year, John and Catherine Bell, who had long

Bell's 'native types' drawings are evidence as much of colonial attitudes to people of different races as of the appearance of Cape Town society in his day. In contrast to the 'Hottentots', who were 'known' to be drunk and disputatious, the people termed 'Malays' were esteemed for their industry, dignity and piety. Although obviously very much more positive, this view is just as stereotyped as the representation of 'Hottentots' in its insistence on a uniform identity. The generalised nature of this image is continued into the landscape which suggests the character of Cape geography without defining any particular place.

provided his 'second home' at the Cape, returned to Great Britain. Taken together, these events represent a change from the carefree days of youth to the assumption of adult responsibilities. But, despite his evident commitment to so many different aspects of life at the Cape – in government, in art and in commerce – there are clear indications that Bell regarded himself more as an agent of British rule than as a settled colonial subject. The prime evidence for this, of course, is his decision, like so many government servants of the time, to retire to Great Britain at the end of his working life. But Charles Piazzi Smyth, who knew him not only during his retirement but also in South Africa between 1836 and 1845, wrote in Bell's obituary notice of 'the fervid love and even ecstatic devotion he always bore to his native land'. And Bell himself, petitioning the surveyor-general, C.C. Michell, in 1846 for leave to return to Great Britain after sixteen years in the Cape, wrote:

> I might further illustrate my feelings by stating that having now found myself enabled, by self denial during many years, to indulge myself honestly in so great a pleasure, if leave were granted, I would decline a bonus of ten years income (or 3300 pounds) if offered on condition of confinement for life to this colony much as I like it as a residence of choice.[14]

To the extent that Charles Bell remained attached to his native Scotland, and to his family that continued to live there, so far was he prevented from identifying completely with colonial life at the Cape. Moreover, his participation in Andrew Smith's expedition into the interior would have impressed on him the enormity of the colonial project of bringing the light of commerce and Christianity to the 'Dark Continent'. The combination of a persistent detachment, on the one hand, with a sense of the tenuous hold of British influence in Africa, on the other, seems to have determined Bell's view of the people he saw around him. Like George French Angas who, visiting the Cape for a few weeks around this time, described the people he called 'Malays' 'foreign', when, of course, it was they who were indigenous and he who did not belong, so Bell, despite his very much longer stay, also seems to have viewed his 'native types' through the eyes of a visitor.[15] The very idea of depicting other racial groups as 'types' served to confirm the existence of racial categories –

figure 13
Lady D'Urban. 1839.
Pencil and wash. 16.5 x 13.4 cm.
Coll: MuseumAfrica

Bell's portrait of the wife of the governor, Sir Benjamin D'Urban, although charming, is a distinctly amateur drawing. The proportion of the arms is manifestly incorrect, and the grasp of both form and character is uncertain. But, unlike Thomas Bowler, Thomas Baines and others of the time, Bell did not intend to make a living from his art. The charm of this drawing, therefore, is that it represents a moment of friendship between the sitter and the artist as members of the same social élite in Cape Town.

and the barrier to communication between them. Moreover, although the accidents of survival suggest caution on this point, it may be possible to interpret the apparent popularity of certain types above others as part of a symbolic language of colonialism.

Amongst Bell's – and John White's – 'native types' there would seem to be a disproportionate number of 'Hottentot' and 'Malay' figures. Statistics are not available for the exact time these drawings were made, but in the first census of 1868, 'Hottentots' numbered 628 out of 28 457 people (or 2.2 per cent) in Cape Town and 81 598 out of 496 381 in the Colony (or 16.4 per cent).[16] And, even in the census of 1904, 'Malays' were considered too few numerically to warrant a separate class. Over and above their supposed exoticism for the European traveller, the reason for the popularity of these two groups in particular would seem to lie in the strong contrast between them. While the one could epitomise depravity, and thus simultaneously the difficulty of the civilising mission and the perils of succumbing to base appetites, the other, in representing the virtues of sobriety, industry and religion, offered an alliance with the colonial power but remained unmistakably foreign. Certain other of Bell's works also suggest the possibility of symbolic readings of more or less stereotypical forms. For example, Bell made several drawings of missionaries at different times of his life which are all very similar. From the many possible points of view, Bell invariably chose to represent the missionary in the act of preaching and to position him high on the left side of the drawing with the congregation spread out below him towards the right (see page 33). These choices, and the left to right reading of the composition, seem to symbolise the bringing of Christian knowledge into Africa. Similarly, the many times that Bell drew transport wagons of one kind or another would seem to be liable to symbolic interpretation (see pages 26, 63, 64 and 109): indeed, his use of the wagon, together with a cornucopia, to symbolise prosperity on the bank note he designed for the Cape Commercial Bank in 1864 (see page 110), suggests that all his drawings of ox-wagons, mail coaches and other forms of vehicular transport may be seen to represent the penetration of commerce through a 'vacant' territory.

figure 14
The Kafirs invade. Grahamstown Corps defeated. Captain Norden left dead. Ap.-May 1846. (Reproduced in the *Illustrated London News* 25 July 1846 as an engraving entitled 'Kaffirs bush-fighting'.)
Pen and wash. 18 x 24 cm.
Bell Heritage Trust Collection, UCT

Bell's project to depict and have engraved in the Illustrated London News *a narrative of the War of the Axe as it was unfolding on the Cape Colony's eastern frontier suggests a certain propagandist quality in the drawings which may be discovered in the choice of both subject matter and style. In this scene, the sympathies of the British viewer would have been stirred on behalf of the colonists by the apparent savagery of the Xhosa soldiers and the somewhat caricatural treatment of their bodies. The monochrome wash medium, chosen for its appropriateness for translation into engraving, reinforces the stark character of this image.*

If Bell made any works for commercial sale it would have been these stereotypical scenes, whether 'native types', wagons, or typical Cape scenes. But it is unlikely that all of these works were sold in the event. Bell is known to have given the Brenthurst 'Cape Slave Sketches' to Lady Frances Cole in 1833; and Piazzi Smyth wrote in his obituary notice that Bell gave away works 'right and left too generously as soon as completed': these gifts would surely have included 'native types' and Cape Town landscapes. Whether sold or given, the works would have been destined for inclusion in album collections, many of which have been lost or broken up over the years. One that remains intact is preserved in the Yale Center for British Art, New Haven. This was evidently assembled over many years by the family of Rear-Admiral Sir George Elliot who was commander-in-chief of the Naval Station, Cape of Good Hope, in 1838 and 1839. The presence in the album of a delicate portrait inscribed 'Cecy Elliot/ by Charles Bell/ Cape of Good Hope 1839' suggests that these scenes would have been acquired as part of a social, rather than commercial, exchange. Coincidentally, Bell's watercolour of 'Table Bay in a South Easter' which was collected by Cecily's older sister, Georgina Maria Elliot for her own album, has recently entered the Bell Heritage Trust Collection (see page 8). Unlike

figure 15 **Burns' Hill.**
Pen and wash and pencil. 18.5 x 25.5 cm. Bell Heritage Trust Collection, UCT

Although he made the War of the Axe drawings in Cape Town, Bell was familiar with the landscape in which the conflict was fought from his tour of duty as assistant surveyor-general in Grahamstown between 1842 and 1844. His desire for both accuracy and topicality is apparent in this drawing in which inscriptions are placed on the lower margin in line with the features they describe in the drawing itself: The Great Place or Residence of the Chief Sandili / Church / Mission houses / Native houses & huts / Wagons shewing the position of the rear of that portion of Major Gibson's Baggage train burned by the Kafirs at the commencement of the War. *The inscription in the bottom right corner of the drawing –* foreground ad libitum *– is an instruction to the engravers to make the foreground as they pleased.*

George Ford, whom Maclear had described as a professional, Bell was clearly an amateur portraitist and most of the portraits that he made can be connected with his close circle, if not to actual family members. Other examples of Bell's work in this genre are 'Lady D'Urban', 1839; and two child portraits (see page 115), possibly of his own children, John Alexander and Catherine Mariann Bell, in the Bell Heritage Trust Collection. They are in pencil and wash, tentative in delineation, uncertain in their treatment of form, and somewhat insipid in their grasp of character.

It is a remarkable fact that Bell's style is more confident when he did not know his subject, even when he had not actually seen it. He made sixty monochrome drawings of the War of the Axe that was fought on the eastern frontier of the Colony in 1846–1847, while he himself was in Cape Town. Bell may have considered the boldness of 'Some Rough Sketches of Scenes Illustrative of Late Events in Southern Africa' appropriate for translation to the medium of engraving for which he seems to have intended the drawings, but this clarity derived in large part also from the strength of the stereotypes that he drew on for many of his renderings of African subjects. Like Thomas Baines and Frederick I'Ons at the same time, Bell occasionally used the idiom of the 'noble savage' in these war scenes, apparently to convey the heroic dimension of the struggle. But also like those two artists, he more often resorted to graphic distortions to communicate his idea of the barbarian savagery of the enemy.

Bell's war scenes are interesting for both how they were done and why they were done. Stationed in Grahamstown between 1842 and 1844 as assistant surveyor-general, he knew well the terrain in which the war was fought, and even some of the people involved. The annotation of a drawing of a group of Mfengu, 'Sketched at Grahamstown', both confirms that this particular drawing was made on the spot and suggests that portraits of Xhosa dignitaries may also have been. Similarly, some of the landscapes must have been informed by his experience in the Eastern Cape. Piazzi Smyth wrote in his obituary that Bell's drawings 'astonished and delighted the soldiers who had been engaged in the operations', but it is more likely that such soldiers were in fact the source of much of Bell's information. He included in the series sketches after military and other artists, notably W.F.D. Jervois. Jervois made an exhaustive survey of the frontier region until his appointment to the garrison in Cape Town in 1846 and professional interests would have brought the two men together then, if they had not met in Grahamstown earlier. The topographical accuracy of the drawings made after Jervois' originals lends a sense of authenticity to the series and Bell clearly took great trouble to situate the conflict in its correct geographical setting. He included elaborate maps in the series, and devised a method for annotating topographically accurate landscapes with notes to indicate the significance of certain sites and, even, the progression of events through space. For the representation of figures, on the other hand, apart from the portraits, Bell concocted his narrative from a combination of oral accounts that he, like Thomas Baines, would have collected 'from many other officers and gentlemen who had visited the frontier' and the stereotypes of savagery that were then in circulation.[17]

Two of Bell's 'Rough Sketches' appeared as engravings over the titles respectively 'Rescue of the Ammunition wagons' and 'Kaffirs Bush-fighting' in the *Illustrated London News* on 25 July 1846. This journal, which had been established only in 1842 as one of the earliest pictorial newspapers, rarely acknowledged the sources of its reports, either verbal or visual, and Bell's work is described simply as 'the sketches of a clever artist in the Colony'. Little is known of this project by Bell, for example whether he was the source of other illustrations of the war in the July and August issues, or just how the drawings left his possession and how they were returned to him. Annotations on several other drawings make clear that Bell intended at least these to be reproduced, but whether in the *Illustrated London News* or elswhere, again is not known. However, the inscription on one drawing, whose vertical design was clearly made with the *Illustrated London News* in mind, although it was not published by that journal in the event, can be seen to confirm the racist stereotypes that the war elicited from many loyal colonists: 'To the Engravers – Please don't make my Bushmen like Niggers – their complexion is not much darker than a withered leaf except when begrimed by dirt.'

The uncertainties surrounding the publishing history of Bell's 'Rough Sketches' are compounded by the artist's own ambitions to reproduce them when he returned to Great Britain on leave in 1847. Piazzi Smyth, who himself had left Cape Town in 1845 to take up the position of Astronomer Royal in Edinburgh, and whose departure seems to have rekindled Bell's desire to return to Scotland, told his printer how Bell had 'brought home an immense number more drawings of the Kaffir War, which he wants to lithograph this Winter, together with his "Expedition" views'.[18] Before leaving Cape Town, Bell had expressed his determination to reclaim his Expedition drawings – and his frustration that Andrew Smith's projected *Journal of an Expedition* had never been published:[19]

> The sketches have been in Dr Smith's hands for the last eleven years – none of them have been published by him, and it is evident that he does not intend to publish them – I think he had better return them to me, and if I can engrave them myself perhaps some of them may appear [words illegible] or at all events, I will value them as recollections of my trip as much as Dr Smith can.

Moreover, Bell's experience of publishing his War Scenes in the

Illustrated London News may have been somewhat contradictory: on the one hand, he was obviously excited to have his work in print; but, on the other, very little had actually seen the light of day in this medium. It may be surmised, therefore, that after spending some time with his uncle and aunt in London, where he would have rearranged his collections of drawings into new narrative sequences, Bell arrived in Edinburgh in November 1847 determined to explore with his friend whatever graphic media were available to permit him to publish his own works.

Piazzi Smyth described to his printer Bell's excitement at being introduced to Charles Hullmandel's patent lithotint process and requested twelve more stones, ink, and 'anything else you think we might require'. In the event, Bell made only a few works in lithotint and the few copies that are known today suggest that the editions were very small. He evidently used drawings from different portfolios to explore the rich tonal possibilities of the medium, for example, the sombre image of 'The Revd Mr Moffat Preaching to the Bechuana' (see page 37), from the expedition collection, and 'The Breakfast Party of Kaffir Marauders Detected' and the nocturne 'Outspan', both of which are re-workings of War Scenes. Bell seems to have moved quickly from the lithotint to the lithograph process for, in his obituary notice, Piazzi Smyth told how Bell had obtained a press and stones from Messrs Schenk & Co. in Edinburgh and immediately produced some South African scenes in this medium also. His first lithograph was evidently the title page 'Scraps from my South African Sketchbooks, 1848' (see page 73) for the copy that was retained by Piazzi Smyth was annotated by Bell 'Hip, Hip – Hoorah', and by Smyth 'First Attempt at Lithography'. Other lithographs bear the same superscription 'South African Sketches' as certain of Bell's lithotints. From this, and from the inclusion of such stereotypical scenes as 'Hottentots' and 'Malays', one can infer that any ambition Bell may have had to produce a sustained narrative sequence of either the War Scenes or the Expedition had been abandoned before he left Great Britain in May 1848, in favour of producing a small heterogeneous collection of sketches. This is how they appear in Piazzi Smyth's album, together with his pen and ink copies after other of Bell's drawings: 'C.P. Smyth's South African Microcosm, or, Sketches Descriptive of the Cape, in all Degrees of Imperfection and Unfinish from Nature and various Travellers there but chiefly after Charles Bell Esq., Surveyor General of the Cape including some of his Lithotints'. Piazzi Smyth recorded in his obituary that Bell took his lithographic press back to Cape Town. The presence in Henry Ebden's album, now in the South African Library, of a couple of lithographs made in Scotland suggests that Bell may have intended to use this medium, and later woodcut, to reproduce stereotypical scenes for sale through the stationers' shops.[20] For reasons that are not known, no more than two lithographs by Bell can be dated with certainty after his return to the Colony.

Bell's failure to take more than a couple of lithographs after his return to Cape Town in 1848 is one indication among many of what appears to have been a crisis in his life in the following decade. The first cause of this crisis was Bell's discovery of his wife Martha's adultery and the bitter divorce proceedings that followed. Thomas Maclear wrote to their mutual friend Piazzi Smyth about the matter, concluding that Bell 'is sadly cut up in health brought on by his misery'.[21] The divorce was granted on 1 July 1850 but the situation was compounded by the opposition of Martha's family, the Ebdens, especially to Bell's determination in October to repudiate as illegitimate the birth of Martha's daughter, Charlotte Margaret. The principal evidence of Bell's state of mind at this time, however, is the correspondence he had with the colonial secretary, Rawson W. Rawson, mainly for the purpose of requesting a second term of leave.[22] In November 1854 he described himself as 'so depressed … physically and mentally' that he could do nothing but sleep for two days. But the extended nature of Bell's condition is clear from a letter of May 1856, two years later, in which he wrote that 'For the last four or five years, I have suffered from my head, whenever I apply myself to lengthened investigation, or intricate questions, and of late, the liability to headache and confusion of mind has increased'. In this letter Bell referred to 'the effect of some slight injuries arising from accident and overwork in Namaqualand about two years ago'. But, in a letter of April 1857, renewing his appeal for leave, Bell wrote that he had 'endured many things within the last ten years that could hardly fail to leave their stamp on the hardest brain'. On this occasion he described himself as losing his 'capability of thinking rightly and steadily and submitting quickly to irritation'.

It is not possible to determine how Bell's state of mind affected his behaviour in general at this time, nor his production of art. There are indications, however, over and above his apparent abandonment of the medium of lithography, that Bell's art was not immune from the crisis he was experiencing. In his address to the Fine Arts Association that was published in *The Cape Argus* on 24 August 1872, Bell told how he refrained from discussing painters and painters' works he had 'known here during the last half century' because 'that would lead to criticism, and artists, owners and donors are very sensitive to all save unmitigated praise'; and he referred to the 'disastrous disunity among our amateurs in times past'. As a member of the committee of the Fine Arts Exhibitions since 1850, Bell was certainly caught up in these disputes, and a close look at his involvement in the exhibition during the 1850s confirms that his own work was indeed affected by them.

The catalogue of the First Exhibition of the South African Fine Arts Association of 1851 shows that Bell committed himself fully to the project that Gilbert MacDougall, the secretary, had described as follows:[23]

> But when it is considered that a knowledge of art is a basis of good taste, to which an honourable distinction in society is attached; and besides, that innumerable advantages are attendant upon it both in a private and popular sense, it assumes a character of serious importance, as a duty which all owe to themselves, to the community in which they live, and the world they inhabit.

From his own collection, Bell lent the exhibition no fewer than eleven works, some of which throw light on his aesthetic and other interests. Thus the J.D. Harding, whose 'Scene from Woodstock' Bell owned, was perhaps the most popular, and well-published, drawing teacher in England at the time. And the 'Bacchanal' Bell lent is probably identical to George Cruikshank's 'Worship of Bacchus', that was later in the collection of his brother-in-law, Daniel Krynauw. Similarly, friends of Bell lent some of his works to the exhibition: for example, George Frere, a colleague on the committee, showed three portraits of children; and Percy Vigors exhibited the statuette 'Dorothea Bathing her Feet', which Bell based on an incident in *Don Quixote*. Bell's loan of his own work was varied in medium, style, date and subject matter. His early drawing of 'Crossing the line on the ship *Lady East*', in which he first travelled to the Cape in 1830, was presumably re-worked for the occasion (see page 13). He showed 'A Mission School, from a sketch in 1836', which can no longer be identified, unknown 'Portraits of Children', an unspecified 'Landscape', and an oil painting, which is now lost, of 'The Boer's Voorhuis': the composition is preserved in two drawings dated 1850 (see page 88). Another subject reminiscent of his earlier stereotyped scenes is 'Hottentots, Klaas en Grietje'; and, despite the scientific function attributed to them in the past, there is nothing to suggest that the 'Model, in pot-clay, of a Hottentot Woman' and another, 'of a Hottentot', were not simply stereotyped heads in three dimensions.[24] Although probably familiar in terms of subject matter, these works are noteworthy as Bell's first works in sculpture. The 'Dorothea', however, was novel in both medium and genre, for this sculpture was of a literary or historical subject. But Bell's most successful work at the exhibition was that in which he adopted both the medium and technique of academic history painting, which still at that time was regarded as the most noble form of art. Bell won the gold medal 'for the best original historical painting' for his oil painting of 'The Landing of Van Riebeeck at the Cape of Good Hope in 1652'. For this work, and for the three sketches of other incidents of

Van Riebeeck's life at the Cape, Bell, like history painters at the Royal Academy in London, provided references to his literary source.[25] In similar vein, Bell exhibited a second major oil painting, 'The Isle of the Holy Cross', illustrating an incident on the voyage of Bartolomeu Dias (see page 94).

In the 1851 exhibition, Bell's amateur status as an artist was confirmed. Unlike Thomas Bowler, for example, who was also on the organising committee, and who won the gold medal for the best landscape, Bell did not offer any of his works for sale. Moreover, he carefully selected the work he put on exhibition. Thus he chose not to show any lithographs; nor did he show any of his 'native types': incidentally, there are no contributions at all from John White, George Duff or any other stationers' shop artist. Furthermore, Bell did not exhibit any caricature or

figure 17 **The landing of Van Riebeeck, 1652. 1850.**
Oil. 75.9 x 92 cm. Coll: South African Library

At the First Exhibition of the Fine Arts of 1851, Bell won a gold medal for the best original historical painting in oil for his 'Landing of Van Riebeeck'.
Although this picture has been used as an illustration of the event in countless history books over the years, it is of course an idealised construction of what happened,
particularly in the representation of the exchange between Van Riebeeck and his companions and the Khoisan inhabitants of the Cape. The heroic quality of the style of the
painting – in the close pyramidal grouping of the Europeans, bathed in light at the centre of the composition – is Bell's response to the challenge in the exhibition
to introduce the academic category of history painting to the Cape.

ethnographical study. The first exhibition of the Fine Arts Association, therefore, represented for Bell quite a radical break with his past and a move, in the several historical works, towards a literary and moral style of painting. The elevated character of the exhibition as a whole is apparent in such classicising and literary work as the 'Psyche', after Westmacott, and 'Ondine', both lent by Bowler, and 'Eve at the Fountain', after Baily, and a cast of 'Laocoon', both lent by MacDougall. Bell's own commitment to the 'grand style' at this time is evident in his loan of a cast of the 'Farnese Hercules'.

However, if Bell's commitment to the grand style principles enshrined in the Fine Arts Exhibition of 1851 represented a break with his past, it was a project that was very shortlived. In the second exhibition of 1852, Bell showed no new work in this genre, although 'The Isle of the Holy Cross' and 'Dorothea' were lent by their owners and Bell himself exhibited 'The Landing of Van Riebeeck'. Bell also lent 'The Boer's Voorhuis' again and three portraits. In fact, although he remained on the committee, first of the third and fourth Fine Arts Exhibitions in 1858 and 1866, and then of the South African Fine Arts Association from 1871 to 1872, his support of them all in terms of loans of his own and other artists' work reduced very quickly.[26] The preference of the committee for his historical works is apparent in the continued loan of the 'Holy Cross' and the 'Van Riebeeck' by their owners in 1858, when Bell himself was in England, and again in 1866. But Bell never attempted new work of this kind, even though three sketches in the first exhibition treated this same historical material. In fact, notwithstanding the continued popularity of his work in this genre, his few published comments on art make it clear that he had little sympathy with the principles of Fine Art.

The claims of high art, that were embraced by the Fine Arts circle in Cape Town from the first exhibition of 1851, were articulated in several lectures in that decade, notably one delivered by the Reverend F. Gilbert White on the occasion of the closing of the third Fine Arts Exhibition on 24 January 1859, that was published soon after by Saul Solomon.[27] In this lecture, White argued that the Fine Arts were important because they tended to 'minister pleasure to the mind', as opposed to the body, through the medium of beauty. However, beauty, for White, was not simply a superficial quality but had a distinct moral dimension: 'The beautiful is not identical with the good and the true but it is suggestive of the good and the true. The beauty of the thing lies not so much in what it *is*, as in what it suggests to the mind…'. White's understanding of the moral sense of beauty is derived from a conventional appreciation of antique art. Thus he spoke of 'the calm majesty which seems to breathe through every limb' of the 'Apollo Belvedere'. In this reckoning, the figure of the artist took on extraordinary significance: 'No one can become great in

any [of the Fine Arts] unless he has within himself noble thoughts to be embodied, or rather to be shadowed forth, in his works'. Thus the purpose of the Fine Arts, according to White, 'is *not* to convey an exact transcript of natural subjects, but to call up in the mind of the spectator, the deep feelings which natural or historic scenes have stirred in their own breasts'.[28]

When Charles Bell eventually delivered his thoughts on art on the occasion of the Fine Arts Exhibition in 1872, the contrast could hardly have been more marked. He started his address with a significant disclaimer:[29]

> I will avoid as far as possible all attempt to lecture on high art. For *that* a better speaker, and one more versed in the subject, must be chosen to lead his audience to a greater height than I can pretend to soar. I will confine myself to a few plain practical observations on the present exhibition and its bearing on art from an educational point of view.

And, instead of the poetic and moral function of art that White and other speakers had celebrated, Bell commended Wilhelm Hermanns' award-winning 'Sunset at Sea Point' in entirely literal terms. Bell praised this representation of 'one of nature's gorgeous scenes' because 'The painter evidently copied what he saw and merely copied it'. Similarly, Bell's understanding of the principles of art concerned not so much ethics or philosophy as mere 'tricks of the trade' for 'cheating the eye'.

In light of these sentiments it is not surprising that Bell made no 'high art' paintings after the exhibition of 1851 and, in fact, very little pictorial art of any kind. However, he did adopt the academic language of 'high art' in his treatment of allegorical figures in several utilitarian designs at this time. For example, both the Cape triangular stamp (see page 95) and the emblem for the Mutual Life Assurance Society (see page 114) depict the allegorical figure of Hope with an anchor. The generalised features and classicising drapery of this figure conform to the idealising principles of academic art. Similarly, the classical figure of Minerva, on the epergne Bell designed for Andrew Geddes Bain in 1853 (see page 99), the allegorical figures (possibly representing Charity) on the wooden plaque for the Orphan Chamber (see page 111), and the Neptune and Triton on the silver trigger made for Prince Alfred (see page 120) all employ aspects of this abstracting, idealising style.

Although Bell was not concerned to practise 'high art' in its own right, his borrowing from it for utilitarian purposes was itself consistent with contemporary ideas about art at the Cape. The 'Introduction to the Catalogue of the Third Fine Arts Exhibition' addressed the matter of the 'useful arts':

> The fine arts, painting and sculpture, minister immediately to our souls or intellect, our immortal part; but we see the useful arts which furnish the

necessaries of common life, everywhere borrowing freely from them a grace and dignity that reconcile their own harsh expression to the perfect forms of nature, relieving the toil of the body by refreshing the nobler appetites of the mind.

Through the 1850s and 1860s, Bell embellished utilitarian objects with decorative and classicising designs for the colonial government and the leading commercial institutions of assurance companies and banks. But his most remarkable work of this type was produced after a second spell of leave in Great Britain in 1857 to 1858, in partnership with Sir George Grey, apparently as part of the governor's ambitious programme of extending the instruments of British civilisation at the Cape.

Bell's creation of the cover for Henry Tindall's translation of the Gospel of St Matthew into the so-called Hottentot language is an extraordinary achievement.[30] Within the carved openings of wooden boards, which are inlaid with decorative designs in paste, Bell has mounted tin plates that are etched with a variety of designs. The front cover is now difficult to read, but includes both figures and heraldic devices. The central scene of the back cover shows an allegorical figure, seemingly 'Faith', clinging to the cross of salvation, while in the openings to each side above it indigenous figures are shown reading holy scriptures and, below, two more figures kneel in prayer. Bell has used the curious medium of etching on tin to describe form with a quality of line whose extreme simplicity puts one in mind of John Flaxman's illustrations of the *Iliad*, a version of which had been shown in the 1851 Exhibition. The idealising quality of these images represents a strong departure from the racist stereotypes of 'Hottentot' subjects Bell had made earlier, and would seem to reflect the interest and concern he had developed for indigenous people while investigating their land rights in the copper fields of Namaqualand in 1854.[31]

A similar idealising treatment of the naked human form is apparent in many of the drawings Bell introduced into the manuscript 'Account of the Korana', also made for George Grey.[32] The title page, for example, depicts classically rendered male and female figures either side of the central inscription, with reclining figures at the top of the page that also seem to have been borrowed from some Renaissance composition. In the manuscript itself, Bell provided witty comments on the text, both in the embellishment of initial letters and at the end of each section. His new attitude to indigenous subjects is apparent in his illustration of the supposed Korana practice of wife-swapping: a puritanical

figure 19
Title page of *An Account of the Korana*. 1859.
Coll: South African Library

Both the design of this title page of An Account of the Korana and the treatment of individual figures within it are reminiscent of the classicising style of Italian Renaissance art and architecture. These products of Bell's interest in the genre of history painting are applied to the utilitarian medium of book design. Like his patron at this time, Sir George Grey, who contributed significantly to the establishment of the South African Library, Bell clearly believed in the civilising role of education, religion and good design.

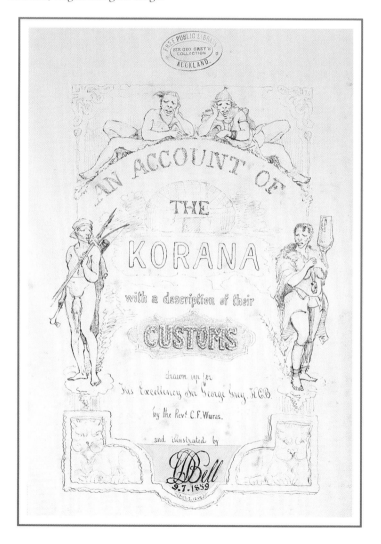

missionary figure is used to convey a sense of outrage at the practice, but Bell chose to render this figure burlesque and the Koranas themselves comical to an extent but also dignified (see page 118).

Bell may have found inspiration for some of his designs in the remarkable library of illuminated manuscripts that Grey had brought to the Cape. His third work for Grey was to decorate a book that actually formed part of this collection (see page 119). He illuminated the margins of several pages and the initial capital letters of the twelve sections of an incunabulum of Martial's *Epigrams* that had been printed at Venice in 1475.[33] The style of these illuminations show that Bell had looked very closely at other Renaissance manuscripts in the Grey Collection.

Another prestigious production at this time was the series of wood engravings he designed, and probably cut, for *The Progress of Prince Alfred through South Africa* in 1860 (see pages 122 and 123). This was a curious choice of medium to embellish the account of the royal visit and, like the decision to use tipped-in photographs for other illustrations, seems to have been as much a demonstration of skill and technical capability as a means of communicating visual information. The superb quality of these woodcuts demonstrates his mastery of yet another medium of mechanical reproduction.

Bell's inventiveness and curiosity, as well as his ongoing interest in different graphic media, almost certainly led him to experiment with the medium of photography at this time. His friend Charles Piazzi Smyth had been one of the pioneers of photography at the Cape and there are photographs in the Bell Heritage Trust Collection that would seem to reflect at least Bell's interest in the medium. While some of the photographs were clearly taken by professionals, others, for example, of the building of the breakwater in Table Bay and a party of surveyors, probably in Namaqualand (see page 104), may well have been taken by Bell himself. The fact of the matter,

however, is that there is neither documentation nor, actually, a substantial enough body of work to decide finally that Bell made these images. However, an extraordinary pair of photographs in the collection does confirm that Bell had a creative interest in the medium. In 1863, Bell had Arthur Green photograph himself with his second wife Helena and their two young children in a conventional *carte-de-visite*. Subsequently Bell covered his own image in this photograph by a detail of himself cut from a much later photograph. Possibly he created this montage as a virtual trick photograph to draw attention to the considerable age gap between Helena and himself. In any event, it is yet another illustration of the playful inventiveness that characterised Bell's mind throughout his life.

The remarkable thing about all these productions at this time,

figure 20
Charles and Helena Bell with two of their children, Alexander and Helena Isabella. 1863.
Photograph by Arthur Green, Longmarket Street, Cape Town. Bell Heritage Trust Collection, UCT

Although there is no indisputable evidence that Bell ever practised photography, this pair of photographs demonstrates his interest in the medium and his recognition of its potential to manipulate reality. The family portrait on the left is a conventional carte-de-visite *by the Cape Town photographer, Arthur Green. In the image on the right, Bell has wittily altered this family group by introducing a portrait of himself taken some time later.*

including the Bell–Krynauw tray and other very substantial work on Cape heraldry, is that they were done in addition to his work as surveyor-general of the Cape Colony. It is clear from accounts of his journeys to Namaqualand and Tsitsikamma, as well as his applications for leave, that this was onerous and time-consuming work. As always, Bell used his artistic skills in composing official reports and, in the case of the Namaqualand commission, he

invented new graphic forms to describe the mining potential of the territory. He had contemplated making a geological chart of the subcontinent with Andrew Geddes Bain and it is possible that his analytical drawings of mining methods and geological deposits in Namaqualand owe something to this venture (see pages 101 and 102). Whatever the case, these drawings also draw attention to the fact that, rather than celebrating the beauties of nature, like the work of Thomas Bowler or Abraham de Smidt, all Bell's representations of the South African landscape, from his very first journey around the Peninsula, were designed to extract information about the geography of the region.

Thus, whether made as part of his official work or after hours, as it were, Bell's production as an artist throughout his life was distinctly amateur in character. By that is meant not simply that he did not charge for work, as far as is known, but also that, fitting his art between other commitments – as well as, incidentally, changing medium and type of work so very often – Bell never had the opportunity to develop any of his aesthetic interests to any degree of professionalism. However, the establishment of the Fine Arts Exhibitions in Cape Town in the 1850s introduced a degree of professionalism even into the practice of pictorial art, both in its exhibition and in the articulation of theory that attended it. The effect of this was to narrow the opportunities of an amateur like Bell to produce pictorial art in any form. It is possible, of course, that the sense of Bell's oeuvre is distorted by the substantial loss of his work. But the surviving indications are that after 1851 Bell produced very little art until he retired from government service at the Cape in 1873. In Scotland, Bell revisited some of his South African subjects, investing them with a new sentimentality (see page 136); and he filled sketchbooks with drawings of local scenery and family excursions (see pages 133 and 135). In these late drawings, Bell communicates a new sense of well-being amongst familiar faces and longed-for places in the soft tonal modelling of his style. His subjects at this stage are no longer the rare specimen on the frontier of knowledge documented for the benefit of others, but people and places of his own familiar world recorded for his own pleasure. In making the change from the exotic to the familiar after twenty years of frustrated production, Bell was reclaiming the freedom of an amateur artist.

NOTES

CHAPTER 1 **THE IMMIGRANT**

1 *Cape Government Gazette*, 27 August 1830.
2 See John Milton (1608–1674), *Paradise Lost*, book 2.
3 Also occasionally known as Malmaison, Hopemille or Mill Gardens.
4 Letter from Lady Catherine to her father-in-law, David Bell, 23 October 1829. Bell Heritage Trust BC 686 (19, no. 18j).
5 *Dictionary of South African Biography*, Cape Town, 1976, vol. 1, p. 66.
6 The genealogy of the Bell clan is traced in detail in *Memorial of the Clan of the Bells …* by Charles Davidson Bell; printed by Saul Solomon, Cape Town, 1864.
7 R.H. Simons, *History of St Paul's Church, Rondebosch 1834–1947*, unpublished manuscript.
8 Bell Heritage Trust BC 686 (19, no. 18f). A passage from a letter, dated 25 December 1834, from Bell to his 12-year-old sister, Christina, reads '… I often think of Newhall, Camboden and Kingsbarns school and many a wish rises in my heart that I saw them again …'. Cambo Den is a small wooded area near East Newhall.
9 See Charles Piazzi Smyth, 'Charles Davidson Bell', obituary in *Proceedings of the Royal Society of Edinburgh*, vol. 12, 1886–1887, p. 15.
10 James Wilkie, *Bygone Fife*, Edinburgh, 1931, p. 309.
11 Bell Heritage Trust BC 686 (23, no. 1a).
12 Dorothea Fairbridge (ed.), *Letters from the Cape by Lady Duff Gordon*, London, 1927, p. 154.
13 The original inhabitants of the Cape, more correctly known as Khoikhoi, or 'men of men'.
14 W. Cowper Rose, *Four years in southern Africa*, London, 1829, p. 4.
15 On this occasion, D'Oyly was at the Cape from 3 April 1832 until the middle of 1833. See A. Gordon Brown, introduction to *The Cape sketchbooks of Sir Charles D'Oyly*, Cape Town, 1968.
16 C. Piazzi Smyth, 'Charles Davidson Bell', obituary, p. 15.
17 Today the South African Cultural History Museum.

18 Cape Archives GH 23/10, 1831. Letters from Sir Lowry Cole to Colonel John Bell.
19 J.B. Ebden (1787–1873), a prominent citizen of Cape Town, was, among other things, a founder of the Cape of Good Hope Bank and of the Cape Town Chamber of Commerce. He was also a director of the first railway company and a member of parliament.
20 Hamilton Ross (1775–1853) was a lieutenant in the British army which took occupation of the Cape in 1795. He married a local girl and remained at the Cape to become a successful entrepreneur with many interests.
21 *Cape Almanac*, 1832.
22 From this institution evolved the South African College School (1874) and the University of Cape Town (1918).
23 Samuel Taylor (*c*. 1748–1811) published his 'Universal System of Stenography and Short Hand Writing' in 1786, after which the method was widely used until the middle of the nineteenth century. As in Pitman's short-hand, vowels were indicated by the position of dots. See H. Glatte, *Shorthand systems of the world*, p. 10.
Correspondence in the possession of Robin Fryde, between him, Monsignor Donald de Beer and Geoffrey Bonsall, 1979 and 1980.
24 Leeuwenhof was built by the fiscal, Johannes Blesius, who was granted the land in 1697. It is now the official residence of the leader of the political party in power in the Western Cape.
25 Built on the farm, Boscheuvel, originally granted to Jan van Riebeeck, Protea was acquired by H.C.D. Maynier, *landdrost* of Graaff-Reinet, in 1805 and later leased by him to the Coles. In 1851 Maynier sold the estate of 213 acres to Robert Gray, first Anglican bishop of Cape Town, who changed its name to Bishopscourt.
26 Bell Heritage Trust Sketchbook no. 1: *Cape Sketches*.

CHAPTER 2 **TOWARDS CAPRICORN**

1 C. Piazzi Smyth, 'Charles Davidson Bell', obituary, p. 15.
2 Ibid.

3 *The Cape of Good Hope Literary Gazette*, 1 July 1833, p. 5.
4 Alexander Michie, *Memoir of Sir Andrew Smith*, Alnwick, 1877, p. 8.
5 Advertising sheet attached to *The Cape of Good Hope Literary Gazette*, 1 July 1833.
6 P.R. Kirby (ed.), *The diary of Dr Andrew Smith*, Cape Town, 1940, vol. 1, pp. 27–32.
7 David S. Evans *et al.* (ed.), *Herschel at the Cape*, Cape Town, 1969, p. 58. Sir John Herschel (1792–1871) visited the Cape from Britain between 1834 and 1838 in order to observe the southern skies. This he did while based at the estate 'Feldhausen' (also known as 'The Grove') in Claremont. An obelisk, erected by the people of Cape Town in gratitude for his considerable contribution to local education, was set up on the site of his 20-foot reflecting telescope and is now a focal point in the grounds of the Grove Primary School.
8 Cape Archives A 515 Maclear Papers. Letter to Sir Francis Beaufort (1774–1857), inventor of the Beaufort Scale, and at that time hydrographer to the Royal Navy.
9 C. Piazzi Smyth, 'Charles Davidson Bell', obituary, p. 12.
10 Cape Archives CO 426.
11 Cape Archives A 515 Maclear Papers, 2 July 1834.
12 Andrew Geddes Bain (1797–1864), explorer-trader, pioneer road engineer and geologist, arrived at the Cape from Scotland in 1816. He made several hazardous journeys into the interior and served in the Sixth Frontier War of 1834–1835 before being appointed inspector of Cape roads. He constructed several mountain passes, including Michell's Pass (Ceres) and Bain's Kloof (Wellington) and, as a palaeontologist, he discovered a number of fossils previously unknown. *The geology of South Africa*, published in 1851, brought him world recognition.
13 The three German missionaries were D.A. Kraut, August Gebel and Johan Schmidt. Sent to South Africa by the Berlin Missionary Society, they left the party at Philippolis to establish a mission station at Bethany on the Riet River.
14 'Shewed him many objects in the 20-feet –

such as η Argus – ω Centauri &c.' Diary, 30 March 1834. Evans *et al.* (ed.), *Herschel at the Cape.*

15 Kirby (ed.), *The diary of Dr Andrew Smith*, vol. 1, p. 58.

16 Ibid., p. 64.

17 John Burrow, *Travels in the wilds of Africa*, ed. P.R. Kirby, Cape Town, 1971, p. 15.

18 William F. Lye (ed.), *Andrew Smith's journal of his expedition...*, Cape Town, 1975, p. 30.

19 Burrow, *Travels in the wilds...*, p. 16.

20 Adam Kok II (*c.*1760–1835) was recognised by the Colonial Government as hereditary chief or 'captain' of the Griquas. In 1824 the missionary John Philip persuaded him to settle at Philippolis where he was ruling over his people when Smith's party reached the area.

21 Margaret Lister (ed.), *Journals of Andrew Geddes Bain*, Cape Town, 1949, pp. 133–134.

22 Lye (ed.), *Andrew Smith's journal...*, p. 53.

23 Jean-Eugène Casalis (1812–1891) helped to lay the foundations of the Paris Evangelical Missionary Society in South Africa. While stationed at Thaba Putsoa he established friendly relations with Moshoeshoe and worked on translating the Bible and the catechism into Southern Sotho. His wife, Sarah Jane Dyke, was the first white woman to enter Basutoland (now Lesotho).

24 'Mountain of the Night', so-called because Moshoeshoe believed that it had supernatural powers during the hours of darkness.

25 Burrow, *Travels in the wilds...*, p. 21.

26 Ibid., p. 22.

27 Lye (ed.), *Andrew Smith's journal...*, p. 90.

28 Burrow, *Travels in the wilds...*, pp. 27–28.

29 Ibid., p. 29.

30 Lye (ed.), *Andrew Smith's journal...*, pp. 131, 133.

31 Burrow, *Travels in the wilds...*, p. 30.

32 Bell Heritage Trust BC 686 (19, no. 18f).

33 Scotland, famous for its oatcakes.

34 Kirby (ed.), *The diary of Dr Andrew Smith*, passim.

35 Bell Heritage Trust BC 686 (19, no. 18g).

36 *The Cape of Good Hope Literary Gazette*, January 1835, pp. 13–14.

37 Robert Moffat (1795–1883), one of the most famous missionaries ever to serve in southern Africa, began his work for the London Missionary Society in Namaqualand in 1817. For many years he lived with his wife and family at Kuruman where he translated the catechism and the New Testament into Tswana and had a marked influence for good over the local people, including the chief, Mzilikazi.

38 Burrow, *Travels in the wilds...*, p. 32.

39 Ibid., p. 33.

40 *The Cape of Good Hope Literary Gazette*, June 1835, p. 93.

41 Kirby (ed.), *The diary of Dr Andrew Smith*, vol. 1, Introduction, p. 46. The son born at this time was John Smith Moffat (1835–1918) who grew up to become a missionary in what was then Matabeleland (now Zimbabwe).

42 Burrow, *Travels in the wilds...*, p. 40.

43 Robert Moffat, *Missionary labours and scenes in southern Africa*, London, 1842, pp. 510ff.

44 Burrow, *Travels in the wilds...*, p. 51.

45 Lye (ed.), *Andrew Smith's journal...*, p. 112.

46 Burrow, *Travels in the wilds...*, p. 55.

47 Hartbeesport, site of the extensive dam built early in the twentieth century.

48 C. Piazzi Smyth, 'Charles Davidson Bell', obituary, p. 16.

CHAPTER 3 CIVIL SERVANT

1 *South African Commercial Advertiser*, 24 December 1834.

2 Bell Heritage Trust BC 686 (19, no. 18j). Letter from Lady Catherine Bell to her father-in-law, 24 August 1830.

3 See C.G.W. Schumann, *Structural changes and business cycles in South Africa 1806–1936*, London, 1938, p. 71.

4 The property is now owned by Rondebosch Boys' High School. Only the foundations of the Bells' house remain.

5 Brian Warner (ed.), *Lady Herschel: Letters from the Cape 1834–1838*, Cape Town, 1991, p. 23.

6 See Brian Warner, *Charles Piazzi Smyth, astronomer-artist: his Cape years*, Cape Town, 1983, p. xiii.

7 Lye (ed.), *Andrew Smith's journal...*, p. 300.

8 Kirby (ed.), *The diary of Dr Andrew Smith*, vol. 2, pp. 212–215.

9 Evans *et al.* (ed.), *Herschel at the Cape*, p. 225.

10 Lee was also patron of the artist, Thomas Bowler, who had come to the Cape with Maclear as a servant.

11 Brian Warner, *Charles Piazzi Smyth, astronomer-artist: his Cape years*, Cape Town, 1983, p. 82; letter dated 15 July 1836.

12 C. Piazzi Smyth, 'Charles Davidson Bell', obituary, p. 16.

13 Ibid., p. 17.

14 Bell Heritage Trust BC 686 (23, no. 2a).

15 Evans *et al.* (ed.), *Herschel at the Cape*, p. 227.

16 Now St Joseph's (Marist Brothers) College in Belmont Road, Rondebosch.

17 Evans *et al.* (ed.), *Herschel at the Cape*, p. 209; Warner (ed.), *Lady Herschel: Letters...*, p. 118.

18 Warner (ed.), *Lady Herschel: Letters...*, p. 118.

19 Francis Darwin (ed.), *The life and letters of Charles Darwin*, London, 1887, vol. 1, p. 268; letter to J.S. Henslow, 9 July 1836.

20 Kirby (ed.), *The diary of Dr Andrew Smith...*, vol. 2, pp. 225–226.

21 Evans *et al.* (ed.), *Herschel at the Cape*, pp. 247–248.

22 24 September 1836.

23 Kirby (ed.), *The diary of Dr Andrew Smith...*, vol. 2, p. 236.

24 The journal was not published until 1975.

25 C. Piazzi Smyth, 'Charles Davidson Bell', obituary, p. 17.

26 Warner (ed.), *Lady Herschel: Letters...*, p. 112.

27 Bell Heritage Trust BC 686 (23, no. 2a).

28 Ibid.

29 *Cape Almanac*, 1839, p. 182.

30 Bell Heritage Trust BC 686 (23, no. 2c).

31 This probably refers to the house 'Westbrooke', now Genadendal, in Rondebosch. It served as a country retreat to which governors escaped to avoid Cape Town's heat and high winds in summer.

32 Cape Archives SG 2/1/1/2.

CHAPTER 4 SURVEYOR

1 *Cape Almanac*, 1841, p. 276.

2 *Dictionary of South African Biography*, Cape Town, 1976, vol. 1, p. 380.

3 Cape Archives SG 2/1/1/2.

4 Ibid.

5 Cape Archives SG 1/1/7/1.

6 Ibid.

7 Ibid.

8 C. Piazzi Smyth, 'Charles Davidson Bell', obituary, p. 18.

9 Cape Archives, St George's marriage records.

10 *Dictionary of South African Biography*, vol. 1, p. 213.

11 *Cape Almanac*, 1842, p. 484.

12 Cape Archives SG 2/1/1/2.

13 'Sour veld'. C. Piazzi Smyth, 'Charles Davidson Bell', obituary, p. 19.

14 Cape Archives SG 1/1/7/1.

15 Ibid.

16 Ibid.

17 Rex and Barbara Reynolds, *Grahamstown: from cottage to villa*, Cape Town, 1974, pp. 13–14.

18 *Cape Almanac*, 1844.

19 Cape Archives SG 1/1/7/1. Letter from Bell to W.F. Hertzog, 14 June 1842.

20 Cape Archives SG 1/1/7/1.
21 *Cape Almanac*, 1846.
22 Cape Archives CO 4922, letter of 16 November 1844.
23 Acts 6 & 7 (1836) of William IV, the so-called Cape of Good Hope Punishment Act.
24 Karel Schoeman (ed.), *The Touwfontein letters of William Porter*, Cape Town, 1992, passim.
25 Ibid., pp. 15–19.
26 Ibid., p. 22.

CHAPTER 5 THE MIDDLE YEARS

1 Mutual Life Assurance Society of the Cape of Good Hope, Annual Report, 1855.
2 Cape Archives SG 1/1/3/11.
3 A town situated on the Kat River about 140 kilometres north of East London.
4 Brian Aldridge, 'Cape Malays in Action', *Quarterly Bulletin of the South African Library*, vol. 27, no. 2, December 1972, pp. 24–26.
5 C. Piazzi Smyth, 'Charles Davidson Bell', obituary, p. 20.
6 Cape Archives SG 2/1/1/5. Letter of 28 August 1846.
7 Cape Archives A 515 Maclear Papers. By 'carbonatjie', Bell means a mutton cutlet usually grilled over a fire and eaten in the open.
8 Phillida Brooke Simons, *Old Mutual 1845–1995*, Cape Town, 1995, p. 23.
9 Cape Archives SG 2/1/1/5. Letter of 6 May 1847.
10 *Dictionary of South African Biography*, vol. 4, pp. 586–587.
11 Crawford Library, Royal Observatory, Edinburgh, quoted by Brian Warner in 'Lithographs by Charles Davidson Bell', *Africana Notes and News*, vol. 24, no. 6, June 1981, p. 196.
12 This volume is now in the possession of the Royal Society of Edinburgh and the story of its discovery is told by Professor Brian Warner in an article published in the now discontinued journal, *Africana Notes and News*, vol. 24, no. 6, June 1981.
13 Warner, 'Lithographs by Charles Davidson Bell', p. 196.
14 Ibid., p. 197.
15 Cape Archives CC 2/17.
16 Cape Archives SG 1/1/1/13.
17 Mutual Life Assurance Society, Minutes, 6 December 1849.
18 Cape Archives CSC 1/1/64, no. 24 of 1850.
19 Cape Archives GH 23/10, 24 June 1833.

20 Cape Archives A 515 Maclear Papers.
21 British civil servants and army officers on furlough from India were generally known locally as 'Indians'.
22 William Porter.
23 Cape Archives A 515 Maclear Papers.
24 Cape Archives CSC 2/1/1/64, no. 24 of 1850.
25 The evidence of this is a portrait of a Khoi boy by Bell which he dated 17 October 1850.
26 Cape Archives CSC 1/1/64.
27 See Simons, *History of St Paul's Church . . .*, unpublished manuscript.
28 Bell Heritage Trust BC 686.
29 Ibid.
30 Cape Archives MOOC 7/1/331.
31 Ibid.
32 *Dictionary of South African Biography*, vol. 1, p. 65.

CHAPTER 6 DIVERSITY IN MATURITY

1 It broke out when a colonial patrol on the Boomah Pass was attacked by Ngqika warriors incensed by the recent deposition, by the British, of their paramount chief Sandile. The following day they went on to destroy three nearby villages settled with British military personnel.
2 F.R. Mitchell, 'Sir Harry Smith's medal for gallantry', *Africana Notes and News*, vol. 11, June 1954, pp. 236–242.
3 Ibid.
4 *South African Commercial Advertiser*, 19 October 1850.
5 *Cape Town Mail*, 5 April 1851.
6 Apparently they were never accepted, those of William White, brother of the headmaster, Henry Master White, being selected.
7 F.K. Kendall, *A short history of the South African Fine Arts Association*, Cape Town, 1941, pp. 5–7.
8 See A.M.L. Robinson, 'Charles Davidson Bell's Bartolomeu Dias painting', *Quarterly Bulletin of the South African Library*, vol. 34, no. 2, December 1979.
9 *Cape Town Mail*, 5 April 1851, 'Report on the first annual exhibition of fine arts in Cape Town in the year 1851'.
10 Kendall, *A short history of the South African Fine Arts Association*, p. 7.
11 Cape Archives CO 611, 10 February 1851.
12 Cape Archives CO 611, 26 July 1852.
13 Ibid.
14 *Cape Times*, 18 June 1993.
15 *Cape Almanac* 1852, p. 180.
16 *Cape Almanac* 1853, p. 338.

17 A.H. Smith, 'Charles Davidson Bell – designer of the Cape triangular stamps'. *Africana Notes and News*, vol. 11, June 1954, p. 83.
18 This may be a reference to Paul's Epistle to the Hebrews, Chapter 6, verse 19, which reads '. . . hope we have as an anchor of the soul, both sure and steadfast'.
19 J. Allis, *Cape of Good Hope: its postal history and postage stamps*, London, 1930, pp. 21–25.
20 Later filed with the Colonial Office papers at the Public Record Office, London.
21 Allis, *Cape of Good Hope: its postal history . . .*, pp. 23–25.
22 D. Alan Stevenson, *The triangular stamps of the Cape of Good Hope*, London, 1950, p. 34.
23 Information provided by Robert Goldblatt, RDPSA, past president of the Philatelic Federation of Southern Africa.
24 Ibid.
25 Bell's dual achievements as artist and as designer of stamps were commemorated during the 1952 tercentenary celebrations of the arrival in South Africa of Jan van Riebeeck. His well-known painting of this event was used as the design for the one shilling special issue stamp.
26 Thos. N. Cranstoun-Day, *The British Lodge No. 334 and English Freemasonry at the Cape of Good Hope 1795–1956*, n.p., n.d.
27 *Cape Town Mail*, 20 November 1852.
28 *South African Commercial Advertiser*, 5 April 1851.
29 *Cape Town Mail*, 21 December 1852.
30 Joyce Murray (ed.), *In mid-Victorian Cape Town*, Cape Town, 1953, pp. 26–27.
31 Cape Archives CCP 1/2/1/1, Report A. 37, September 1854.
32 It was on Robben Island that Nelson Mandela and many other anti-apartheid activists were imprisoned for lengthy periods between 1948 and 1990.
33 Simon A. de Villiers, *Robben Island: out of reach, out of mind*, Cape Town, 1971, p. 48.
34 Edmund H. Burrows, *A history of medicine in South Africa*, Cape Town, 1958, p. 307.
35 Ibid.
36 Cape Archives CCP 1/2/1/1, Report A. 37.
37 Burrows, *A history of medicine . . .*, p. 308.
38 *Dictionary of South African Biography*, vol. 1, p. 38.

CHAPTER 7 A MAN OF GOOD REPORT

1 Ralph Kilpin, *The romance of a colonial parliament*, London, 1930, p. 80.

2. Schumann, *Structural changes and business cycles...*, p. 77.
3. R.F.M. Immelman, *Men of Good Hope*. The Cape Town Chamber of Commerce, Cape Town, 1955, p. 138.
4. 'The hamlet of the Cape'. It was not until the governorship of Ryk Tulbagh (1751–1771) that Cape Town acquired its name. See P.W. Laidler, *A tavern of the ocean*, Cape Town, n.d., p. 120.
5. John M. Smalberger, *Aspects of the history of copper mining in Namaqualand 1846–1931*, Cape Town, 1975, p. 36.
6. G.8 – '54. The report was also published in various newspapers, including *The South African Commercial Advertiser and Cape Town Mail*, 26 August 1854.
7. G.8 – '55, p. 37.
8. R.W. Murray, *South African reminiscences*, Cape Town, 1894, p. 17.
9. G.8 – '55, pp. 18–19.
10. Ibid.
11. See Phillida Brooke Simons (ed.), *John Blades Currey 1850–1900*, Johannesburg, 1986, p. 91.
12. G.8 – '55, Annexure 1 B8.
13. G.8 – '55, pp. 6–7.
14. Unnumbered government report 'of a select committee to [investigate] the establishment of regular communication by steam or otherwise between this colony and the mother country'.
15. R.W. Murray, *South African reminiscences*, p. 18.
16. Ibid.
17. Joyce Murray (ed.), *In mid-Victorian Cape Town*, p. 75.
18. Christopher C. Saunders (ed.), *An illustrated history of South Africa*, Sandton, 1994, p. 169.
19. See Sir George Cory, *The rise of South Africa*, London, 1913, vol. 4, p. 196.
20. Cape Archives CO 666.
21. Ibid.
22. Approximately 82 hectares.
23. Unnumbered report of a select committee to investigate 'the alienation of a piece of land called The Camp Ground; proceedings of 16 April–2 May 1855'.
24. Cape Archives CSC 2/1/1/64. In the words of the summons served upon Lestock Wilson Stewart on 11 April 1850, he 'did wrongfully, wickedly and unjustly debauch and carnally know Martha Antoinetta Bell' on 10 January 1850 'and at divers other times ... at the Camp Ground in the District of Wynberg'.
25. Cory, *The rise of South Africa*, vol. 6, p. 54.

CHAPTER 8 'A MULTIFARIOUS LIFE'

1. C. Piazzi Smyth, 'Charles Davidson Bell', obituary, pp. 20, 21.
2. Bell Heritage Trust, D.W. Manning, unpublished paper: 'Charles Davidson Bell: F.G.S., F.R.S.E', 1903.
3. See *South African paper money 1782–1921*, catalogue, Africana Museum (now MuseumAfrica).
4. Eric Rosenthal, *A century of service: 1856–1956*, Cape Town, 1956, pp. 11–12. This well-known trust company was absorbed by Syfrets in 1971.
5. Cape Archives CO 687, 12 May 1856.
6. Cape Archives CO 709, 8 April 1857.
7. Colonel John Bell was made KCB in 1852.
8. See Brian Warner, *Charles Piazzi Smyth...*, Cape Town, 1983, pp. 115–120.
9. Information from David Rhind, Cape Town.
10. Letter from Ms A. Morrison-Low of the History of Science section of the National Museums of Scotland, 19 May 1992, to Ms Leonie Twentyman Jones, principal librarian of the Manuscripts and Archives Department, University of Cape Town Libraries.
11. Cape Town became a city upon the consecration of its first bishop, Robert Gray, in Westminster Abbey on 29 June 1847.
12. Cape Archives CO 749, 14 April 1859.
13. J.J. Oberholster, *The historical monuments of South Africa*, Cape Town, 1972, pp. 10–11.
14. Cape Archives CO 749, 29 March 1859.
15. Cape Archives CO 749, 25 February 1859.
16. Cape Archives CO 750, 31 October 1859.
17. Cape Archives CO 4576, vol. 5, case no. 1562.
18. *Cape Almanac*, 1855.
19. See Robert A. Laing of Colington, 'The Bell–Krynauw tray', *Africana Notes and News*, vol. 27, no. 1, March 1986, pp. 16–23. The tray is in the holdings of MuseumAfrica, Johannesburg.
20. W. Ritchie, *The history of the South African College 1829–1918*, Cape Town, 1918, vol. 1, pp. 181, 183.
21. Among other accomplishments, Pilkington was also responsible for the design of the Roeland Street Gaol, now repository of the Cape Archives.
22. C. Piazzi Smyth, 'Charles Davidson Bell', obituary, p. 20.
23. Cape Archives CO 5325, no. 250.
24. Government notice, no. 337, 18 November 1861. This state of affairs continued until 1904 when, following years of confusion between the stations of D'Urban Road, Cape, and Durban in Natal, the name of the former was changed to Bellville.
25. The Grey Collection consists of rare works personally collected by Sir George Grey and presented by him to the South African Library after his departure from the Cape in 1861. Grey presented another valuable collection to the Public Library in Auckland, New Zealand, where he also served as governor.
26. Grey Collection, South African Library.
27. Son of one of the founders of the colony of South Australia, George French Angas (1822–1886) was an artist, traveller and zoologist who, between 1843 and 1846, took part in expeditions to the wildest parts of both Australia and New Zealand, making sketches as he journeyed. Early in 1847 he arrived in South Africa where he travelled widely for about a year and painted watercolours depicting various ethnic types as well as contemporary scenes. He published several collections of his paintings, one of which, *The Kaffirs illustrated*, contains lithographs of his South African watercolours. Angas later became director of the Australian Museum in Sydney.
28. *Dictionary of South African Biography*, vol. 2, p. 10.
29. Grey Collection, South African Library. Carl Friedrich Wuras of the Berlin Missionary Institute, was also a Korana linguist.
30. Grey Collection, South African Library.
31. See E. Capps (ed.), *Martial: Epigrams*, The Loeb Classical Library, London, 1919, Introduction, p. xiv.

CHAPTER 9 YEARS OF RESPONSIBILITY

1. Paolo Gaffodio, described as a silversmith and jeweller, is mentioned in various issues of the *Cape Almanac* from 1855 onwards. In that year his address is given as No. 2 Darling Street, but nothing else has been discovered about him.
2. See Cecil Skotnes and F.R. Bradlow, *Charles Davidson Bell 1813–1882, wood engravings*, privately published by the John and Charles Bell Heritage Trust, Cape Town, 1984.
3. *The progress of Prince Alfred...*, p. 12.
4. R.C. Fryde, 'Africana books and publisher's cloth': C. Pama, (ed.), *Bibliophilia Africana IV*, pp. 111–120.
5. See article on Heraldry by C. Pama, *Standard encyclopedia of southern Africa*, Cape Town, 1972, vol. 5, pp. 486–487.
6. Marischal Murray, *Under Lion's Head*, Cape Town, 1964, p. 25.

7 Cape Archives MOOC 6/9/107.

8 The children of Charles and Helena Bell were Helena Isabella (born 31 May 1860), Alexander (born 15 September 1861) and Anthony (born 9 February 1863), all of whom survived to adulthood. David Duncan Traill was born on 21 April 1864 and died on 14 December 1865; and Catherine Susan was born on 11 May 1865 and died on 13 September 1865.

9 See C. Pama, 'Die Bell–Krynauw-versameling' in C. Pama (ed.), *The South African Library: its history, collections and librarians 1818–1968*, Cape Town, 1968, pp. 166–168.

10 *Memorial of the Clan of the Bells...*, p. 47.

11 C. Piazzi Smyth, 'Charles Davidson Bell', obituary, p. 21.

12 Cape Archives A 515 Maclear Papers.

13 Commission into the Law of Inheritance in the Western District, April 1866. G.15 – '65.

14 Bell Heritage Trust BC 686 (28, no. 1).

15 It closed in 1882 at a time when there was a general failure of banks at the Cape.

16 The correct identity of this Jan Hendrik Hofmeyr has not been discovered. Like eight other men of this name known to be alive in the mid-1860s, he was almost certainly named after the family's South African progenitor, Johannes Heinrich Hofmeyr (1721–1805).

17 *Correspondence between J.H. Hofmeyr Esq., and C. Bell*, privately printed by the latter for the information of the shareholders of the Cape Commercial Bank, and of the Umzinto, and the members of the Mutual Life Assurance Society, Cape Town, parts 1 and 2, Cape Standard, Cape Town, 1866.

18 In 1872, after having been widowed three years earlier, Richard Southey (1808–1901) married Bell's sister-in-law, Susanna Maria Hendrika Krynauw. He was knighted in 1891.

19 Cape Archives CO 864.

20 Cape Archives SG 1/1/3/1/2, 16 August 1866.

21 See article by A.C.G. Lloyd in *The South African Quarterly*, September–November 1915; also F.R. Bradlow, 'Sixty-seven years later in Africana', *Quarterly Bulletin of the South African Library*, vol. 37, no. 2, p. 204.

22 Kendall, *A short history of the South African Fine Arts Association*, p. 10.

23 *South African Advertiser and Mail*, 3 November 1866.

24 The 'Eureka', 21¼ carats, discovered on the farm 'De Kalk' near Hopetown.

25 C. Piazzi Smyth, 'Charles Davidson Bell', obituary, p. 21.

26 Cape Archives CO 881, 27 July 1867.

27 See Marjorie Bull, *Abraham de Smidt 1829–1908*, Cape Town, 1981, pp. 58–61.

28 Kendall, *A short history of the South African Fine Arts Association*, p. 11.

29 See G.W. Eybers, *Select constitutional documents illustrating South African history 1795–1910*, London, 1918, pp. 63–64.

30 Molteno's strong personality combined with the fortune he had made from sheep farms in the district of Beaufort, now known as Beaufort West, gave rise to this sobriquet.

31 Cape Archives SG 1/1/3/50, 29 November 1872.

CHAPTER 10 RETURN TO SCOTLAND

1 Bell Heritage Trust BC (24, no. 10a).

2 *Dictionary of National Biography*, vol. 4, p. 170.

3 B.H. Strahan, 'Charles Bell in Scotland', *Africana Notes and News*, vol. 25, March 1982, pp. 96–97.

4 Ibid., p. 96. To this day, the ancient stone may still be seen in Crail kirk.

5 C. Piazzi Smyth, 'Charles Davidson Bell', obituary, p. 21.

6 See a long and learned paper by Charles Bell, published in the *Proceedings of the Society of Antiquaries of Scotland*, 13 December 1880.

7 Piazzi Smyth, in his obituary to Bell, erroneously claimed that the second harp had belonged to Brian Boru, king of Ireland, who defeated the Danes at the battle of Clontarf in AD 1014. Bell knew of the existence of Brian Boru's harp and that it was preserved in the library of Trinity College, Dublin.

8 Minutes of the South African Fine Arts Association, 19 February 1879.

9 Bell Heritage Trust BC 686 (28 no. 3; 28 no. 4). Letters from Charles Bell to Margaret Bell, 30 April 1879 and 8 March 1882.

10 Bull, *Abraham de Smidt...*, p. 80.

11 Cape Archives MOOC 6/9/166.

12 Charles Bell sold Canigou on his return from Scotland in 1865. After it had changed hands several times, it was bought in 1900 by Robert Ramage, first headmaster of Rondebosch Boys' High School, and completely reconstructed as a hostel. The fate of the decorated ceilings and doors, as well as of the stained glass windows, has not been discovered.

THE ART OF CHARLES BELL: AN APPRAISAL

1 F.R. Bradlow, 'The John and Charles Bell Heritage Trust', *Jagger Journal*, 2, December 1981, pp. 16–29. In writing this appraisal, I have drawn on three main sources for the life of Charles Bell: Charles Piazzi Smyth, 'Obituary: Charles Davidson Bell', *Proceedings of the Royal Society of Edinburgh*, vol. 12, 1886–1887, pp. 14–22; Michael Lipschitz, *The Charles Davidson Bell Heritage Trust Collection: a catalogue and critical study*, unpublished MA thesis, University of Cape Town, 1992; and Phillida Brooke Simons' biography in this volume. My thanks to Sandra Klopper for comments on a draft of this essay.

2 See Brian Warner, *Charles Piazzi Smyth, astronomer-artist: his Cape years*, Cape Town, 1983.

3 Edna Bradlow and Frank Bradlow, *Thomas Bowler of the Cape of Good Hope*, Cape Town, 1955, pp. 26–31.

4 Bell Heritage Trust BC 686.

5 William F. Lye (ed.), *Andrew Smith's journal...*, Cape Town, 1975, pp. 5–10.

6 C. Piazzi Smyth, 'Charles Davidson Bell', obituary, p. 15.

7 Bradlow, *Thomas Bowler...*, p. 38.

8 Lye (ed.), *Andrew Smith's journal...*, p. 212.

9 Bell Heritage Trust BC 686 (19).

10 Warner, *Charles Piazzi Smyth...*, p. 82.

11 Margaret Lister (ed.), *Journals of Andrew Geddes Bain*, Cape Town, 1949, p. 134.

12 A. Gordon-Brown, *Pictorial Africana*, Cape Town, 1975, p. 153.

13 Gordon-Brown, *Pictorial Africana*, pp. 36–39.

14 Cape Archives, SG 2/1/1/5: in Lipschitz, *The Charles Davidson Bell Heritage Trust Collection*, p. 15.

15 Frank Bradlow (ed.), *George French Angas: The Kafirs illustrated*, Cape Town, 1975, p. 5.

16 For nineteenth-century census reports, see Rosemary Ridd, 'Creating Ethnicity in the British Colonial Cape: Coloured and Malay Contrasted', unpublished seminar, University of Cape Town, Centre for African Studies, 31 March 1993.

17 R.F. Kennedy (ed.), *Thomas Baines, journal of residence in Africa, 1842–1853*, Cape Town, 1961, vol. 1, p. 9.

18 Brian Warner, 'Lithography by Charles Davidson Bell', *Africana Notes and News*, vol. 24, no. 6, June 1981, pp. 195–199.

19 Cape Archives, A 515 Maclear Papers: in Lipschitz, *The Charles Davidson Bell Heritage Trust Collection*, p. 66.

20 R.R. Langham-Carter, 'Dr Henry Ebden's Album', *Quarterly Bulletin of the South African Library*, vol. 31, no. 3, March 1977, pp. 60–69.

21 Cape Archives, A 515 Maclear Papers: in Simons, this volume, p. 75.

22 Cape Archives, CO 687 and 709: in Simons, this volume, p. 111.

23 The catalogues of all but one of the Fine Art Exhibitions of this period are preserved in the South African Library, SABP 111. I am grateful to Anna Tietze for this reference.

24 Piazzi Smyth in his obituary notice wrote that 'the object of most of these artistic works "in the round" was to preserve the physiognomy, manners, customs, tastes, and traditions of the native races of South Africa', but this seems to be a confused memory of Bell's work for, while Bell did start a series of lithographs on 'Tribal Types', he is not known to have made any more figures in pot-clay.

25 It is generally assumed that Bell invented these Van Riebeeck compositions in response to the committee's decision to promote work in the category of History Painting. But Bell seems to have been thinking of this subject matter as early as 1847 in Scotland, for the three heads that Piazzi Smyth described Bell as sketching rapidly on the margin of the stone on which Smyth had already designed a landscape seem to represent seventeenth-century figures.

26 F.K. Kendall, *A short history of the South African Fine Arts Association*, Cape Town, 1941.

27 Rev. F. Gilbert White, *Address delivered at the closing of the Fine Art Exhibition on Monday, January 24, 1859*, Saul Solomon, Cape Town, 1859.

28 Although in rather different terms, Piazzi Smyth also believed that art should not simply copy nature: 'The object of painting as well as of literature, is to present something more perfect than that which is commonly seen; to give a local name and habitation to those abstract images of ideal & perfect beauty; which, though derived from nature herself, are never to be seen entire in any one of her forms'; in Warner, *Charles Piazzi Smyth...*, p.111.

29 *The Cape Argus*, 24 August 1872.

30 South African Library, Grey Collection. Although the inscription on the cover gives only the etching on tin to Bell, it is likely that he also designed and carved the wooden covers.

31 Charles Bell, *Reports of the Surveyor General Charles Bell on the Copper Fields of Little Namaqualand*, Saul Solomon, Cape Town, 1855.

32 South African Library, Grey Collection. *An account of the Korana with a description of their customs drawn up for His Excellency Sir George Grey, K.C.B., by the Revd C.F. Wuras and illustrated by C.D. Bell.*

33 South African Library, Grey Collection.

1813	22 October	Charles Bell born.
1830	23 August	Arrives in Cape Town.
1832		Joins the civil service at the Cape.
	April	Tours the Cape Peninsula.
	November	Transferred to office of the Master of the Supreme Court.
1833		Becomes second clerk in the Colonial Audit Office.
1834	3 July	Leaves Cape Town as second draughtsman on Andrew Smith's Expedition for Exploring Central Africa.
	12 August	Smith's party sets off from Graaff-Reinet.
	August–December	Explores mountains north of Orange River and, in October, meets Chief Moshoeshoe on Thaba Bosiu.
1835	30 January	Arrives Kuruman, where Smith attends to fever-stricken missionary Robert Moffat.
	February–May	Explores region north of Kuruman.
	May–October	Travels northeastward, to explore Magaliesberg and Pilanesberg; in June meets Matabele king Mzilikazi; in September Tropic of Capricorn reached and party turns for home.
1836	January	Smith's Expedition returns to Cape Town. Bell's sketches and paintings from the Expedition exhibited in Cape Town, with those of fellow-draughtsman, George Ford. Bell promoted to first clerk in the Colonial Audit Office.
1837	July	London exhibition of Expedition artefacts, specimens and artworks by Bell and Ford.
1838		Bell qualifies as land surveyor and joins office of surveyor-general.
1840	July	Promoted to second assistant surveyor-general.
	November	Undertakes first commission, to survey the Kamiesberg, in Namaqualand.
1841	March	Completes survey in Namaqualand.
	3 June	Marries Martha Antoinetta Ebden.
1842	April	Bell and Martha depart for Grahamstown; Bell is to investigate land claims on Eastern Frontier.
1843	25 January	Their elder son, John Alexander, born in Grahamstown.
1844	March	Bell and family return to Cape Town. Bell turns down post of surveyor-general at Port Natal.
1845	May	Accompanies Sir Peregrine Maitland's expedition to Touwfontein, Transorangia.
	1 August	Second son, Charles David Ebden, born.
	September	Bell takes out his first policy with newly-founded Mutual Life Assurance Society.
1846	March	Seventh Frontier War (War of Axe) breaks out; Bell executes sketches of war events for *Illustrated London News*.
	April	Promoted to assistant surveyor-general.
1847	May	Bell and family depart for 15-month leave in Britain.
	November	Bell's first attempt at lithography, at Piazzi Smyth's home in Edinburgh.
1848	July	Bell appointed surveyor-general of the Cape Colony.
	August	Bell and family return to Cape Town.
	16 December	Daughter Catherine Mariann born at Canigou, Rondebosch.
1850		Bell appointed a director of Mutual Life Assurance Society.
	1 July	Granted divorce from Martha.
	17 October	Martha gives birth to a second daughter, whom Bell refuses to accept as his child.
1851	February–March	Cape Town's First Exhibition of Fine Arts held; Bell awarded gold medal for his oil painting 'Arrival of Van Riebeeck'. Designs medal awarded by Sir Harry Smith for gallantry in the Eighth Frontier War.
1852		Designs Cape triangular stamps. Becomes a Justice of the Peace, and a member of the Central Board of Public Roads.
	November	Cape Town's Second Exhibition of Fine Arts opens.
1853	December	Bell heads commission of enquiry into conduct of surgeon-superintendent of Robben Island's General Infirmary.
1854		Designs banknotes for Cape Commercial Bank, of which he is a director.
	August	Travels to Namaqualand to report on copper mining in the area and investigate land claims.
1855	September	Travels to Tsitsikamma region to investigate land claims of Mfengu people.
1856		Travels to Eastern Cape to report on arrival of new settlers of the British German Legion. Appointed chairman of General Estate and Orphan Chamber.
1857	May	Leaves Cape Town with his family for extended leave in Scotland.
1858		Returns to Cape Town towards end of year.
	October	Cape Town's Third Exhibition of Fine Arts opens.
1859	7 July	Bell marries Helena Krynauw. Commissioned to design coat of arms for South African College. Commissioned by Sir George Grey to embellish books from his famous library.
1860	31 May	Daughter Helena Isabella born. Bell designs silver trigger for inauguration of Table Bay breakwater by Prince Alfred. Bell and Helena move into second home, Belton, in Green Point.

1861	15 September	Their first son, Alexander, born.
1863	9 February	Second son, Anthony, born.
	16 July	Bell's daughter from his first marriage, Catherine, dies.
1864	21 April	Third son, David Duncan Traill, born; dies 14 December 1865.
1865	11 May	Daughter, Catherine Susan, born; dies 13 September 1865.
		Bell appointed chairman of Mutual Life Assurance Society.
1866		Takes brief holiday in Scotland, without his family.
	31 October	Cape Town's Fourth Exhibition of Fine Arts opens.

1867	June	Bell's request to retire as surveyor-general is refused.
1871	August	South African Fine Arts Association established; its first exhibition held on 4 December.
1872	21 August	Bell delivers speech at opening of second exhibition.
	1 December	Officially retires as surveyor-general.
1873		Bell, Helena and their three children leave Cape Town to settle in Scotland.
1875		Bell elected to Society of Antiquaries of Scotland.
1878		Bell's eldest son, John, dies in England.
1878–1879		Bell and Helena visit Cape Town.
1881	10 September	Helena Bell dies unexpectedly.
1882	7 April	Charles Bell dies in Edinburgh.

SELECT BIBLIOGRAPHY

Published books

Allis, J., *Cape of Good Hope: its postal history and postage stamps*, Stanley Gibbons, London, 1930.

Anonymous, *The progress of Prince Alfred through South Africa*, Saul Solomon, Cape Town, 1861.

Becker, Peter, *The pathfinders*, Viking Penguin, New York, 1985.

Bradlow, Edna and Frank Bradlow, *Thomas Bowler of the Cape of Good Hope*, A.A. Balkema, Cape Town, 1955.

Bradlow, Frank (ed.), *George French Angas: The Kafirs Illustrated* (facsimile reprint), A.A. Balkema, Cape Town, 1975.

Bull, Marjorie, *Abraham de Smidt*, 1829–1908, published by the author, Cape Town, 1981.

Bunbury, Charles, *Journal of a residence at the Cape*, 2 vols., John Murray, London, 1848.

Burrow, John, *Travels in the wilds of Africa*, (ed.) Percival R. Kirby, A.A. Balkema, Cape Town, 1971.

Burrows, Edmund H., *A history of medicine in South Africa*, A.A. Balkema, Cape Town, 1958.

Chapman, James, *Travels in the interior of South Africa*, 2 vols., Bell & Daldy, London, 1868.

Chase, J.C., and Wilmot, A., *A history of the colony of the Cape of Good Hope*, Juta, Cape Town, 1869.

Cory, Sir George, *The rise of South Africa*, 6 vols., Longmans, Green & Co., London, 1913.

Cranstoun-Day, T.N., *British Lodge no. 334*, privately printed, Cape Town, 1937.

Darwin, Francis (ed.), *The life and letters of Charles Darwin*, 3 vols., John Murray, London, 1887.

De Brett's Peerage, Baronetage and Knightage, De Brett's Peerage Ltd, London, 1970.

De Villiers, G.G., and C. Pama, *Geslagregisters van die ou Kaapse families*, 2 vols., A.A. Balkema, Cape Town, 1981.

De Villiers, Simon A., *Robben Island: out of reach, out of mind*, C. Struik, Cape Town, 1971.

Evans, David *et al.*, *Herschel at the Cape*, A.A. Balkema, Cape Town, 1969.

Everson, G.R., *The South Africa 1853 Medal*, Samson Books, London, 1978.

Eybers, G.W., *Select constitutional documents illustrating South African history, 1795–1910*, Routledge, London, 1918.

Fairbridge, Dorothea (ed.), *Letters from the Cape by Lady Duff Gordon*, Clarendon Press, London, 1927.

Gordon-Brown, A., *Pictorial Africana*, A.A. Balkema, Cape Town, 1975.

Gutsche, Thelma, *The microcosm*, Timmins, Cape Town, 1968.

Kendall, F.K., *A short history of the South African Fine Arts Association*, South African Fine Arts Association, Cape Town, 1941.

Kennedy, R.F. (ed.), *Thomas Baines, journal of residence in Africa 1842–1853*, Van Riebeeck Society, Cape Town, 1961.

Kilpin, Ralph, *The romance of a colonial parliament*, Longmans, Green & Co., London, 1930.

Kirby, P.R. (ed.), *The diary of Dr Andrew Smith*, 2 vols., The Van Riebeeck Society, Cape Town, 1940.

Kirby, P.R. (ed.), *Robert Moffat's visit to Mzilikazi in 1835*, Witwatersrand University Press, Johannesburg, 1940.

Kirby, P.R. (ed.), *Sir Andrew Smith, M.D., K.C.B.: his life, letters and works*, A.A. Balkema, Cape Town, 1965.

Lister, Margaret (ed.), *Journals of Andrew Geddes Bain*, Van Riebeeck Society, Cape Town, 1949.

Lye, William F., *Andrew Smith's journal of his expedition into the interior of South Africa 1834–1836*, A.A. Balkema, Cape Town, 1975.

Moffat, Robert, *Missionary labours and scenes in southern Africa*, John Snow, London, 1842.

Murray, Joyce, *In mid-Victorian Cape Town*, A.A. Balkema, Cape Town, 1953.

Murray, Marischal, *Under Lion's Head*, A.A. Balkema, Cape Town, 1964.

Murray, R.W., *South African reminiscences*, Juta & Co., Cape Town, 1894.

Oberholster, J.J., *The historical monuments of South Africa*, The Rembrandt Van Rijn Foundation for Culture, Cape Town, 1972.

Pama, C. (ed.), *The South African Library: its history, collections and librarians 1818–1968*, A.A. Balkema, Cape Town, 1968.

Reynolds, Rex and Barbara Reynolds, *Grahamstown from cottage to villa*, David Philip, Cape Town, 1974.

Ritchie, W., *The history of the South African College 1829–1918*, Maskew Miller, Cape Town, 1918.

Rose, W. Cowper, *Four years in southern Africa*, Henry Colburn and Richard Bentley, London, 1829.

Rosenthal, Eric, *A century of service: 1856–1956*, General Estate & Orphan Chamber, Cape Town, 1956.

Saunders, Christopher C. (ed.), *An illustrated history of South Africa*, Ibis Books, Sandton, 1994.

Schoeman, Karel (ed.), *The Touwfontein letters of William Porter*, South African Library, 1992.

Schumann, C.G.W., *Structural changes and business cycles in South Africa, 1806–1936*, P.S. King & Son, London, 1938.

Simons, Phillida Brooke, *Old Mutual 1845–1995*, Human & Rousseau, Cape Town, 1995.

Simons, Phillida Brooke (ed.), *John Blades Currey 1850–1900*, The Brenthurst Press, Johannesburg, 1986.

Smalberger, John M., *Aspects of the history of copper mining in Namaqualand 1846–1931*, C. Struik, Cape Town, 1975.

Smith, Alexander, *The third statistical account of Scotland: The County of Fife*, Oliver & Boyd, Edinburgh and London, 1952.

Smith, Andrew, *Illustrated zoology of South Africa*, 5 vols., Smith Elder & Co., London, 1849.

Stevenson, D. Alan, *The triangular stamps of the Cape of Good Hope*, H.R. Harmer Limited, London, 1950.

Viney, Graham, and Phillida Brooke Simons, *The Cape of Good Hope 1806–1872*, The Brenthurst Press, Johannesburg, 1995.

Warner, Brian, *Astronomers at the Royal Observatory, Cape of Good Hope*, A.A. Balkema, Cape Town, 1979.

Warner, Brian, *Charles Piazzi Smyth, astronomer-artist: his Cape years*, A.A. Balkema, Cape Town, 1983.

Warner, Brian (ed.), *Lady Herschel: Letters from the Cape 1834–1838*, Friends of the South African Library, Cape Town, 1991.

Wilkie, James, *Bygone Fife*, Blackwood & Sons, Edinburgh and London, 1931.

Journals

Africana Notes and News: March 1947, June 1954, March 1965, March 1971, June 1981, March 1982, March 1986.
Bibliophilia Africana IV, C. Pama (ed.), Friends of the South African Library, Cape Town, 1981.
Cabo: 1982.
Cape Almanac: 1830–1883.
The Cape of Good Hope Literary Gazette, Cape Town: 1830, 1832, 1834, 1835.
The *Illustrated London News*: 1846–1848.
Jagger Journal, University of Cape Town: December 1981.
Quarterly Bulletin of the South African Library: September 1971, December 1972, December 1979.
The South African Quarterly: September 1915.

Pamphlets and articles

Bell, C., *Correspondence between J.H. Hofmeyr, Esq., and C. Bell*, 2 parts, Cape Town, 1866.
Michie, Alexander, *Memoir of Sir Andrew Smith*, H.H. Blair, Alnwick, 1877.
Papers in Reference to a Plan for an Expedition into Central Africa from the Cape of Good Hope, George Greig, Cape Town, 1833.
Smyth, Charles Piazzi, 'Charles Davidson Bell', *Proceedings of the Royal Society of Edinburgh*, vol. 12. Obituaries, 1886–1887.

Newspapers

The Cape Argus
Cape Monitor
The Cape Times
Cape Town Mail
The Government Gazette of the Cape of Good Hope
South African Commercial Advertiser

General reference works

Dictionary of National Biography, 63 vols., Smith Elder & Co., London, 1885.
Dictionary of South African Biography, Human Sciences Research Council, Pretoria, 1972.
Standard Encyclopaedia of Southern Africa, 12 vols., Nasou Ltd, Cape Town, 1976.

Official reports

The Royal Commission on the ancient and historical monuments and constructions of Scotland, HMSO, Edinburgh, 1933.
Bell, Charles, *Reports of the Surveyor General Charles Bell on the Copper Fields of Little Namaqualand*, Saul Solomon, Cape Town, 1855.
Report on the Robben Island establishment, A 37, 1854.
Smith, Andrew, *Report of the expedition for exploring Central Africa*, published for subscribers only, Government Gazette Office, Cape Town, 1836.

LIST OF SUBSCRIBERS

SPONSORS' EDITION

G.K.H. Anderson • E. Bertelsmann SC • The Brenthurst Library
Jim Gerard Paul Broekhuysen • Leslie F.G. Frankel • John & Nakkie Hoffman
Jack Koen • Anthony Dumaresq Manning • Lee Manning • Robin Moser • Old Mutual
Steve Phelps • Mike & Norma Rattray • Jean Turck • Dr Dieter Waibel

COLLECTORS' EDITION

Joan S. Bortnick
Ivana Katarina Bucalina
Chris Calitz
Elsie Calitz
Carl Schlettwein Foundation
S.W. Caroline
Aubrey Christie
Donald & Rosemary Currie
Christo de Wit
Jalal & Kulsum Dhansay
Leicester Dicey
Fritz G. Eckl
Fernwood Press (Pty) Limited
Eugene & Lalie Fourie
Adrian Gardiner
V.H. Gebers
Peter & Claire Goosen
Lydia Gorvy
Timothy Griessel
Basil Hersov
M.J. Hyde

H.E. Jean-Richard
G.E. Jewell, New Zealand
Donn Jowell
Quentin Keynes
J. Kogl
Harold L.E. König
G.G. Leslie
Morris Lurie
John H. Martin
Peter & Megan McGregor
John-James McHardy
Ian McPherson
Robin Moser
Jan & Elizabeth Nel
Danie, Anet, Daniel, Christiaan,
   Loren & Rita Olivier
Petersfield Nurseries
Joanna Pickering
Jan Willem Pont
Beryl & Lawrence Posniak
Herbert M.J. Prins

Peter G.S. Radford
C.H. Rance
J.C. Rance
Philip Read
Hymie Sibul
June Stannard
David & Isolde Stegmann
Michael Stevenson
Pieter & Pam Struik
University of Stellenbosch Library
   Service
J.A. Janse van Rensburg
N.P. Janse van Rensburg
Paul van Schalkwyk
Dr H.J. van Wyk
Willy C. Vandeverre
Hylda Weinstein
Christopher Robert White
Derric H. Wilson
J.A. Windell
Robin Wissing

STANDARD EDITION

ABC Bookshop
Rob & Eveline Abendanon
Stanley P. Abramson
Gareth & Amanda Ackerman
J.N. Ahmad
Keith Allen
Amfarms
Philippe Andersson
Peter Apsey
Marion Arnold
Brian Askew
Robert Assure
P.D. Attenborough
Hennie Aucamp

Shuli Babus
Paoletta Baker
David & Linda Baldie
Marijke & Ken Ball
Doreen Barendse
Guy John Barker
C.J.A. Barratt
Marius Basson
Yvonne Becker
Alan & Sonja Begg
Thomas Behnisch
Dr B.C. Benfield
M.D. Berman
Giulio Bertrand
Christine Beyers
Albert Blake
M. Blersch
Colin Blythe-Wood
Ortwin Bock
J.C.A. Boeyens
Dr J. Bolt
Richard Booth
C. Botha
Frikkie & Monica Botha
Mrs F.E. Boustred
E.P. Bowker
Dr Frank R. Bradlow
John Bridgman
Nigel & Hillary Bruce
Anton Bryant
Dr H.J. Brynard
Barbara Buntman
Fay & Roy Burrett

Alan & Joanne Calenborne
Alec Campbell
Dr Philip C. Candy

Vincent & Jane Carruthers
M.J. & T.A. Chapman
R.W. Charlton
Laurie & Rita Chiappini
C.J. Chorlton
Christison Rare Books
P.J. Cillié
G.B. Clapham
Margaret M. Clapham
Clarke's Bookshop, Cape Town
Seán Michael Cleary
P.A.G. Cloete
Coach House
M.J.R. Coetzee
Nicolaas Abraham Coetzee
Pieter & Elna Conradie
Paul Cooper, St. Martin's School
H.M. Corder
Covers Interiors
Graham & Jillian Cox
Mark & Clare Cresswell
Lynette Croudace
Simon Crutchley

Arthur & Elizabeth Davey
Bill & Jean Davidson, Zululand
Neill Davies
Henrietta Dax
Gerhard C. de Kock
D. de Milander
Pierre de Reuck
Ingrid E. de Villiers
William de Villiers
Dr Nic de Wet, Somerset West
Helen & Wal Dean
Stef en Meredith Delport
Martin, Lisa & Vincent Di Bella
Hendrik & Coba Diederiks
E.J. (Ted) Dowling
John & Lisa Doyen
E.P. du Plessis
Durban Metropolitan Library Service
Mr & Mrs Gavin Durell
Pieter & Louise Duys

Jon Eagar
B.R. Eastman
Etaine Eberhard
Fred Egan
George, Brenda, Kathleen & Bronwyn
    Elliott
Jean Elworthy

Schalk Engelbrecht
Joan Evans

Pauline Farquhar
M.J. Farrell
G.T. Ferreira
P.T. Fewell
Liz & Alex Fick
M.L. Fielding
E.C. Folli
D.J. Fölscher
Thora Ford
Malcolm Foster
Andries Fourie
Dalray Fox
K.R. Fraser
Jonathan Freedberg
R.M. Friedlander
Malcolm Funston
Susan Funston

Paul James Galpin
J.J. Gauntlett
E.G. Gearing
H.W. Gebers
David & Gaby Gess
F.W. & S.K. Gess
M.M. Glyn
Robert Goldblatt
Joy & Roger Goodwin
Belinda Gordon
J. Gordon Dyer
Murray Graham
Alan & Patricia Graham-Collier
Michael Graham-Stewart
Alec & Catherine Grant
F.E. Graves
Dr & Mrs Ryno Greenwall
John Groenewald
G.G. Groenwald
Marié-Hendrine Grotepass

Dr Anthony Hall-Martin
Neville Harden
Wolf-George Harms
Harold Strange Library,
    Johannesburg
Derek Harraway
Mrs M.A. Harrison
J.O.C. Hart
Alan McA. Harvey
R.A. Harvey

Eduard C. Haumann
James R. Hersov
Birgitta Hope
N.S.H. Hughes
Stefan Hundt
Ian B. Huntley
Erika Huntly
Henry J. Hustle
ICS Holdings Limited (Imperial Cold
    Storage & Supply Company)

Clare Ions

David S. Jack
John & Ann Jarvis
R.G. Jeffery
N.R. Jenkinson
Theodore Johannes
Johannesburg Historical Foundation
Vaughan Johnson
Jean Jordaan
Phyllis Jowell

Brian & Dil Kalshoven
Kristofer Kenneth Karner I
Dr T.J. Keegan
Eileen Kent
Owen Kinahan
Michael W. King
Menno Klapwijk
T.L. Klapwijk
Dick Klein
Gerald P. Klinghardt
David & Noleen Knott
P.A.F. Knowlden Snr
Gerry & Zoë Kock
Walter & Colleen Köppe-Schwager
Errol & Fredia Kreutzer

Greg & Jean Labuschagne
Robert A. Laing
N. Lambourn, Christie's
William N. Lane III
P.J. Latham
S.K.A. Laursen
Paul Lee
Carol Leigh
John Lennard
Letaba Arts and Crafts
R.E. Levitt
Oscar Lockwood
Steve Lombard

Gill & Rupert Lorimer
J.E. Loubser
Betty Louw
H. Louw
Percy A. Lugg

Mrs D.B.R. Macaulay
Keith MacMullen
Ian & Diana Madden
K.D.H. Maisels
Ian R. Marais
Dr Paul Marchand
Amy, Sue & Don Marshall
Liz McGrath
M. Peter McGregor
H.S. McKenzie
David & Karen McLennan
Mrs C. McNeill
Adv. Abri Meiring
Walter Middelmann
Professor C.J. Mieny
M.E. Elton Mills
John Milton
P.D. Minnaar
Mrs S.L. Mitchell
Buddy & Jenny Mockford
S.L. Moorcroft
Dr D.G. Mordant
Mrs Rhona Morris
Robin Moser
Edwin Moses
Therese Mourier
Roger & Maaike Murphy
Lyndall Murray

Héloïse Naudé, Worcester
J.H. Neethling
Hylton Nel
T.M. & J.W. Newsome
Douglas Newton
Sarah Newton
Mrs G.A. Nikschtat
P.A. Nisbet
Marilyn Anne Noakes

T. Ogilvie Thompson
Old Mutual
Lida & Peter Oldroyd
M.J.L. Olivier Library, OKB
Robert Ornduff

R. Pampel
Mary & Elizabeth Paterson

C.E. Peacock
Graham S. Peddie
Roydon C. Peden
Jonathan Pennefather
P.N. Pentz
Ernst J.V. Penzhorn
Jeffry Perlman
Mrs Wendy Pickstone
D. Picton James
Colin & Charmaine Pinker
John Pitout
Bertram & Cecilia Poole
George & Penny Poole
Noel Potter
Henriëtte Prince
Carla Prinsloo

Coenraad J. Raath
Rand Afrikaanse Universiteit
    Biblioteek
Cicero Rautenbach II
Sally Reunert
Cassius Rhode
Dr & Mrs F.D. Richardson
Marion Ellis & Stephen Richardson
F.G. Richings SC
R.B. Ritchie
J.E. Rivett-Carnac
G.M. Roberts
Cedric Roché
Christo Roets
David L. Rose
Annabel Ross
Catriona Ross
Marsaili Ross
Mr & Mrs W.G.M. Ross
Royal Museum of Scotland
Robert M. Rubin
Dr Brendan Ryan

S.A. Cultural History Museum
I.E. Sacks
M.J.V. Samuels
H.L. Schaary
A. & P. Schaefer
Isobel Scher
Daan W. Schoeman
Nicholas Schofield
Jacqueline Heaton & Johann Scholtz
Koning Scholtz
Jonathan Schrire
Sylvia Schrire
Bruce G. Schulze

Dr G.J. Schutte, Hilversum
Ian F. Scott
Rossall Sealy
P.W. St. L. Searle
R. Searle for Eugéni Searle
Frederick R. Sellman, London
Melanie Sharp
Phillip & Gillian Sher
Douglas Simons
Richard Simons
C. Singels
Genard & Heather Sizer
D. & H. Skawran
Karin M. Skawran
Cecil Skotnes
Dennis, Ansie, Jennifer & Ryan
    Slotow
A.O. Smit
Professor Andrew B. Smith
J. Smith
James R. Smith
Jay Smith
Keith & Dorothy Smith
Laurie & Barbara Smith
South African Historical Journal
Sheila Southey
Cheryl Spence
Ian & Joyce Spence
St John's College, Zimbabwe
Lilla & Wald Stack
Nicholas Stamatiadis
Marius Stanz, Fairland,
    Johannesburg
Ines & Basil Stathoulis
Stellenbosch Museum
Michael Stevenson
Leonore Strobos
Patricia Sullivan
David Susman
Suzelle Interiors
Dr M.B.E. Sweet

Carla Dayna Tanner
Arthur Tassell
J. Terry-Lloyd
Gaby Thinnes
M.J.H. Tonking
Townshend van der Walt & Partners
Transnet Heritage Foundation
Rhodes & Diana Tremeer
Oliver & Michelle Trevor
Professor Elizabeth Triegaardt
Di & Bill Turner

UNISA Library
Universiteit van Pretoria Biblioteek
University of Stellenbosch Library
    Service
W.E. Uÿs

Dick & Liz van der Jagt
Dr Gerdrie van der Merwe VDM
S.W. van der Merwe
Maria M. van der Ryst
Raoul van der Westhuizen
Hendrik J. van Eck
M. van Eyndhoven
Anne & Errol van Greunen
Johannes van Heerden, Klein Withoek,
    Brits
Danie van Niekerk
Edna van Niekerk
Fébé van Niekerk
Louis & Joyce van Rensburg
M. & M.A. van Rijswijck
Dr Natie & Mrs Erna van Vuuren
Deon Viljoen
Klaus von Ludwiger
Dr & Mrs P. Vorster

Wartenweiler Library
Phyllis Wasdell
A.F. & S.J. Watermeyer
Anne Watt
Professor Ian B. Watt
Dr A.G. Wesley
J. Wessels
Wessel P. Wessels
T.F. Wheeler
Derrick Willett
William Humphreys Art Gallery
Annette Wilsenach
Derric H. Wilson
Hilda & Jürgen Witt
B. Nigel Wolstenholme
R.A.C. Wood
G.W. Woodland
Lloyd A. Wright

B.E. Yarnell
Alan & Ameli Trantina-Yates

Maurice Zunckel
Mr & Mrs Stan Zway